Lilya's Journey

A RUSSIAN MEMOIR

KSANA AND BOHDAN NATALENKO

LILYA'S JOURNEY: A RUSSIAN MEMOIR
First published in Australia in 2004 by
Simon & Schuster (Australia) Pty Limited
Suite 2, Lower Ground Floor
14–16 Suakin Street, Pymble NSW 2073

A Viacom Company
Sydney   New York   London   Toronto   Singapore

Visit our website at www.simonsaysaustralia.com.au

© Ksana and Bohdan Natalenko 2004

All rights reserved. No part of this publication may be reproduced, stored in a retrieval system, or transmitted, in any form, or by any means electronic, mechanical, photocopying, recording or otherwise, without the prior permission of the publisher in writing.

National Library of Australia
Cataloguing-in-Publication data

Natalenko, Ksana.
Lilya's journey: a Russian memoir.

ISBN 0 7318 1133 X.

1. Makarova, Ludmila, 1914- . 2. Refugees - Soviet Union - Biography. 3. World War, 1939-1945 - Personal narratives, Russian. 4. Russians - Australia - Biography. 5. Immigrants - Australia - Biography. I. Natalenko, Bohdan. II. Title.

305.906914092

Cover design by Melissa Keogh
Internal design and typesetting by Adam Hodson, Fly Design
Typeset in Lomba Book 11 pt on 15 pt
Printed in Australia by Griffin Press

10 9 8 7 6 5 4 3 2 1

CONTENTS

Prologue	1
Chapter 1	2
Chapter 2	15
Chapter 3	26
Chapter 4	39
Chapter 5	65
Chapter 6	72
Chapter 7	93
Chapter 8	111
Chapter 9	134
Chapter 10	145
Chapter 11	164
Chapter 12	188
Chapter 13	206
Epilogue	225

*To our beloved parents Lilya and Boris,
as a tribute for everything you mean to us*

ACKNOWLEDGMENTS

A huge thanks to my mentor, friend and agent, Selwa Anthony, for your unstinting support and encouragement. Without Selwa, this book may not have been published. A huge thanks to all my editors: Jody Lee, Anouska Jones and Siobhán Cantrill. Your suggestions, help and critiques made this book come alive.

Thank you to: Anton Gurchenko, for your assistance in translating the manuscript from Russian to English—you passed away much too soon; Ina, my cousin, for helping transcribe Lilya's tapes; Pam Ricketson, for your assistance in interviewing Lilya in the early stages of the manuscript; Rie Natalenko, for your insightful suggestions and editing assistance; my dear friend Sue Williams, a prolific author, for your continued friendship, support and encouragement; Julia Morrell, dear kindred spirit, for artistic suggestions and believing in me; Carol Smith for advice and loving support; David Corbett—the Photo Fixer—for a great job in restoring Lilya and Boris's old family photos; Olga and Nina, current administrators of the Smolensk Drama Theatre, for your generosity in assisting Bob and me with archival research; Margot Allott-Rodgers, journalist and dear friend, for your love and support, especially during late-night phone calls; Dr Matthew Crawford—my wonderful pain specialist—for keeping me going through intense pain; and to Doug and Chris, my four-legged children's surrogate parents, for minding Oscar, Coco, Bobbie and Toby—my beloved dogs—on many occasions when I needed quiet time to write.

There are many other friends and colleagues to whom I owe heartfelt thanks and gratitude for discussing the book with me over numerous cups of coffee and glasses of wine. You all know who you are.

Thank you.

Ksana Natalenko

PROLOGUE

This is the story of my mother, Ludmila Gavrilovna Natalenko, known always as Lilya. A talented actress, a wonderful wife and an incredibly dedicated mother, Lilya was born in Russia and lived through the dreadful atrocities of the Stalinist era and the turbulent years of World War II.

Her very promising career as an actress was cut suddenly short by the outbreak of war, during which she lost her family. Occupying troops overran her village and she was forcibly taken to Germany to face an unknown future.

In Berlin, she met, fell in love with and married Boris, a Red Army soldier who was a prisoner of war. As the war drew to a close, she and Boris went on the run through Germany and Czechoslovakia. Capture by either the Allies or the Red Army would have meant deportation to Russia, followed by imprisonment in Siberia's labour camps, or death.

Not until many years after the war did hope of a secure future present itself to them, when millions of displaced persons throughout postwar Europe were relocated through Assisted Migrant schemes. So eventually, my mother and father, together with me and my brother Bohdan, succeeded in reaching Australia and making a new home.

My mother Lilya always considered herself to be a very ordinary person. However, her experiences, her indomitable spirit and her courage shaped her life in a way that made her anything but ordinary. It is a privilege to celebrate the life of this remarkable woman by sharing her story with you.

CHAPTER ONE

Born on 29 September 1914, I was named Ludmila like my mother. My birthplace was the village of Ilovitsa in the shire of Roslavl, in the Smolensk region. Smolensk is in the far west of Russia, about midway between Minsk, the capital of Byelorussia, and Moscow. My father, Gavril Lavrentievich Makarov, was a secondary school principal, and taught mathematics and physics. My mother, Ludmila Michaelovna Makarova, taught Russian language and literature.

There were only two children in my family, myself and my brother Alec, who was five years younger. We loved one another very much—we were inseparable—and our relationship remained extremely close as we grew to adulthood.

Mother came from generations of clergy. Her father, my grandfather Michael Vorobyov, was a minister who died very young and in tragic circumstances. He was an alcoholic and committed suicide at the age of 33. His wife, Neonila Alexandrovna Murashkina, also the daughter of a minister, found herself widowed at the age of 27 with two children, Seryoja and Ludmila (my mother), and expecting a third. This was my uncle, Vanya, who became my godfather. Fortunately, Grandmother had a profession—she was a midwife—and so somehow managed to raise her children, but life was very difficult. To make ends meet, she worked for an estate owner and his wife as a nursemaid for their 22 children. With the help of friends she enrolled both sons in theological college in the family tradition, and my mother in the Parish school. Uncle Seryoja soon abandoned the college, however, running off with a troupe of itinerant actors and disappearing to God knows where for twenty years. He eventually returned home with his wife, having become an accomplished actor. He was a fine baritone but I have only a very dim recollection of him singing. He died of typhoid in his late thirties. Uncle Vanya also abandoned the college, teaching at first but later enrolling at university, reading history and philology. He graduated, only to re-enrol in the Faculty of Medicine, and became a doctor.

Father came from a poor peasant background. My grandfather on my father's side, Laurentiy Yegorovich Makarov, was very poor. His father, my great-grandfather, built himself a cabin on the bank of the River Vorenitsa. As other peasants settled around him, little by little the small community grew into an entire village, called Makarovka, named after my great-grandfather. My grandfather had a big family: four sons and three daughters. He couldn't afford to educate his children, so it was with great difficulty that my father managed to complete primary school. He was needed at home to look after his two younger sisters, so his parents tried to keep him from attending school by hiding his boots. But, barefoot and wearing only a shirt and trousers, he would run off to school, even when it was snowing. Later, when he was conscripted into the army, one of the officers wondered about this clever fellow who had such attractive handwriting. An interest was taken in him and he was given books and educated to the point of sitting for an external exam for graduation from secondary school. His success gained him promotion to sergeant, and eventually to first lieutenant. On his release from the army he became a primary school teacher, married, and continued his self-education. Studying mathematics and physics by correspondence, he became a secondary school principal.

My father's sisters didn't receive any education and all got married. I remember Auntie Khretiniya and Auntie Aldona very well, but not my third aunt. I also remember Auntie Aldona's children, Maryusa and Ilya, my cousins. They both lived in Smolensk and studied at the Institute of Medicine. I often visited them. Auntie Khretiniya lived about thirty kilometres away from us, on the edge of an enormous forest, in the village of Dengubovka.

The entire Smolensk region was surrounded by enormous, dense and very ancient forests, made up mostly of birch trees. The red brick wall of ancient times stood protectively around the city itself. Even though I had never travelled anywhere, I couldn't imagine a more beautiful place. Ghostly white in the winter, the many man-made ornamental lakes in the parks would be frozen over, children skating on their glassy surfaces. In summer, the parks turned to masses of colour as tulips and other flowers jostled for prominence in the sun. The buildings were tall and stately, and there was always an air of great serenity. I absolutely loved the place.

The tiny village of Roslavl where Alec and I grew up was, by contrast, a dusty place, boasting an undistinguished collection of thirty or so wooden huts, painted green or blue or ochre—it seemed that the colour depended on whatever paint the owner could obtain. No matter, this was home to me and I couldn't imagine ever leaving it.

I always knew I would be an actress. At the age of three I loved to recite short pieces of poetry to our guests; once I learned to read I would recite entire poems which I memorised in lightning-quick time. I had a phenomenal memory. I would stand on the table as though it were a stage, and would subject the poor guests to my recitals. They would listen out of politeness and exclaim, 'Oh, what a wonder-child, what a prodigy!' I recall memorising a poem called 'A Christian' which I gave a theatrical presentation. I would play the part of the unfortunate Christian, while the roles of the lions which devoured her were taken by Alec and his friends. They attacked me, roared and bit me to death with great passion and fervour. But when one of the lions actually drew blood when he bit my ear, and I screamed with genuine emotion, I was banned from playing this part and moved onto more sedate and peaceful roles—Cleopatra, Aspasia or Penelope from Homer's *Odyssey*. I would remove tablecloths and sheets from Mother's cupboard, tie them across my shoulders tunic style, take a sword in my hands, that is, some stick or other, and torture my slaves, beheading them should they displease me. But here again a misfortune occurred. I once hit one of the boys so hard across the head that he screamed violently, and Father gave me a thrashing and forbade this game as well.

We had a dog called Druzhok (meaning 'friend'), a loveable mutt of indeterminate ancestry, who was also forced to take part in these theatrical proceedings. We would offer him as a sacrifice to Moloch in Flaubert's *Salammbô*. Druzhok would be tolerant for a long time, but eventually would start to bite and run off. We tried to offer our cat as a sacrifice as well, but with somewhat less success—he once gave me such a scratching that I was forced to dispense with his services.

I once got the idea to dig a hole, right in front of the steps leading to our front door, put Druzhok in there, cover it up and camouflage it—and then visitors would fall in, whereupon Druzhok would attack them. No sooner said than done. Alec helped me. We took Father's newly sharpened axe and began chopping a hole, but because the spot was rather littered with stones the axe did not fare too well. The hole was almost ready. Father took one look at the axe and at me, grabbed a bunch of nettles and gave me the biggest thrashing of my life.

'What has our daughter grown up to be?' my mother would exclaim in anguish. 'An absolute scoundrel!' I lived in a fascinating world of illusion and make-believe, amongst imaginary characters, and forced others to share my world with me. I even convinced Mother, who was a teacher, to put on plays with her students. She was the prompt, while I directed them and of course had to play a leading part myself. Later on, when these friends and assistants became students of medicine, education, science and the like, we would gather at our old alma mater during holidays and present plays and extracts with rather more professionalism. Mother and Father were understandably quite proud of what we had all achieved.

Our childhood was very happy but passed by all too soon. One of my fondest memories is of the times Papa, Alec and I went blackberry-picking in the forests around home. We used to bring back berries by the bucketful and baskets full of mushrooms—a great variety of mushrooms. Their fragrance filled the little makeshift kitchen at the back of our house. Mother would prepare jams, marmalades and pickled vegetables for the entire winter and store them on top of the huge stove. Russian stoves are truly enormous, occupying half a room. They look like bakers' ovens, but the top is a flat surface, often used for sleeping. Thus, the stove not only served as a cooking utensil, it also provided me with a warm bed during the bitterly cold winters. Mama would put down a blanket on top and I would lie on the stove thinking that it must almost be heaven.

Father and I would sometimes visit our relatives together. How well I remember those journeys. Alec didn't always want to come with us, complaining that his legs couldn't carry him so far. So Papa and I would start out before first light, walking through the lush meadows and forest paths, while I recited to him poems which I had learned by heart, or passages from famous Russian writers such as Gogol, Chekhov, Nadson and Tutcher. The twenty kilometres to Papa's birthplace of Makarovka would pass almost unnoticed. In Makarovka we would sleep over at one of his nephews' houses and the next day walk the last ten kilometres to the village of Dengubovka. My cousins would accompany us on this second day and a merry group of travellers would arrive at Auntie Khretiniya's house. She would be expecting us, though I'm not sure how she always knew we were coming. Such were the wonderful, never-to-be-repeated, unforgettable days of my youth.

I can recollect events from very early in my childhood. For example, I remember very clearly how Mother and I farewelled Father when he went to war in 1916. That was World War I and I was only two years old at the time. Father was 33 years old so he was in one of the later batch of conscripts to be called up. He looked so handsome in his uniform: black hair slicked back and long, thick whiskers, brushed into perfect order. In the days before his departure, I remember my parents looking for ever so long at one another and whispering to each other for ages at a time. When Mama cried, he would gently wipe her eyes and pat her hair and tell her not to worry, he would be coming home soon. Mother later told me that my description of his departure was extremely vivid. I remembered how a great red smoke-breathing monster arrived at the station and swallowed up my beloved Father. I really believed it had eaten him. I became very ill, refused all food and in my delirium thought the monster wanted to eat us.

The war with Germany ended with the Bolshevik revolution of October 1917, but because of the enormous confusion and disarray of the time, soldiers returning from the war took some time to get back home. Many were immediately absorbed into the Red Army, supporting the Revolution. Others joined the White forces (Mensheviks), who opposed the Revolution and supported a return to monarchic rule or parliamentary democracy. During those incredibly turbulent and unstable years, all the usual services such as mail delivery were completely disrupted. Mother received one letter from Father shortly after he left for the front, then didn't hear from him at all until his return some two years later. Luckily, he was able to disengage from his unit somehow and make his way home by early 1918.

That day, as usual, I was playing outside. It was a cold winter day, the gently falling snow creating a white cloak for the spindly branches of the many birch trees growing around our house. The tiny schoolhouse in which we lived sat in the middle of a large area of partially cleared land, with only the birches dividing us from the surrounding countryside. When anybody visited us we were able to spot them amongst the trees from some distance away. On schooldays our house was very busy, but the rest of the time we didn't see visitors very often, as we were fairly isolated from the nearest village. So when I saw a distant figure approaching, even though I couldn't make out who it was, I ran towards the house calling excitedly, 'Mama, Mama, someone's coming!'. Mother came to the doorstep and peered at the person trudging towards us through the snow. I couldn't tell whether it was a man or a woman, but Mother's expression changed from vague curiosity to astonishment and disbelief. She gasped, 'Oh my God, it can't be, it can't be!' and started running, at first slowly, then as fast as the snow would allow her, towards the speck in the distance. She was crying and calling out and all I could do was follow, calling out in exasperation, 'Who is it, Mama?'.

Finally I was close enough to make out my father's features. When I at last reached him, he picked me up in one arm and held me so close I had to say, 'Papa, don't squeeze me to death now that you're home.' The three of us stood there, hugging and crying, for a long time. He was much thinner than I remembered and his hair greyer, but it was so good to see him again.

When I was five I remember waking up in the night because of my mother's screaming. My room was dark, I was all alone and I also screamed, in fright. Babushka (Grandmother), my Mama's mother, ran in and tried to calm me down. She told me Mama had had a very sore tummy, but she was better now—and I now had a brother. The next day this new brother was shown to me, but I didn't like him at all, because he was all red, and said I'd rather have a puppy or a rabbit. Little by little I got used to his presence and before long I loved Alec more than anything. My love for my little brother remained for the rest of my life.

In 1921, at the age of seven, I began elementary school. In Russia, children usually start school at the age of seven and continue their education for ten years. The school in Roslavl, where Father taught, and in which we lived, was built at the turn of the century of wood and stone with a thatched roof. The main building was two storeys high, with extra classrooms at the back laid out as a series of adjoining self-contained cabins. Each cabin had a large enclosed fireplace for heating during the very cold winters. The chairs and desks in the classrooms were very simple wooden ones. Each desk had an inkwell and the top lifted up so that most of the books could be kept at school rather than being taken home each night.

Russian schoolteachers enjoyed a very high standing in the community. Their pay and conditions were meagre but at least they held a position which was highly respected, a respect shared by their pupils. I cannot remember a single incident in which a student spoke rudely to a teacher or engaged in any serious misbehaviour in class. There were many reasons for this but primarily it was because the school was an instrument of the Soviet State for training and educating young people to become good Soviet citizens—and absolute obedience to the State was the duty of every citizen.

Every day we would devote time to some aspect of our political system, which was variously referred to as Communism, Marxism, Marxism-Leninism or Socialism. Although there were formal differences between each of these terms, most ordinary citizens used them quite interchangeably. Our education included social, economical, historical, philosophical and political perspectives on our everyday life. We were constantly told how wonderful life was in the Soviet Union and how terrible it was elsewhere in the world, where Capitalism was the dominant system of economic organisation. Not knowing any different, we believed that Capitalists were evil millionaires who stalked around in black suits and top hats, exploiting common workers and treating them as slaves. Marxism, on the other hand, gave to people 'according to their needs' and asked that in return they give back 'according to their abilities'. It seemed to make perfectly good sense at the time and we were all encouraged to admire the heroes of the Great October Revolution and the founder of the Soviet State, Vladimir Ilyich Lenin.

I was saddened, like everyone else I knew, when news reached us that our great leader Lenin had died in 1924. We were assured that the leadership would pass to an equally worthy successor who would continue to look after all Soviet citizens as though they were his own children. None of us could possibly have imagined what the future had in store for us under the 'tender loving care' of Joseph Stalin.

I was, like most of my friends in the school, a keen and capable student, especially in the humanities and social sciences, although I also loved biology. But my life was not that of a junior academic, closeted away for hours on end. It was that of a free-spirited rapscallion who could readily separate the disciplined requirements of school life from the youthful demands of adventure and freedom.

Our school stood on the banks of a mighty river, surrounded by huge groves of birch and fir trees. It had lodgings for the principal and a large orchard of apples, pears, cherries, black, red and white currants, raspberries and strawberries. In the vegetable garden were potatoes, tomatoes, peas and cucumbers. All of these had to be weeded and watered, but mainly guarded so that children from the village wouldn't raid the crops. I was forever somewhere in the orchard or garden, waging the next battle in a continuous war with the village children and covered with bruises and scars from numerous fierce encounters. This didn't bother me at all. I raced madly about the village, tanned by the sun, dirty, my nose peeling from sunburn, climbing trees—wilful, overflowing with youthful energy and naughtiness. I was perfectly happy until Father came to find me—if he could—and fetch me home to help Mother with chores, which I really disliked doing. I dearly loved horses, loved bathing them in the river, and would swim across and back again by hanging onto their manes. Since we had no saddles, I would often fall off, whereupon the horses would either bite or kick me. I was a complete and utter tomboy.

During the winter, the river froze over. One day all the village children were tobogganing down the hill onto the ice when I fell through a hole cut by the villagers, from which they used to draw water. Luckily, my friends pulled me out in just a few minutes, but I was already frozen stiff and starting to turn blue. Father thawed me out on top of the kitchen stove.

When Alec had grown up somewhat, I made him part of my adventures. We would go rafting on the river, go horseback riding, play cowboys and Indians, pirates, cops and robbers. A whole gang of village children obeyed me as their leader. I was known as Chief Redskin, Alec was Paleface Brother and the rest were variously named Eagle's Eye, Snaketooth, Running Water, Mustang Ear and Coyote Heart, names I borrowed from the pages of Fenimore Cooper, Jules Verne or Robert Louis Stevenson. We had an extensive library and I was a voracious reader, even by Russian standards. One of the few real benefits of Communism was the extraordinary improvement in the country's literacy rate. It was no surprise to find that the humblest farmer or manual labourer was familiar with the works of Tolstoy, Dostoevsky, Pushkin, Chekhov and so on. Besides that, many ordinary Russians were more familiar with the works of Shakespeare than many English-speaking people.

In any case, the important thing was that I learned to read at a very early age. In the evenings we would gather on the hillsides above the river and light campfires, and I would tell my obedient followers of all the things I had read about. Armed with bows and arrows or slingshots, we would have battles with one another or with children from the neighbouring village. We trampled down crops of rye and wheat, raided the orchards and gardens of our enemies and forever walked about with blackened eyes and faces bruised from the bee-stings we received during our frequent pranks in the vicinity of bee-hives. Our gang was the curse of the village, and on many occasions other parents complained to Mother and Father about that uncontrollable rascal Lilya who had taken possession of their children and was leading them astray. Father was driven to despair and would give me a thrashing with his belt, but to little avail. I would cry and nurse my sore bottom—and almost immediately forget about it. I was constantly up to mischief. It is impossible to recount all the misdeeds of which I was the perpetrator and for which I had to pay. I always wondered how Mother and Father immediately knew that I was the culprit. But I didn't resent the punishments, quickly going on to the next creative idea. My imagination had no limits.

Apart from my parents and Alec, the person I loved most was my 'other father', Uncle Vanya, my godfather. Uncle Vanya had married while he was still a teacher, before enrolling in the Faculty of Medicine at the university in Smolensk. His wife, Auntie Panya, remained in the village and continued to teach at the elementary school, which was some fifteen kilometres from where we lived. Godfather would visit us during the holidays and we would go to Auntie Panya's together to see his two little girls. I simply adored him. He and Mama looked so alike. They shared the same brown, wavy hair, hers worn in a loose chignon, his cut short. They had similar hazel eyes and the well-sculpted cheekbones of those Russians with Tartar heritage. Gradually, Uncle Vanya and Auntie Panya had grown apart, and had separated for some months. He was a well-educated person, an extraordinarily good storyteller, knew masses about all manner of things; we called him the walking encyclopaedia. Auntie Panya, on the other hand, was mean-spirited, self-centred and haughty.

I loved to listen to Uncle Vanya's stories. He introduced me to classical Russian literature and I so loved to be with him that my own father was jealous of his relationship with me and with Alec. My darling father was a generous, intelligent man, but somewhat austere. I knew that he adored both Alec and me by the many kind gestures he made rather than by his words. Whenever he went anywhere without us, he would bring back a memento for the two of us: an especially pretty leaf, a book given to him by a friend or a small piece of sala (pork fat) for which he had stood long hours in a queue and traded some other meagre goods in his possession. In contrast to Father's strictness, our mother was sweetness itself. Should we, or I, as was usually the case, have been punished by Father for some misdemeanour or other, Mama would quietly seek me out, hold me tightly against her plumpness and give me a huge kiss, telling me that Father did indeed love me, but I should show him more respect. I can't ever remember her losing her temper with us, although I'm sure we would have tested her patience a million times. Uncle Vanya shared Mother's stoic, tranquil nature. How patiently he told and re-told accounts of Russian history to Alec and me.

I'm certain that my loving and secure family background shaped me into the survivor I grew up to be. Even in the early days of Stalinism, however, my parents and Uncle Vanya always warned Alec and me never to talk openly to anyone, not even in jest. The oppressive clouds of Stalin's rule blotted the landscape and touched every part of our lives. The population lived in fear of saying the wrong thing, no matter how trivial, in case they were informed on to the authorities.

After I completed elementary school in 1927, my life underwent a dramatic change. Our school in Roslavl was fairly small with an enrolment of only 170 pupils or so and the teachers, though competent, were not as highly qualified as they should have been. The Soviet State had been in existence for less than a decade and was considerably short of capable administrators. During the pre-revolutionary era the population had been largely illiterate, so that when the Soviets came to power there was a massive shortage of qualified people in all sorts of areas needed for building a new nation. Many schoolteachers were drafted into government service, leaving huge shortfalls of trained teachers in the education system. These shortfalls were particularly acute in rural areas.

Mother and Father wanted me to pursue a career in medicine, which would require my completing secondary school at the highest possible level of achievement. Fearing that I might not receive from our small school the kind of tuition this would require, they decided it would be best that I complete my secondary education in Smolensk. So I moved to Smolensk with my maternal grandmother, whom I called Mailichka for some strange reason, since this is just a nonsense word. I was thirteen. Mailichka and I lived with my beloved Uncle Vanya, but I missed home profoundly and went home for holidays without fail. Returning to Smolensk was always a tragedy that caused me to weep bitterly. Mailichka and I lived very poorly, dependent on Uncle Vanya's student scholarship and my parents' monthly contribution of a few roubles.

After some ten months in Smolensk, my darling Mailichka died of dysentery. In those days in rural Russia, illnesses such as dysentery were difficult to treat because the necessary drugs were just not available. So my grandmother gradually grew weaker and weaker until she became so dehydrated that she fell into a coma from which she never awoke. Auntie Panya moved back to Smolensk from where she had been staying in the country to join Uncle Vanya, and life changed for the worse. Instead of a loving grandmother I was now under the control of a virtual stranger, of whom I knew little except that she didn't like me. I think she was jealous of my close relationship with my uncle. She managed to keep all the food locked up unless she was there to dole it out herself. And dole it out she did, so that I was forever hungry. Occasionally Uncle Vanya—who was aware of the meagre rations thrown my way—would slip some of his portion to me, but if Auntie Panya noticed she would nag him for hours about my unwanted presence. I was extremely unhappy and longed for the warmth and comfort of home, where I was loved and cared for.

Despite my unhappiness I remained a good student throughout secondary school, although not altogether at ease with mathematics. In literature, I was dux of the school. My background in reading amazed even my teachers. I tutored students who were struggling with the subject and conducted classes in literature and Russian language for adult students as part of our Soviet community service ethos. My teacher read my compositions to the whole class and I was very proud of my achievements, both personally and as part of my contribution to my country. Looking back, I realise how incredibly naive young people of my age were in those times. On a daily basis we were fed propaganda about the wonders of Communism and the evils of Capitalism. Our beloved leader, Joseph Stalin, was revered like a god. At least that's what all our textbooks told us.

Stalin had come to power following Lenin's death in 1924. Of course we didn't know it at the time, but Lenin had left a document proposing Stalin's removal from the position of Secretary of the Communist Party, being well aware of Stalin's flaws, particularly his craving for personal power. Nonetheless, Stalin continued to strengthen his position until he became the absolute dictator of the

Soviet Union. Throughout my school years, Soviet propaganda grew and grew until it permeated every aspect of life. Our lives, we were told, were only worthwhile inasmuch as they contributed to the welfare of the Soviet State and to building world Communism. We really knew very little about the West or indeed about any other way of life elsewhere, so we had little reason to doubt what we were told.

Russians are, by nature, very patriotic and I, like all of my friends and colleagues, wanted to contribute what I could for the good of my country. As a school student, my patriotism was largely confined to study, in order to be a good citizen as much as for the sake of my future career. So it was with some considerable pride that I received the news in my final year that the local committee of the Regional Division of National Education wanted to interview me concerning my 'literary interests'.

Having just written an examination essay on the poetry of Sergei Esenin, my favourite poet, I was fully expecting to be approached with a view towards using my essay as a model of student writing and having it published, perhaps even nationally. At the very least I would get some sort of commendation or other to recognise my work as an example of educational achievement under the magnificent leadership of Stalin and according to the doctrines of Marxism-Leninism. This naive young schoolgirl was about to receive her first real lesson in the realities of Communism.

CHAPTER TWO

The night before my interview I thought over what I had said in my exam response to the poetry of Esenin. I knew that his poetry was considered to be politically incorrect and subject to continual censorship of one kind or another because it was deemed to be representative of 'depressing and negative attitudes, not in conformity with the spirit of the age, and for its blatant lack of love for Soviet realism'. But although Esenin was censored, his works were still available. Primarily, the State tolerated them as examples of 'misguided' literature.

At the age of eighteen I had written with considerable passion for his poetry but had not commented in my essay on the political nature of the debate surrounding his work. I wrote of his gentle but tormented love for Russia; of his anguish for the way of life that was passing by; of his love towards animals and people. Although rather naive, I was not stupid. I knew that being 'misguided' could be considered a serious matter.

Under the constant influence of propaganda, we generally came to believe that the State did indeed protect ordinary people like us and that, in turn, it was our duty to support the State in every way we could. This included being a good student with respect for the authority of people such as teachers. Of course, the real strength of this system lay in the power of the State to coerce people into compliance if they deviated in any way from the expected norms of behaviour. For example, if a student were to neglect their studies for any reason and their grades showed a marked decline, they would be asked to explain why they were letting down the State, their families and themselves, in that order of importance. Furthermore, the student's parents would have to attend an interview by a committee of school personnel and members of the Communist Party to explain why they were not exercising the principles of good Soviet parenting. They could end up in a lot more trouble than their children for failing to uphold the ideals of the Soviet State. If they had personal problems, such as difficulties with their relationship or with excessive drinking, the State could simply remove their children from their care, since under Communist ideology it is held that children are not the private property of their parents. They belong to the collective known as the State and parents are merely delegated by the State to be caregivers. All of this reduces to a simple equation: any deviation from ideal Soviet behaviour is a crime against the State and if the offender is unwilling to comply then the full power of the State can be invoked to re-educate or otherwise control the offender. The concept of personal freedom was viewed as a dangerous and subversive idea.

I had avoided the political issues in my essay and was sure that my stress on the beauty that Esenin saw in Russian life was what must have impressed my literature teacher to refer my essay to the Committee. How clever I had been, I thought to myself as I went off to sleep.

The next day as I prepared to attend the interview I proudly announced that I was about to leave and would my family like to wish me luck. Father looked at me with an expression of such despair and fear that I have never forgotten it to this day.

'Just remember one thing,' he said. 'Whatever the Committee says is without question correct. Do you understand?'

I didn't realise what he was getting at, so I simply replied, 'Yes, I guess so, Papa.'

'No! Not I guess so, but absolutely so. For all our sakes. Understand?'

Suddenly I was really frightened. Up to this point it hadn't occurred to me that I had put not only myself, but also my teacher and certainly my family in jeopardy. I now knew that something was terribly amiss. As I walked towards the building where I was to be interviewed it became more and more apparent to me that I had been just a foolish and stubborn child. What could I have been thinking? Our teacher had stressed again and again that there was a great danger of being seduced by the aesthetics of the language of

Esenin and of many other writers, both Russian and foreign. Everybody knew what comments like this were intended to convey. In essence one simply needed to refer to 'good' literature as conforming to Communist ideals and 'bad' literature as being opposed to them. But my problem was that I had praised Esenin's work even though it was officially deemed 'bad'. Now I, my family and my teacher were all under scrutiny. How was I to extricate us from the mess I had created?

The building loomed before me like a mausoleum. It was an ugly, square, three-storey building, painted in a dismal grey, although much of the paint had peeled off, probably because it was of inferior quality. The windows were also painted so that I couldn't see what sort of interior I was about to enter. We weren't aware of it at the time but Soviet citizens were to learn over the next few decades that our Government had very little interest in providing us with any of the comforts of modern living. Soviet architecture seemed to lack any aesthetic merit whatsoever. It was all bleak and box-like.

Trying to steel my nerves in anticipation of the coming ordeal, I slowly, and apparently nonchalantly, pulled open the heavy wooden door and went inside. I looked around furtively. Along to the side, a dimly-lit corridor led off the dingy foyer where a desolate-looking figure in a drab coat—whether man or woman I couldn't tell—was seated, staring straight ahead. With some trepidation, I approached this official at the front desk. I say 'desk' but it was actually a small wooden table with a chair, and both had seen better days. Seated at the table was a fat, very stern-faced man holding a pencil, with a small bundle of papers in front of him. He said nothing. I shuffled my feet, waiting to be asked what I wanted. Still nothing.

'Excuse me, sir,' I began, 'my name is Ludmila Makarova and I'm here to…'

'We know who you are, Student Makarova, and we know why you are here,' said the man, without looking up.

I stood there for ages before venturing to continue, 'Yes, of course. So should I…?'

Again I was cut off mid-sentence, but this time by a finger pointing past me towards the wall, against which stood a very uncomfortable-looking chair. I sat down as demurely as I could, trying desperately not to show how nervous I was.

It is interesting how, when you are sitting or standing around in a waiting area, you eventually make observations of everyone else, but without ever making direct eye contact. If someone looks up and sees that you are looking in their direction they go to great lengths to show that they are not in the least concerned by this. You, in turn, go to equally great lengths to indicate that you were not, in fact, observing them at all but simply happened to be casually glancing in their direction when they just happened to look up. So it came as something of a shock to me to find, during one of my 'accidental' glances towards this official, that he didn't avert his eyes at all. Indeed, he kept staring directly at me. Even more disconcerting was his behaviour, for I couldn't help noticing that he was scribbling down notes from time to time. These were not just randomly timed notes, either. He would stare in my direction for an interminably long time and then scribble. I realised that he was assessing me.

If I had been nervous before it was nothing next to the panic I was now feeling. Did they think I was a spy? Would those confounded notes he was taking somehow reveal some terrible secret about me that I was not even aware of? Perhaps the itch on my chin that had been bothering me would provide them with incontrovertible evidence that I was an enemy of the Soviet Union. All my life I had loved an audience, but this sort of attention and this sort of audience I could certainly do without. After all, I was just a schoolgirl who had been rather foolish, but nothing more sinister than that. Perhaps I should just try to make sure they clearly get that impression of me? This thought kept whirling around in my head as I continued to wait. I smiled to myself as I formed a mental image of a play in which a silly little child was being confronted by this enormous committee of sombre-faced interrogators, all dressed in black. They would ask ridiculous questions like, 'Who is your favourite political economist, and why?'. The little girl would answer something like, 'The Big Bad Wolf, because he can at least imagine what it's like to eat pork,' and the audience would giggle with delight at this impish youngster's put-down of her protagonists.

As I sat and waited the concept percolated more and more through my mind. I was indeed here to play a part. I was to face an audience that I would have to please more than any audience I might have pleased in the past. But most importantly, I could play the part badly, with God knows what consequences, or I could play it well. My rebellious, independent nature might have got me into this predicament, but it could also help me get out of it. Once this conviction had taken hold there was no turning back. My nervousness began to dissolve as if by magic. After all, what does a silly schoolgirl have to be nervous about?

'Hhmm,' I rasped in my best attention-seeking voice. No response.

'Hhhuumm!' I repeated, more emphatically. Still no response. 'Excuse me, but could…'

'Yes, yes, don't be so impatient,' came the mid-sentence interjection.

So, someone is still anxious to play the role of Sentence Interrupter, are they? Very well! I continued: 'Could you tell me…'

'I said, don't be so impatient and…'

'…where the ladies' room is? If I…'

'Just wait until your name…'

'…don't go to the toilet soon I'll wet my pants and then you'll be sorry.'

'Look girlie, the toilet's just along the corridor there through the first door on your left and you won't have to wait long when you get back.'

'Oh, I don't mind waiting. I like this place,' I said with the greatest sincerity I could muster. As I walked past the table there was an awful lot of note-taking going on.

When I came back I was just about to sit down again when a woman's voice suddenly announced: 'Makarova—room three—now!' I turned around to see a figure in a shawl beckoning me.

'Hurry up, hurry up, we're very busy,' she said. I went in and took a look around the room. The decor was obviously by the person responsible for the front desk layout. There was just one, larger table behind which sat three men, with a single chair in front of it. Otherwise the room was bare. The man in the middle had a face like a pickled herring while the other two had rounded, bland, vegetable-like faces. I chuckled to myself at the thought of being interviewed by a platter of herring and potato, which is a very popular Russian dish. I felt it was going to be even easier to play my part opposite these characters, who looked more like escapees from the Commedia del Arte of the Italian theatre than Education and Party officials. And the concept I had formed—that they too were somehow merely acting out a role—helped to dispel some of my remaining anxiety.

'So…you are Ludmila Makarova—student,' said Herring-face. 'Please, sit down and make yourself comfortable. We'd just like to have a little chat with you.'

'Yes sir!' I replied, bursting with enthusiasm. 'I just love chatting. In fact my friend Galya and I can chat for hours about anything at all or sometimes about nothing in particular and we're always…'

'Yes, all right,' said Potato Number One. 'This is somewhat more serious than that and we would like your full attention, please. Tell us about your family background!'

'My father is from a family of poor peasants and my mother is the daughter of a minister. But she doesn't remember her father. He died when she was two.'

'I see. And do you have any relatives abroad?'

'No, certainly not. Why do you ask such a thing?'

'Never mind. So you like the poems of Sergei Esenin, do you? Can you tell us why?'

I explained as well as I could, constantly trying to stress the point that Esenin's poems were full of beautiful-sounding phrases that I found very emotive and that inspired me to think more about how other people thought and felt about life so that I could understand them better.

But the questioner kept on at me and succeeded in making me feel uncomfortable once again.

'Gentle and sad you say his poems are, do you? What has he got to be sad about? And you—what have you got to be sad about, may I ask? I don't understand. You live under the Soviet regime. You want for nothing. Tovarish Stalin cares about children like no one else in the world. And you entertain yourself with sad poems. How is one to understand this? Incidentally, are you a young Comsomol [member of the Communist Youth Organisation]?'

'No.' I was sweating now.

'Why not?'

'I don't know, somehow it just never worked out that way. I submitted an application, but my local peers didn't accept me, I guess because I had always fought with them when we were little. And after that I didn't apply again.'

The commissioners laughed. Herring-face looked at me for a long time, then suddenly asked, 'What if an enemy of the Soviet Union were to speak to you with beautiful words? Would you listen to him also?'

Although the sweat was now forming rivulets on my forehead, I tried to adopt a look of repugnance at such a thought.

'No, of course I wouldn't. I wouldn't listen to an enemy of my country. But I didn't think Esenin was an enemy. He...he...' Now I was stuck. Obviously the official viewpoint was that Esenin was an enemy and his writings should be seen in that light. But I had judged his work to be of literary merit and I couldn't see how to justify my interpretation on political grounds.

'Yes, yes, go on. He what?'

I thought very quickly. What was it that I ought to say to these officials? What would a silly schoolgirl who listened to her teacher but liked pretty language be likely to believe about Esenin? The answer came quite readily, much to my relief, for the runnels of sweat had started dripping down my nose.

'He is a bad citizen, but I didn't think that made him an enemy of our country.' I tried to wipe my nose as delicately as I could with the back of my hand.

'It's not up to you to judge such things—whether he is or is not an enemy. But even if you thought he was simply a bad citizen, and we certainly have enough of those, why is there no mention of this in your essay?'

'Because it was the last question on the paper,' I replied in as matter-of-fact a tone as I could, though my voice was betraying what was dangerously like a snivel. They looked at each other in perplexity.

'What has that got to do with anything?' one of them asked.

'Well, you see, before I could get to the important task of analysing

Esenin's faults, such as his problem with alcohol…'

'So you do admit he has faults?'

I tried to put on a look of utter incredulity. 'Of course he has faults. Many faults. I made a full list of them and studied them very carefully, just like our teacher told us to. But because…'

Suddenly Herring-face shot up out of his chair as if he had been fired from a cannon and, with a look almost of rapture, completed my sentence for me in a way I could never have foreseen. 'But because it was the last question on the paper…' He paused dramatically, then in a fit of inspired logical deduction and melodrama, carefully concluded by slowly sounding out each word, 'and because you had wasted so much time being seduced by the pretty-sounding words and phrases, you didn't have time to address the most important part of the whole question. Don't you see? That's what we've been trying to tell you all along.'

He sat down with a gasp of self-satisfied smugness. His colleagues were delighted with him. But their delight was as nothing compared to the exhilaration I was feeling. In a single stroke of brilliant Soviet logic and rigorous scientific deduction, old Herring-face had got me—and themselves—off the hook. There was nothing embarrassing that they would have to report about the failure of the education system or the questionable views of any of the major characters involved. In fact, the entire matter could be used as an outstanding confirmation of the dangers posed by the seductive nature of non-conformist writers.

I began to cry. It was obviously a cathartic response to the whole nerve-racking episode I had just been subjected to. No one said anything for quite some time. Then one of them, in his most patronising tone, summed up: 'So you see, my dear, your job is not to entertain yourself with pretty poems, but to build a beautiful future world—Communism.'

'Oh yes! I will build it. Of course I will.' I continued sniffling.

'There you have it. Go and study and don't be led astray by the lure of pretty poems. Study to be a real Soviet girl, a fighter for world revolution and for the triumph of Communism. And as for Esenin, and like-minded others who do not have the good of the Soviet Union at heart, you are well advised to stay clear of them as they will lead you to no good whatsoever. Be uncompromising and learn to identify our common enemies.'

'Oh yes, I promise I will.' Hiccups now took over.

'Go and read rather the works of Lenin and Stalin and not those of Esenin or Blok.'

I left hurriedly, flushed and shaken, my face streaked and looking awful. When I got home, Father was sitting at the table with his back to me, his head in his hands. He didn't look up but asked quietly, 'Well, my dearest, how are things?'

'Fine, Papa. Just fine,' I replied.

He rose slowly, studied me carefully and put his arms around me. We cried together for some time. Mother came in and joined us, repeating 'Thanks be to God' over and over. An evil shadow had passed us by. God knows what would have happened to us if I hadn't passed this 'test'. People under suspicion of anti-Soviet sentiment just disappeared, without a trace. It had happened to friends of my parents. The husband was at a local gathering and recounted a harmless joke about Stalin. Within a week, officials took him away at night and his family hadn't seen him since. That had occurred over six months ago and there was still no news of his fate. What was even more frightening was that someone in his circle, pretending to be a friend, had obviously reported him to the authorities.

The entire incident had been a valuable lesson to me in many ways. Yet there was an aspect of my behaviour that I found extremely disturbing: I had been willing to denounce my favourite poet in order to appease the immoral bureaucrats and protect myself. In the years to come, however, Stalin's reign of terror would so pervade Soviet life that even family members would betray one another to save themselves. I discussed this thought with Father and Mother, who had never been very willing to talk about anything political. They began to confide in me, but only to a limited extent, believing that the less I knew the safer I would be.

I did discover, however, that during the rise to power of the Soviet regime after the Revolution of 1917, my parents had lived in constant fear. Because my mother had come from a family of clergy, we had many religious artefacts in our possession—various editions of the Bible and numerous icons, amongst other things. Marxism propounds the view that since 'religion is the opiate of the masses' it is not only outmoded and unnecessary, but also subversive. Under Soviet rule, religion was not only discouraged but suffered the most severe repression. In the early 1920s, when it was clear that the Bolsheviks would triumph over their adversaries, Father had secretly taken every item associated with religion and buried it deep in the forest. He understood me completely when I told him of my revulsion at betraying Esenin.

'My crime is much worse, dear one,' he said. 'I have betrayed God. But what is a father to do?' he continued. 'Surely God would want me to protect my family. And whatever else they may be able to do, they can't stop my believing in what I want.'

The Russian people have had a bitter history and endured many invasions. My family believed that we would endure this evil as well, even though the enemy was from within Russia and more evil than any before. The instinct to survive is very strong in the Russian people and so it was with me. The end of my schooldays thus marked the beginning of my awakening to the true nature of the blight that had descended on my country.

In due course I received my leaving certificate in 1932, aged eighteen, although my report stated that I had a tendency towards individualism and was not entirely disposed towards collectivism. I did well academically, achieving a high pass in all my subjects except mathematics, which I loathed and barely passed.

Finally the time came for the graduation ball. Mother had made me a beautiful dress. My first party dress! She found some lace in a local market and stood in a queue for two days to buy it for me, trading a pair of her shoes for it. Darling Mama. She only had that one pair of shoes for going out and an old worn-out pair for everyday. How I loved her. Still, the selfishness of youth didn't allow guilt to mar my happiness. I pirouetted around the house, singing at the top of my voice. I had set my long hair in rags the night before and now it cascaded thickly down my back. How wonderful my life was! Even Alec, usually totally uninterested in balls and dresses, commented rather dryly that I looked quite pretty. I had written some lyrics for the occasion and one of the teachers wrote the music to accompany them. The school choir presented the piece during the evening. It was a success. I was a success! Even though there was no special boy in my life, I returned home tired and happy, having danced every dance. On the horizon the dawn was breaking and ahead, life was waiting. Long, full of joy and happiness, full of promise... Farewell school! Welcome a wonderful future!

CHAPTER THREE

My parents had already mapped out my future career path. They gave me two choices—enrol in either the Institute of Philosophy, Literature and History in Moscow, or the Faculty of Medicine in Smolensk. I was interested in both choices, but it was medicine that appealed to me more. I also didn't want to leave my family to go to Moscow, which was many kilometres away.

I had often accompanied my uncle to his clinic where he was the Assistant Professor. I followed him on his rounds and he tutored me in diagnostic medicine. However, in Russia the entrance examinations for university consisted of all the subjects taken at secondary school. Since I had always struggled with mathematics I sought permission from my parents to spend a year in preparation to come to grips with it, especially since I had failed the subject in year nine and had had to sit a re-examination—although the circumstances had been rather unusual, to say the least.

My schoolfriend Zhenya had suggested we go to the monthly ballroom dance at the local hall on the evening before the mathematics examination. I was very glad to do so after a whole year of dreary studies. Everybody would be there. I changed quickly into my only non-school outfit, a skirt and blouse, and Zhenya and I were off. Near our lodgings grew some flowers. I broke off a bunch of blossoms, putting them up to my face before pinning them to my blouse. Something stuck to my cheek. Thinking it was a petal, I lifted it off and put it to my nose. A sharp pain suddenly shot through me—it wasn't a petal, it was a bee, and it had stung me right on the tip of my nose. My eyes flooded with tears and I screamed like a madwoman.

'Zhenya, take out the sting!' But Zhenya was killing herself laughing. Within half an hour my face was transformed into a hideous mask—swollen and deformed. Worst of all was that no one believed it had happened by accident. They all thought I had planted the bee on my nose deliberately so that I would have an excuse to miss the examination. Uncle wanted me to do the exam but I stated categorically that I would rather repeat a whole year than appear anywhere with a face like a football. He went to the school principal, who was also sceptical that it was an accident, to ask that my exam be deferred. Out of respect for my uncle he allowed me to postpone the exam for two weeks, by which time, fortunately, the swelling had subsided and I managed to pass.

And now, were I to enrol in medicine, I would be faced with the unfortunate prospect of once again having to do battle with my nemesis. Notwithstanding my liking of medicine, there was another, deeper love which had been in my heart since childhood—the theatre. This calling appealed to me even more strongly, but how would I ever be able to get my parents' permission? I had tried talking about it with them but they didn't want to listen. They were convinced that a career as an actor would be full of difficulties, disappointments, bitter tears and poverty.

'We don't even know if you have any talent, whereas medicine is dependable—it will always provide for you…' Their words echoed on and on. Privately I knew that I would never be worn down by any argument, however valid.

That same year, 1932, our school in Roslavl burnt down in a fire started accidentally by the school's general assistant. He had left for the night after tending the fire in the oven. Father had gone to the club for a general meeting and Mother, Alec and I were in bed. Somehow some embers from the fire must have got onto the wooden floor. We awoke to the acrid smell of smoke to find the fire well underway, having already engulfed the classrooms, and now almost upon us. It was already too late to get out through the doors, so we broke the windows and escaped in our nightclothes, in bare feet. It was impossible to rescue any of our belongings and by the time Father and the townspeople arrived, the school was totally ablaze.

While the school was being rebuilt and the few things not destroyed by the fire were being collected, our family moved into another house in Roslavl. I went to work at the local publishing collective as a proofreader. The printery produced six local newspapers and I proofread all six. The work was reasonably interesting but it was night work. I began about three in the afternoon and finished just before dawn, when the first editions came out. Neither Mother nor Father could get school positions because the school year had already begun and all positions were filled. So Mother taught literature and Father taught mathematics as home tutors, preparing students for entry to university.

That year the local theatre hosted presentations by a number of touring companies and my brother Alec and I never missed an opportunity to see these productions. Even though Alec had no inclination to make theatre his career choice, preferring literature and language studies, he had always shared my love of the art and was a very talented amateur actor, often participating in my school productions. Since I now had a job, I had my own money to buy tickets so Alec and I went to see productions of Ibsen, Gorky, Tolstoy, the operettas of Lehar and Kalmasun, amongst others, and the magical world of illusion overtook me. Bewitched by the artistry of so many wonderful people, I became totally convinced that only the theatre would give me that satisfaction of creative endeavour that I had desired since childhood. I decided I would embark upon a theatre career no matter what, and fate moved to meet me in that desire.

Meanwhile I was involved in the mundane task of proofreading in order to make a living. When I arrived at the printery each afternoon I would find the individual printed columns which required checking before a first composite proof could be run off. There was constant communication between proofreader, compositor and editor while the tedious work of newspaper production went on. This was in the days of monotype, when each individual letter and word space had to be placed in the printing block by hand. By early morning, only the compositor and proofreader were left. If any mistakes were discovered at this stage of production the compositor would actually have to climb into the machinery, carefully locate the offending piece of lead type on the typeset block, remove it and replace it with the appropriate one.

During this process, there would be a two- to three-hour period during which the proofreader was not required. I used this time to go to the theatre, but I could only do so when the procedure ran smoothly. If, for example, anyone happened to drop the typesetting blocks, they had to be reconstructed letter by letter, punctuation mark by punctuation mark, and everyone's schedule was totally altered. On more than one occasion, an urgent message would reach me in the theatre audience to return at once—the usual 'emergency' had occurred, and I was needed to assist with this manual recomposing.

As well as all that, the work of a proofreader during Stalin's regime carried with it some special difficulties and dangers. As I said, the type was all manually composed, as was the rolling-out process, whereby ink was distributed across the blocks and pressed out onto the proofing paper. This often involved smudging and consequently the possibility of illegible or distorted characters, so mistakes were frequent and seldom picked up immediately—sometimes not at all. If the mistake changed the nature of the political message involved—and in those days virtually every sentence had political import—it could mean a forced sojourn of several years in Siberia. My predecessor in the position had missed just such a mistake. Instead of 'the historical decisions of the Party', he had inadvertently allowed 'the hysterical decisions of the Party' to be printed. He was, of course, immediately dismissed from the position and arrested. He simply disappeared and was not heard of again. No one dared to ask about him—he simply didn't exist and it was safest to assume he had never existed. There was thus a premium on care and accuracy, as well as on having a keen eye.

Besides that, in the Soviet Union, our supposed Eden of freedom and justice, no one knew what tomorrow would bring. Any one of the Party leaders whose praises were being sung today might be arrested overnight. All was well if the editors around the country were informed of the change. Then late at night they would ring the production staff directly, who would rush to the printery, stop the presses, and amend the relevant articles. But if Moscow didn't contact the regional media, was it Moscow that would have to answer for the consequences? Not at all. The editors, together with the production staff, would be labelled traitors and saboteurs and have to suffer the usual dreadful consequences, irrespective of their total innocence of the political changes that had transpired.

However, most Russian editors, having become somewhat skilled at deciphering the machinations of the Moscow leadership—that is, Stalin—would be aware that, in general, prior to the removal of a high-ranking Party official, certain indicators would have been circulated to give some sort of credibility to the forthcoming denunciation of that official. Accordingly, careful and forward-looking editors of provincial newspapers would reproduce articles from Moscow papers word for word, without editorial comment or amendment, in an attempt to protect themselves from the dangerous uncertainties of Party politics.

There were many other dangers involved in the world of newspapers. All editors were members of the CPSU (Communist Party of the Soviet Union) and many were appointed solely on the basis of their long-term Party membership, not because of any editorial skills or qualifications. As a rule, most of them were, in fact, poorly educated. The newspaper editorial was generally written directly by the editor. So, on the proofreader's desk would appear an editorial, not only grammatically but also stylistically incorrect. It required major amendments. The grammatical errors were generally easy to deal with but not so the stylistic ones. The proofreader had to hold over the production staff for an extra hour or two while the editorial was being rewritten. Who had to pay for the overtime? You might think the newspaper itself. Not so! I, in fact, had enormous arguments with the editor over his insistence that any overtime due to the production staff caused by the delay in amending the editorial should come directly out of my own wages. It was futile to insist that my job entailed the production of correct copy and that I was not responsible for the inferior quality of the original article.

'Why do you think this phrase or sentence is ungrammatical?' the editor would ask me. I could hardly reply that he should go back to school and learn the basics of the Russian language. He would have sacked me immediately, at the very least. On one occasion I became so frustrated I appealed to my colleagues from a nearby newspaper.

They wrote to Moscow. One Friday, in *Pravda*, there appeared a special article called 'The Responsible Proofreader and the Irresponsible Editor', which detailed my difficulties on this matter. My editor was carpeted by Party officials, and given a warning: leave your grammatically capable proofreader alone and give her the opportunity to do the job she is properly qualified to do, and either learn the Russian language yourself or resign. After that I commanded some respect and authority. But the editor told me, 'Don't worry—I'll get even with you for this.' Fortunately, I left the position before he could keep his word! The Russia of the early 1930s was no place to become the target of a Communist official's enmity.

The nation at this time was faced with ever-darkening clouds of terror. Stalin's personal reorganisation of the Soviet Union's resources involved successive Five Year Plans—but these suffered many industrial and agricultural setbacks. The most significant of these was the resistance by the peasant proprietors, known as the kulaks, to enforced collectivisation. Stalin's response to the resistance was brutal and murderous. Between 1932 and 1933, opposition to his will resulted in death by execution or forced starvation of up to ten million people.

Ukrainian peasants appeared on our doorstep, having walked hundreds of kilometres in search of food, and their stories were filled with the most dreadful and horrific experiences imaginable. These included cannibalism. We ourselves were so short of food we were forced to make bread of a kind by crushing dried grass seeds into a rough flour. The bread was black and really heavy. Newspapers spoke of the happy life of the Russian citizen while we knew only too well the real truth—a life of hunger, terror and death.

I remember a very young man came to our house one day. We woke to a cold and bitter morning. Everything was covered in frost. The ground looked as though it were made up of little icicles. The trees appeared ghostly and stunted. A chill wind was blowing. A figure approached, bent almost double to the wind. He stumbled to our house, but was so weak he collapsed near the front doorstep.

'Oh my God, poor soul,' cried Mama. 'Quick, Gavril, take him in and warm him near the stove.'

Father rushed to the figure slumped in the doorway and carried him into our little kitchen. Mama gave him some bread and milk, which he devoured in seconds. Alec and I stood at the back of the room, frightened by the half-crazed look in the stranger's eyes. Between racking sobs he told of the starvation endured by his family. We listened in horror. At times, Mother took Alec and me and hugged us against her, putting her hands over our ears. After months of hunger, the first to die was his little sister—the surviving members of his family ate her. But his mother and father and two brothers died of hunger anyway; only he was left. Finally he had come this far and was asking for some kind of food, any kind at all. He stayed with us for a week or so and then, with the meagre provisions packed for him by Mother, went away. I never knew where. I saw this with my own eyes.

I remember how my father ground his teeth and said, 'Those bastards, those incredible bastards,' while my mother, as pale as a sheet, said, 'Be quiet, be quiet. Even the walls have ears. Be quiet for the sake of the children.'

That entire year passed very quickly. I had been studying very hard and all too soon the time had come when I had to sit for my university entrance exams. But in what faculty should I enrol—was it to be Medicine or Theatre? I was no closer to deciding.

A troupe from the Smolensk Regional Drama Theatre was playing in Roslavl at that time. After much deliberation I decided to try my luck with them. I harnessed some courage and went to the Railway Workers' Club where the troupe was holding auditions, although I didn't know that. I was simply going to ask if I could join them—I was really naive. A rehearsal was under way but many of the actors not involved at that moment were sitting in the garden, reading, playing chess or just engaged in conversation.

I went up to one group and, stammering with fear and trepidation, asked if I could see their director. They looked me up and down and after a long silence asked me who I was and what I wanted. 'Pretty one, why do you want to see the director? Surely you can't wish to join our theatre,' they smirked good-naturedly.

I was ready to melt into the ground but with mock bravery replied, 'Yes, I do, if I possibly can.'

'Oh, without a doubt, a place will be found for someone like you. We need interesting young girls like you in our theatre. Have you seen any of our productions? Which ones did you like most of all? Did you notice me? I played V.'

'What about me? I was in…'

'And how about me? I was in…' I didn't know what to say to all this. I was perplexed by their attitude.

'Hey, listen—leave the poor child alone!' said an elderly gentleman approaching the group that had surrounded me.

'Don't pay any attention to them, dear child. They're all no-hopers and hangers-on. The director is currently at the rehearsal but will soon be free, and then I'll introduce you to him.'

I recognised this man as an actor whom I had seen in many classical roles, and told him that his performances had impressed me enormously by the depth of feeling he conveyed and the artistic mastery he commanded. He was very flattered.

'Do your parents know of your intentions?' he asked.

'Well, that's the trouble,' I said. 'They don't approve. They want me to be a doctor.'

'And you, of course, don't want to be one,' he replied.

'It's not that I don't want to be one—it's just that I want to be in the theatre even more. The theatre can't be compared to anything else. It's magical, it's some kind of sorcery.'

'My dear,' he said, 'in the first place, it's primarily just plain hard work—and that work lasts your whole life. Occasionally it brings rewards, and at times it doesn't, but if it does, then the rewards are sweet and intoxicating—that's true. But look, there's a rehearsal break now. I'll find the director for you.' He went over to one of the people who had emerged from the theatre and then called me over.

'This is our artistic director, Boris Nikolayitch Zaitstein, and this is Lilya. I'll leave you two alone now. Goodbye Lilya, and good luck.'

Boris Nikolayitch sat on a bench and beckoned me to do likewise. He said that at the moment he was busy, as the break was only a twenty-minute one, but tomorrow I could come again between eleven and twelve and then we could discuss things in detail. He wanted me to prepare a piece—a short poem or a prose reading—and he would give me his opinion. Needless to say I was in a terribly excited and agitated state all day. That night I couldn't sleep. I chose one of Blok's poems for my selected piece.

The following day, with my heart ready to leap out of my chest, I returned to the club's garden. I again met the hangers-on from the previous day and they took me to see the artistic director. They encouraged me but I felt even more apprehensive. Surely I wouldn't have to do my reading in their presence, I thought. Fortunately Boris Nikolayitch understood my feelings and chased everyone out of the hall.

'Well, what have you prepared for me?' he asked.

'A poem by Blok,' I replied.

'No, my dear, you are not ready to read Blok,' he said. 'Blok won't be for some time yet. So, for now, read me one of Krilov's fables, "The Fox and the Raven."' (Krilov rendered Aesop's fables in poetic form, in Russian, and these are widely known throughout the country.)

"The Fox and the Raven"?' I exclaimed, disappointed. 'But that's for children. That's not interesting.'

'Not interesting? On the contrary, it's extremely interesting. If you don't know the poem, here's the book. You can read directly from that.'

'No, it's all right, I remember it from childhood days.' I recited the first four lines of the poem.

'Wait, wait, my dear,' exclaimed Boris Nikolayitch. 'So where's the raven? I don't see the raven.'

'I don't know,' I said, somewhat sullenly.

'Exactly. You don't know. That's because you don't think. Don't you get it? You yourself are the raven. The raven is stupid, isn't it? But I can't see any stupid raven. I see you saying words, but I want to see a raven, an actual raven. And that raven is you. Now, make yourself feel like a stupid but happy raven, contented because it was lucky enough to come by a piece of cheese.'

I made my eyes as big and round as I could, and started again. When I got to a particular line, I stretched it out as awkwardly as I could to indicate the raven's stupidity. When I got to 'pauses to consider', I tilted my head sideways and closed one eye, as if contemplating where to put the cheese for safekeeping to eat later on in comfort. But 'with the cheese in her mouth' I pronounced with my teeth closed, trying to mimic the raven's problem in having to hold onto the cheese with its beak.

Boris Nikolayitch laughed at my revised attempt and said, 'Well done, girl. You learn quickly. Now do the fox.'

'At just this time a fox was running past.' This line I read in the manner of a storyteller. On the line 'The fox smells the cheese, the cheese beckons the fox', I began to smell the cheese and made a glint in my eye to show the fox's plan to obtain the cheese.

When I had finished the whole piece Boris Nikolayitch said, 'There you have the first lesson of the actor's craft. Now listen carefully to what I have to say. Of course I could include you in the company right now, based on your looks and youth and so on, but that path is long and uncertain. You have to go to school first. That will be the correct path to take. There they will teach you to understand what you are doing and why you are doing it. To go on stage without going to school first is like trying to read without learning the alphabet. This year a theatrical institute is opening in Smolensk with acting and directing departments. I will be one of the teachers in the acting department. Besides me there will be some of the best actors from the stage and directors from the National Institute of Dramatic Art. Present yourself for the entrance examination, and I guarantee you will get in, do well and have an interesting career. The course lasts for four years. What do you say? As for your parents, I will speak to them personally. I promise to convince them—is it a deal?'

'Yes, it's a deal. But what will I live on?' I said rather forlornly, saying goodbye to my dreams of becoming an instant actress.

'You will receive a stipend, perhaps rather small, but manageable. Sometime you can get some work on the radio. Once you're there, things will sort themselves out. Put in your application. I'm a member of the enrolment panel, and I promise to give you my support, even though the number of applicants will be very large. You have a very good chance.'

'But four years is a long time,' I said.

'A long time? No, my dear. That's not a long time, and it's not really four years anyway. You will have to spend the rest of your life learning and working at your craft if you want to achieve mastery. But think very carefully before you step onto this road, because it is a very long and difficult one. You will need to acquire bravery and patience and be prepared not only for success but for adversity as well. You will fall, get up again and continue to strive for the heights of artistry. Don't lose faith in yourself and above all, love what you are doing, love your art, and then this thorny road may become a road of flowers, and give you moments of such pure joy as no other person on earth ever enjoys. Let the theatre become the meaning of your whole life, now and forever. If you ever happen to achieve some success, don't lose your head, don't rest content with it, don't think that you are now a complete master of your art. Remember that if you have played a part well, even extremely well, it is still possible and in fact necessary to play it even better. Then and only then you will be able to say yes, I am a professional actress. For now, go home and relax. I will see you at enrolment time. I have to go to rehearsal now. The actors are waiting while I am here romanticising about things. Would you like to see the rehearsal?'

'Oh yes, if I could, very much so,' I said.

'Then come with me.'

All the actors were gathered together. I recognised many whom I'd seen in public performances. I found a spot in a corner and tried to be inconspicuous. The men looked at me with good will, but the women were rather antagonistic and gave me funny looks—or so it seemed to me at the time. I huddled even more into the corner and focused my gaze on the stage.

They were doing a run-through of *Guilty Without Guilt*. The actors all seemed like gods to me, capable of performing miracles, but Boris Nikolayitch sat with a grim, dour expression, letting forth with highly critical, sarcastic, even poisonous comments from time to time.

What does he expect of them? I thought they were acting marvellously. But Boris Nikolayitch suddenly jumped onto the stage, grabbed a stool which he flung onto the floor and yelled, 'You've messed up everything. You've smeared my mise-en-scènes all over this stage. Rubbish! Amateurs!'

To Neznamov, the hero of the play, he said, 'Why are you flapping your arms about like a windmill? Do you think by doing that you can make me believe you? And you, Kruchinina [the heroine], what's with you? Why are you spinning around on that chair as if you were on an anthill? Why doesn't your face express anything? It's like an underdone pancake. From the beginning—the whole scene from the beginning.'

But at this stage Kruchinina raised her voice, and almost crying, called out, 'I am spinning because I have needed to go to the toilet for the last half hour but I am too afraid to ask you because you are so angry today.'

Boris Nikolayitch laughed and said, 'Well go, then. Let's have a ten-minute break.'

I didn't wait for the continuation of the rehearsal and sneaked away. Boris Nikolayitch had so alarmed me with his treatment of the actors that even much later, as a student of the academy, I tried to avoid being in his group. I felt that if he yelled at me that way I would die of shame on the spot and be unable to continue. But the actors had behaved as if nothing unusual had happened. They walked up to Boris Nikolayitch, laughed and joked with him as if this was the way they interacted all the time. I didn't even say goodbye, and went home in a sort of daze. Arriving home I collapsed into bed. Fortunately it was the weekend and I didn't have to go to my newspaper work that day. I slept like a corpse until eleven the next morning.

August was approaching. In all tertiary institutions across the country, entrance examinations were taking place. The academic year began on 1 September. To enrol, one needed to apply to the Admissions Committee. How was I to tell my family that I had decided to go to drama school instead of medical school? I wouldn't get their permission anyway, and I might miss the opportunity to lodge my request for admission. Moreover, what would I do if I failed the entrance exam? No matter how hard I thought about it, I couldn't come up with any solution to the problem. In the end I decided not to say anything, but simply do the exam. Only if I got in would I confront my family with the fact that I had passed the entrance exam to the new Institute of Dramatic Art in Smolensk. I was certain of one thing—I wanted to be an actress more than anything else on earth. I submitted my application and waited to learn the time and date of my exam. What will be, will be. Finally the day arrived…the day that would determine my future forever.

CHAPTER FOUR

The windows of the recently built Institute sparkled like mirrors. The Institute beckoned and enticed me, but at the same time frightened me with its uncertainties and fear of the unknown. What awaited me on this road? Failures, tears, disappointments, intrigues? Or perhaps success and fame? Full of hopes and anxieties, I crossed its threshold.

It was a beautiful building. Roman columns greeted me at the entrance to a large and majestic foyer. The auditorium, just off the foyer, was full of hopeful young people. On the first-day about a hundred were to be examined. As I discovered later, there were about 700 applicants, 80 of whom were to be enrolled in the first-year intake. It was decided to divide these into two classes. The second-, third- and fourth-year enrolments were partly drawn from overcrowded courses elsewhere. The examinees were called up in alphabetical order. Some came out quickly from the examination room; others took somewhat longer. The emerging students related some strange things. I was tired and hungry and becoming rather pessimistic about the outcome.

At last, around 3 pm, I heard my name called. By now suffering dreadfully from nerves, I entered the examination room. Near the wall was a long table with many people seated at it. Of them I recognised only Boris Nikolayitch Zaitstein and one of the leading actors of the Smolensk Drama Theatre. Boris Nikolayitch winked at me like an old acquaintance. I responded with a weak, rather limp smile. They started to ask me questions. Why did I want to enrol at this particular institute? What plays had I seen? What plays had I read? Who was my favourite author?

Apparently my answers were to the panel's satisfaction as one of them said, 'You are a well-read and well-educated young lady. Who are your parents?'

Before I could answer, Boris Nikolayitch suddenly said, 'Yes. But she doesn't like Krilov—she only likes Blok.'

I was ready to fall through the floor. Everyone laughed and I was directed to turn my back on them. Then I was asked how many people were at the table. I thought about it, imagined the scene, and said, 'Fourteen.'

'Very close,' said Boris Nikolayitch. Then he asked, 'What am I wearing?'

'A suit,' I answered.

'What colour?'

'Grey!'

'Good. Now, please light the stove.'

'What stove?' I said. 'I don't see any stove.'

'We know that,' he said, 'but you do see a stove, don't you? So bring some wood and light it, please.' I realised what they wanted and, as well as I could, carried out the undertaking, even managing to burn my finger on the imaginary fire. I was pleased with that little improvisation.

'And now, show us some movement in keeping with this music.' One of them sat at the piano and started playing in different rhythms, sometimes fast, sometimes slow. 'Do you dance?'

'Yes,' I answered.

'Okay then, show us how you dance a waltz or a tango.'

I was feeling a little bolder by now. 'Excuse me, but it's a bit hard on my own—would you mind?' I asked, beckoning the person who asked me the question. Everyone laughed again, but he walked over, bowed and we started to dance a waltz. The others began to make jokes.

'Enough, enough! Look at him, will you. Trying to impress the young lady.'

The atmosphere had lost its tension and was now very friendly. Then they asked me to sight-read an unfamiliar and difficult text. Interrupting me halfway through, they said that was enough.

'Thank you. You are accepted.'

I couldn't believe it. I was partly overjoyed and partly in shock. From amongst the hundred or so applicants on day one only two men and two women were accepted—and I was one of them. I thanked the examiners and said something insipid, like 'I won't let you down.' One of them responded with, 'You may live to curse us all one day.' They reminded me that I still had to sit for exams in geography, history, literature, biology and, of course, that old faithful—political economy. Fortunately I was able to gather my wits and the exams went by very easily and successfully.

There was of, course, one more obstacle to be overcome. I had not yet told my parents. They still thought I intended pursuing a medical career. Just as he had promised, Boris Nikolayitch Zaitstein had discussed my theatrical aspirations with them, but the results had been inconclusive. My father had grudgingly relented to the extent that if I were unsuccessful in gaining admission to medical school or were to fail the first year of the course, then I would have his blessing to choose this other so-called career. As the time for applications to the medical school to be lodged drew nearer, and I still hadn't told them, I found it more and more difficult to muster up the courage to broach the subject. Now there was no way out. I had been accepted at the Institute and the theatre was the future I wanted more than anything. My parents had to be told.

As I had expected, Mother took the news fairly well. She simply wanted whatever was best for me and, though she shed a few tears at first, finally agreed that my passion for the theatre was a good indication that this was the path fate had decreed for me. Father was very angry. According to him acting was not a serious career, and unreliable at the best of times. Moreover, he and Mother would not be able to support me and I would have to depend almost entirely on a very modest student stipend. This didn't worry me at all, I told them, as I had already realised I would need to supplement my wages with part-time jobs. Father kept insisting that the difficulties of getting through Drama School would continue afterwards.

'Acting is not a proper vocation,' he kept saying. 'What do you need to become a professional actress for? You've been an actress ever since we can remember.'

'That's just it, Papa,' I said. 'Acting isn't just a career I want to pursue for the rest of my life. It is my life. I can't imagine doing anything else.'

Father finally resigned himself to my decision. 'No, in all truth, neither can I, my precious one,' he said slowly. Then looking across at Mother, and allowing a smile to cross his face, he admitted, 'Neither can we.'

I hugged and kissed my beloved parents. My joy was now complete. Not only was I able to follow my dream, I had my parents' blessing to do so.

'Someday you'll be proud of me,' I said, drying a few tears of joy. But when my parents replied as one, 'We don't have to wait for that, dearest one,' there was no holding back the flood.

We spent the rest of the evening lovingly reminiscing about old times—especially all the pranks and 'stage productions' I had been responsible for. I kept apologising for having been such a worry to my parents, but they dismissed it as normal childhood energy and fancifulness. My parents cherished their children and we both loved and respected them. Despite being hungry and poor and living in a country under the sinister shadow of Stalinism, I could not imagine being any happier than I was at that moment.

And so, on the morning of 1 September 1934, student of the Smolensk Institute of Dramatic Art, Ludmila Makarova, aged all of twenty years, ascended the steps of her future alma mater. What youngster has not experienced that feeling of freshness mingled with anxiety as they start a new school year or go from primary to secondary school? Neatly done hair, clean clothes and shoes; freshly sharpened pencils; a new notebook with crisp new margins ruled in on the first few pages and one's name on the cover in the neatest of neat handwriting. Well, that was me. A whole new world lay before me and I was desperate to explore and embrace it.

There were thirteen disciplines to be undertaken: Acting, Voice, Narrative, Technique, Dance and Rhythm, Theatre History, History of Fine Arts, Make-up, Russian Language and Literature, German, History of the CPSU, Political Economy and Sport. Lectures were from 9 am to 3 pm. In the evening and on Saturdays we undertook practical classes in groups, pairs or individually. The only break we had was Sundays. The instructors were actors and directors of the Smolensk Regional Theatre and the Government Institute of Theatrical Art. Many of them had the best possible qualifications, as they had studied under or even worked with the great Constantin Sergeievitch Stanislavsky and/or with his collaborator, Vladimir Nemirovitch-Danchenko. So our mentors and teachers were all intimately acquainted with the outstanding work of the foremost authorities on the theatre in Russia and we were very lucky to gain the benefits of their experience and training.

I immediately realised I had embarked upon the right path. This was what I had dreamed about, what I loved to do so much; I knew it was a love that would never fade away. I was not mistaken. Even now, over sixty years later, for me the theatre remains a place where miracles are performed. The nature of this miracle is transformation. I lived many different lives in the theatre. I have been a duchess, a witch, a prostitute in Gorky's *Lower Depths*, a snow queen, and the grandmother in *The Trees Die Standing* by Alesandro Cassena. Who haven't I been? Many different characters have I internalised; many different souls, both good and evil, have I uncovered for the audience in this house of wonders called the theatre. Is it not a miracle that the thoughts, feelings and actions of fictional beings who have never existed can so affect the everyday existence of real beings, their actual feelings, actions and thoughts; can force them to re-evaluate their outlook, their lives and their beliefs? I have always profoundly disagreed with a tendency in Western culture to treat the theatre quite often purely as a vehicle of entertainment rather than an extremely important means of education, helping formulate and define human thoughts and relationships. But the meaning of the theatre is inexhaustible. One could speak about it endlessly. Many people have devoted their lives to it. I was one of them, and I have no regrets.

Within the walls of the school I spent the best years of my life. They were years of great hopes, unlimited expectations, bitter tears and fiery achievements. Little by little I came to understand the movement of the human spirit during the most complex moments of a person's life; the mysterious reasons for the actions of individuals; and at last the treasured ability to express this understanding through words and actions, even silent looks and gestures.

It does not come easily or quickly and sometimes not at all. However, sometimes it is illuminated for you and you begin to feel easy and comfortable on stage. Within you, some sort of magical power is evoked which affects the people in the audience, causing them to share your thoughts and emotions and live through what you are living. Everything you do is the way it should be and this gives you inexpressible satisfaction. You may be speaking or silent, you may be looking at the floor or standing with your back to the audience and you are not afraid or anxious. Your arms and legs don't bother you and your body is composed but not tense. Every word is thoughtful and expressive—you live the character. You are Nora or Maria Stewart or Anna Karenina. For these few moments of such sublime illumination one does not regret so many long years of hard work.

But an actor can only be said to have achieved mastery when such movements come not by accident but whenever the actor sets foot on stage—so teaches Stanislavsky and so I believe to this day. To achieve this level of skill is only possible through constant and untiring work. At the Institute I understood that talent alone was not enough. One had to also achieve technical mastery; and that was a kind of science. And just like students at high school struggling to understand the intricacies of the Periodic Table of Elements (which in Soviet Russia was always referred to as Mendeleev's Table) or trying to cope with those confounded logarithms, so we at the Institute faced the same kind of confusion and frustration trying to understand the mysteries of dramatic art.

Imagine, if you will, that you have just sat through a series of classes on characterisation. You have been told that it is necessary to get inside the character; to invent a new life behind the fictional one, so that you can believe in the role you are undertaking and not merely pretend to be that character. Very well. You internalise and invent. You think you have become the character. Now for the practical demonstration of what you have learnt. The instructor asks you to perform a short scene in which the character is, let us imagine, extremely angry. You dig down into your own feelings and let forth with such real anger that you actually tremble and shake. You are really pleased with yourself and the other students are very impressed. Surely the teacher must be impressed as well? Wrong.

'What do you think you are doing? Who told you that Ludmila Makarova was in this play? I did not ask to see an enraged Ludmila Makarova, though I must say that your anger was very believable. No. I asked to see an enraged Nora, our heroine—remember? Ludmila, you are an actress, yes? So why did you forget all the mise-en-scènes you were meant to follow?'

'I'm sorry. I got caught up in the role and in the anger so much that…'

'…that you lost control! Precisely my point. But control is what you must have even while you are the character. You must be both simultaneously. Understand?'

Of course most of us didn't really understand at first because the task seemed impossible. If you were conscious of yourself as an actor on stage you had difficulty really getting into the role. Laughter seemed forced. Tears came only with intense concentration. It was all too artificial-looking. On the other hand, becoming the character as fully as possible made it difficult to concentrate on the technicalities of stage movement, keep to the script and so on. How could we ever hope to perfect this seemingly insurmountable paradox of a dual life, we asked our instructors.

'Perfect it? Who said anything about perfecting it, my dears? My goodness! No one has ever done that. Haven't we told you over and over again that it is a lifelong learning process that you merely improve upon for the rest of your professional life? And that is only if you are a true artist with genuine ability. I can say with complete confidence that many of you will leave here believing that you are a finished product, as many have done before you. I can only advise that you will be mistaken, for if you do indeed ever reach the end of your artistic development, from that moment on you will begin to stagnate. We do, however, understand your perplexity. It is certainly true that in reality one person cannot be two people at the same time, and we are not asking you to perform this impossible task. But one can, with intense work in learning the techniques involved, artistically simulate the presentation of one life on stage while remaining totally in control of this simulation. After all, you are, as a matter of fact, the actor—not the character.'

Indeed, as time went on, this seemingly paradoxical and extremely demanding duality became easier and easier to evoke and sustain. There was indeed a profound difference between my real tears, when tragedy entered my own life, and theatrical tears, which all good actors can turn on like a tap whenever the occasion demands it. But this difference is invisible to the audience because it is not a physiological difference but a psychological one. They believe in the tears and they are moved by the accompanying emotions. In fact the audience is as much a part of the miraculous nature of the theatre as the actors. The miracle is that although the audience knows it is observing a fiction, it nevertheless reacts with completely real, not fictional, emotions. And when the actor knows that this effect has been induced, there is an intense and exquisite satisfaction. It is not the self-centred satisfaction of having been successful or well liked on stage, though doubtless there are many actors for whom this is of primary importance. Rather it is a much deeper, far more profound satisfaction that transcends mere performance. It is a kind of intimate and intense bonding. The actor's humanity has bonded with that of the audience. At its very best, the theatre is a celebration of the human spirit. The actors and the audience become a blending of all that is good about human beings.

It is small wonder that I saw my life as a student of dramatic art as the most challenging and most rewarding period of my entire life. But there were more personal sides to my life at the time which evoke both bitter-sweet and tragic memories.

It was during that period that I met someone with whom I fell in love. I was 22 when we met, a slim and attractive young woman, with long, dark brown, curly hair, intelligent grey eyes and several potential suitors wanting to take me out. From the moment I saw this man, I was smitten. Extremely handsome, tall and muscular, he was one of the most talented painters in Smolensk. I met him through mutual friends in the theatre when he was designing a set for a play. I will never forget the night we met. My friends and I had decided to go to a restaurant after our performance. It was a small out-of-the-way place where the staff were friendly and, knowing our hours as actors, served us even when we came in late. We sat down and ordered drinks and *zakuski* (snacks). I didn't really drink then, or smoke, but would have a glass of whatever was ordered with my friends.

He was sitting at a table to the left of us, and I caught him looking at me when we came in. He was with a well-known theatre director whom we all knew and they seemed to be involved in an intense conversation. I was enjoying myself, laughing and joking, but couldn't help looking over in his direction. Our eyes met several times, but I thought no more about it other than to admire his appearance. His slightly haughty demeanour made him even more attractive. The women at my table gossiped about him, telling me that although he was married, he was known to have had an affair with one of the leading actresses of the Smolensk Theatre. Within twenty minutes or so, he and the director, Sergei Ivanovich, sauntered across to our table.

'May we join you?' Sergei Ivanovich asked, smiling at everyone.

'Please do,' replied Volodya, one of the actors at our table. 'Do you and Tolya know everyone here?'

'Yes, except this fascinating creature,' answered Tolya, extending his hand to me. Anatole Michaelovich Sokolov held my hand—it seemed for hours—as I melted into his gaze. At last I broke the hold, flushing and casting a quick glance around to see whether my friends had noticed anything. But everyone was talking animatedly and asking Sergei Ivanovich about his new production.

Tolya sat down next to me, pulling up a spare chair and good-naturedly asking one of the girls to move a little to make room for him. I didn't notice the drinks when they arrived, nor the food placed on the table in front of us. I was oblivious to the conversations around me. We seemed to have so much in common: love of the theatre and literature, taste in food and similar sense of humour. I knew even before he asked to see me again that I had fallen in love.

He was 36. We would meet up almost every evening, either before or after my performance. He was working just as hard on designing the set of a new production. We usually met at my little apartment in Matrosova Street, where I had moved after leaving Uncle Vanya's. In fact, it was only a few kilometres from my uncle's, just over the bridge spanning the River Dnepr. Despite moments of guilt about his wife, with whom I was slightly acquainted, I was deliriously happy and more in love than I had ever been in my life. He seemed to reciprocate all my feelings. We had been lovers for a little more than four months when I began to suffer extreme nausea and stomach pains, which I put down to ulcers from which I suffered. At first I denied that there was anything amiss, but when I began putting on weight, I made an appointment to see a doctor.

The tests ordered by the doctor confirmed my suspicions. I was eleven weeks pregnant. I had a big decision to make. I couldn't ask Tolya for help, as he was married and had a child of his own, and I didn't want to give up drama school. I didn't even consider the option of abortion. This wasn't necessarily on moral grounds; I had always dreamt of having children, even when I was a child myself. My dream had not included being a single parent, but if this was the way it was going to be, then so be it. I was ecstatic that I was going to be a mother. A week after the diagnosis, I decided to tell Tolya. We had returned to my little room after the performance as usual. I had gone to a lot of trouble to buy a bit of food and half a bottle of wine. He listened quietly while I told him my news. If he seemed a little distant, I was pretending not to notice.

My happiness very quickly turned to despair, however, when he informed me that his wife, also an actress, was being relocated to a provincial theatre in the far north. Of course he still loved me, he said, but he had already agreed to the relocation with his wife. He didn't feel he could leave her while their son was still so young. And anyway, he owed her a lot of gratitude for introducing him to many important people in the theatre who had given him work. I didn't listen to any of this. I pleaded with him not to go, to leave his wife and to stay in Smolensk with me. Between us we could make enough of a living to raise a child. I was always doing some extra work when I wasn't studying. My entreaties came to nothing. He kissed me gently for what was to be the last time and left.

I was in a daze. I couldn't believe that it had ended. I loved him so much that it physically hurt. I was convinced I couldn't live without him. The sobs racked my body. I cried all night, then fell into a tortured half-sleep. I remember dreaming that I was by a beautiful dark blue lake, so enticing that I wandered in. The water was freezing. I wanted to get out but I couldn't move. Suddenly something began pulling me down into the water. I was waist deep and going further under. 'Help, help me, Tolya! Where are you?' I screamed, as the water rose higher and higher. I was struggling to breathe, and now was taking gulps of water. My nose and throat burned. I couldn't see and my lungs were bursting. A dark form floated past me, ghastly green. It was laughing grotesquely at me. I screamed and as I did so, began losing consciousness. Obviously the dream was a metaphor for my life. Two weeks later, Tolya left Smolensk, promising to stay in touch with me. But of course, that was the last time I heard from him.

I thought of killing myself, but the thought of hurting my beloved unborn child stopped me. In utter despair, I turned to my parents. They hadn't known about the affair, as I had kept it from everyone. But I was very lucky. My family was supportive and encouraged me to go through with the pregnancy and keep my child. They would help me in any way they could. Uncle Vanya was also wonderful and visited me almost daily to ensure I was eating as well as I could in the face of the poverty we all experienced. I continued at drama school during my entire pregnancy. I couldn't stop because it would mean losing my stipend, and that was all the money I had to live on.

At that time in Russia it was common for women to be single mothers. One reason was that divorce was obtained very easily. The church had virtually disappeared from public life due to the State's suppression of religion so church weddings were a thing of the past. The State's view of marriage as an institution was in accordance with the Marxist view of private property, that is, private property was an historical aberration that had served the purpose of justifying and maintaining the personal wealth of a few and depriving the masses of their fair share. Marriage was seen as an extension of this phenomenon. Ideally, under Marxism, everyone belonged to the State, including children and spouses. So marriage ceased to be an expression of romantic attachment and became a merely legal device of little significance. The opprobrium previously associated with having a child out of wedlock simply wasn't a factor any more. Though the burden of supporting a new addition to our family was going to be severe, I revelled in my state of impending motherhood. The earlier nausea had passed, and I felt healthy and serene. I still mourned the loss of my relationship with Tolya, however, and despite what he had done to me, was still madly in love with him.

I threw myself into my work with even more passion than usual until the last month of my pregnancy, when I became very tired. In hindsight, the difficulties were enormous, but because life was extremely difficult for so many people, I saw my existence as normal. It was the way things were.

Born during one of the darkest periods of Russian history, my beautiful little girl, whom I named Ina, was my treasure. People even told me that she looked like me. I would hold her for hours, talking and singing to her. I could hardly bear being parted from her while I attended classes. Either Uncle Vanya or, when she could get to Smolensk, Mother, would look after my angel. As soon as I got home, I would run to her, covering her perfect little body with my kisses. I couldn't get enough of her. But I feared for her future with an intensity that only a parent can fully comprehend.

I was also worried about Alec. He had finished school and was contemplating his future. He was interested in literature and was going to apply to university when the new term began. But I had noticed that he'd begun drinking—not just occasionally, at family gatherings, but almost daily. He visited me in Smolensk often and I would notice a distinct smell of alcohol about him. He often asked for money, which I just didn't have to give him. Whatever stipend I received went on rent and food for Ina and me. I asked him to stop drinking so much and he always promised he would, but they were empty promises. Mother and Father had little or no influence on him either. We prayed that this was just a juvenile phase he was going through and that when he began university he would come to his senses.

In the years since my entry to Drama School, something terrible had happened to our country. I had been so happy and so full of hope in 1934, looking forward to my future in the naive hope that the excesses of Stalinism of the early 1930s would somehow fade away. But during the ensuing four years it became more and more apparent that the excesses had become a permanent feature of Soviet life. Following the imposed famine of 1932–33, Stalin continued to strengthen his power and extend his web of terror. Show trials became commonplace. The government was forever denouncing nests of 'traitors' and then conducting trials where these alleged traitors were convicted and sentenced.

The nation was faced with an ever-thickening fog of terror. These were the years of forced collectivisation, the destruction of the rural economy, and the destruction of the very basis of Russian life; the years of mass murder of Russian and Ukrainian citizens. Everywhere one looked—in the army, in the Party itself, in government and in all its agencies, in educational establishments—people were being arrested and shot or sent to concentration camps in the far north. The newspapers were full of headlines such as 'Conspirators Discovered—25 Enemies of the Nation Apprehended'.

The papers demanded the death penalty and blood, blood, blood. All this was served up as if it were on behalf of the general population, and for their good. Everyone knew it was a pack of terrible lies, fabricated by Stalin, Beria—head of the dreaded Secret Police, the NKVD or, as it is now known, the KGB—and their cronies, but everyone kept silent. Kept silent and prayed only in secret. 'Dear God, let this horror pass us by,' was a daily thought.

People lived in constant fear and dread. There was continual official encouragement to act as an informer. It was impossible to trust anybody. In Smolensk, the First Secretary of the Regional Committee of the Party was arrested—his name was Rumyantsev. The Chairman of the City Council was arrested. Kovtyukh, a hero of the Civil War, was arrested. The Army generals Uborevich, Primakis, Yakir, Yegorov and Gamarnik, and 35000 other officers, were found to be traitorous enemies of the people. Even one of the nation's highest ranking officers, Marshal Tuckachevsky, was suddenly denounced as a traitor. The country overflowed with the blood of its own people.

Just as in the days of the Spanish Inquisition, it was enough to have an anonymous informer denounce you in order to bring about your downfall, as well as that of your family and friends. Brother informed on brother, husband on wife, children on their parents. Churches were closed. Ministers were shot or sent to concentration camps in Siberia where they died of hunger or the terrible conditions. Children were raised in the corrupt atmosphere of lies, godlessness and eternal vigilance in relation to enemies of the people. Meanwhile the newspapers spewed out endless proclamations concerning the achievements and successes of the Party and of the Government under the wise direction and guidance of the Communist Party and the Father of all Nations, Joseph Stalin. Everybody was so affected by fear and mistrust that we all praised this sadistic fiend of a leader, his executioners and the murderous Party they belonged to. 'Ave Caesar, morituri te salutant.' ('Hail Caesar; those who are about to die salute you.')

The effects of the purge even reached within the walls of the Smolensk Institute of Dramatic Art. First a student named Volkovich was arrested. At 36, he was the oldest person in our course. We found out later that he was accused of being a foreign intelligence agent and of taking part in a conspiracy against the government. Specifically, he was accused of organising the derailment of the fast train, the 'Arrow', on the line between Moscow and Poland. Party members were scheduled to use this train for some occasion or other but alert patriots had found out about the plot and the disaster was averted. Such was the ridiculous nature of the accusation. How and when he could have managed to organise this, when he had to attend lectures each day like the rest of us, was of course never explained. He simply disappeared and no one ever saw him again.

Soon after his disappearance each student was systematically questioned by the NKVD. I was duly summonsed to appear before them, so on the designated day, while Uncle Vanya looked after little Ina, I entered the dreaded NKVD building. It was typical of Soviet architecture—ugly grey brick exterior, blacked-out windows, formidable wooden door guarding the entrance. I gave my name to the guard, he made a call, and an officer came downstairs and asked me to follow him. On the second floor he knocked on a door and opened it for me. I entered a large room with an enormous window. Seated with his back to the window was an NKVD officer of the security branch. I waited just inside the doorway and looked around, admiring the rich red carpet on the floor. I had never seen such a thing. There were heavy velvet curtains on the windows, a divan and some lounge chairs. The person behind the desk continued to write, paying no attention to me. At last he looked up, smiled politely and rose. He looked about 35 or a little older. He was good looking and had an extremely attractive smile. I was surprised, because I had imagined that all Secret Service police would look dour and sinister.

'Pardon my rudeness,' he said, 'but I needed to finish this paperwork urgently. Please be seated.' He moved a lounge chair over for me to sit in, opposite his desk.

'Let's get acquainted. My name is Filipov—Igor Nikolayitch. And your name is…?'

'Lilya, Lilya Makarova.'

His voice had a rich soft timbre, and I thought he must be a good singer. He took out a packet of cigarettes, offered me one, and lit one for himself.

'Thank you, I don't smoke,' I replied.

'That's good,' he said. 'It's a dreadful habit. I wish I could give it up myself but somehow can never manage to do so. Lilya—is that short for Elena?' he asked.

'No—Ludmila,' I answered.

'Aha—Ludmila. And is there a Ruslan?' (in reference to Pushkin's epic poem 'Ruslan and Ludmila').

'No, there's no Ruslan,' I said bitterly.

'Why not?' he said. 'Such a lovely girl and she can't find a Ruslan. What sort of fellows do you have at the Institute, missing out on this sort of opportunity? What idiots! Never mind. There'll be lots of Ruslans in your life yet, I'm telling you that for a fact.'

'I don't mind,' I said, rather impatiently. 'I'm perfectly happy without a Ruslan.'

'Please don't be offended, I was just joking. It's just that looking at you improved my mood. Young, pretty faces do that to me.'

'Well, you're not exactly old yourself, are you?' I retorted.

'In comparison to you, yes,' he replied. 'Everything in the world is relative, as Einstein says. You are probably no more than eighteen, are you?'

'No, you're wrong. I'm already over twenty.'

'Yes, that certainly is a very respectable age,' he responded seriously. 'And how old do you think I am?'

'Oh, about thirty-two or thirty-three,' I replied, wondering where this conversation was leading.

'You're wrong too,' he said. 'I'm almost forty.'

'You're fishing for compliments, aren't you?' I said, rather bravely. 'I'm sure you know that you look younger than your age.' As I said this, I was surprised at my own boldness. After all, this was the enemy—the NKVD, who could dispense with you by a stroke of the pen.

'Really?' He seemed genuinely surprised. 'I swear I hadn't thought that. But I'm very flattered that you think so. Apparently my wife doesn't share your view. You see, she left me.' His face seemed to darken, with a sadness apparent in his eyes. I began to feel uncomfortable, even to feel sympathy for him. I knew exactly how being left by someone you loved hurt. And he was so unlike what I had expected.

'Igor Nikolayitch, forgive me. I'm very sorry if I caused you to remember those unpleasant memories.'

'Don't worry, Lilya. I stopped feeling sorry for myself long ago. It's all in the past. You know what, tell me about yourself. Who you are, who your parents are, what you like to do, what you wish for. That will be more interesting than talking about my past, okay?'

'Igor Nikolayitch, you asked me here for some reason other than listening to my life story, didn't you?'

'Don't be too sure,' he replied. 'Your life story, if not directly then indirectly, has a bearing on the matter which we have to discuss. All right, I'm listening. Do you mind if I smoke a pipe?'

'No, please do,' I answered.

He listened attentively, without interrupting, gazing steadily into my eyes. He looked very serious. Had I not been so miserable about Tolya, I know that I would have found this man attractive.

'Well, that's it,' I concluded.

'Thank you very much,' he said. 'I wasn't mistaken when I said you were a fine young lady. I'm very pleased to have met you and that there are still people such as you in this world. I wish you every success in your career. Now please answer a few more questions and then you may go. I won't need to interrogate you a second time, even though that doesn't mean we'll never meet again. I will find some time and place to meet with you. That is, of course, if you don't mind.'

I protested, telling him that I didn't have the time to see anyone outside my studies, but he gently wore my reservations down.

'Lilya, please don't be alarmed. All I want from you is your company whenever you may have the time or the inclination. We will be friends only, if that's what you would like.'

I mumbled something about it being fine with me and left it at that.

Then he started to ask me questions about Volkovich, the student accused of being a traitor. What role did Volkovich most like to play? The hero or the villain? That is, a friend or an enemy of the Soviet Union? Did he ever say anything in opposition to the general line of the Party? Did he ever tell any anti-Soviet anecdotes—and if so, which ones? I told him that I personally had never heard such things from him. Students did not choose the roles themselves but merely played those that our instructors gave them. Then I asked, 'What was he arrested for and what will become of him? Will he be returning to the school?'

Igor Nikolayitch looked at me and sounded a humourless laugh. His tone hardened. 'You must understand that I am not in a position to discuss such things with you and, in any case, you should forget that you have ever been here. Forget it completely—understand? It's a good thing I got to interview you rather than someone else. It's best that you don't tell anyone about our conversation. Here is your release pass. Goodbye. We will meet again somehow, I'm sure. I'll phone you at the school.'

I took the pass and with a great sense of relief left the building. A few steps further on I turned around. Igor Nikolayitch was standing on a small iron balcony, looking down at me.

He did in fact call me at the school, and on more than one occasion. We went together to see a number of plays, which he enjoyed as much as I did. He also took me to restaurants. I felt that he liked me. He conducted himself very properly but was always very sensitive and somewhat withdrawn. In all respects, he was a thorough gentleman, never pressuring me to go to bed with him. He brought me flowers and small gifts and when we parted he kissed my hand. I got to like him more and more, even though I was still very cautious about allowing another man into my life.

What endeared him most to me, however, were his feelings for my Ina. He absolutely doted on my beautiful little girl and had grown to love her enormously. She, in turn, looked forward to his visits, particularly as he never arrived without something for her. She was walking now and used to run to Igor each time he entered the room.

'Dada, dada' (her version of *dyadya* which meant 'uncle'), she would gurgle delightedly as he picked her up and kissed her.

One night, as we put her to bed and sat down at the other end of the room, Igor turned to me with a serious look on his face. 'Lilya, my dear, you don't know how much joy you and Ina have brought into my life. I didn't think I could ever feel this way again after my wife left me. Would you consider marrying me so we could be a family? I would look after you and Ina so that you wouldn't have to work as hard as you do. What do you say?'

I was silent for quite a long time, remembering my last love affair and how painfully it had ended. 'Igor dearest, you know how fond I have grown of you. And Inotchka would be devastated were she never to see you again. Would you let me think it over for a while?'

'Take as long as you need, just make sure the answer is yes.' He smiled and we held each other in a long and warm embrace. I was beginning to trust this relationship because everything had begun so beautifully between us and was continuing to do so.

The reign of terror continued to affect our school. The Director was relieved of his position and in his place was appointed a Party official who knew nothing of the theatre—he was a former bathhouse keeper. The lecturer in Acting Technique was also removed for unknown reasons. Soon after that, the whole school was shut down. First-year students were simply sent home. Second- and third-year students were sorted into those who were discontinued immediately and those who could take up a place in various other dramatic schools. Of the 28 or so in my year, third year, eight of us were allowed to join other schools, four boys and three other girls beside myself. We were sent to Kalinin until the situation settled down. But in Kalinin, as in the rest of the country, the fear and suspicion felt by everybody was evident.

Our lecturer in Theatre History in Kalinin was a young man who had recently graduated from GITIS (Government Institute of Theatrical Art). His name was Avshtolis. He was very erudite—a very well-educated and talented person. He gave extremely interesting lectures but not everyone could understand him; only the best-read and best-prepared students were able to keep up with him. But soon he too was arrested and just disappeared. Of course none of us knew why. At that time, several other actors from the Kalinin Drama Theatre were also arrested. They simply disappeared, as if they had never existed. Everyone behaved as if nothing unusual had happened and no one even asked what had happened to them. No one could be sure that they themselves wouldn't disappear the next day.

At one time I asked Igor what he had meant when he told me at our first meeting, 'It's lucky that I got to interview you rather than someone else.'

He told me in the strictest confidence that some students were asked to act as informers within the ranks of the students and lecturers at the school, listening to all that the others had to say and even trying to engage them in 'provocative' or 'questionable' conversations. This included the incredibly odious technique called 'fishing', which is similar in many ways to what is nowadays known as entrapment. A person who was known to others in a group might tell a questionable joke or anecdote. It was deemed to be questionable if it in any way implied or even hinted at the suggestion that the Government was not perfect in every way, let alone that it had shortcomings. If you had listened to the joke you were now in a dilemma. If you informed on the person you could be responsible for sending an innocent victim of an evil regime to their death. However, if you didn't inform on them but someone else did, then you would most surely find yourself at the receiving end of Stalin's Siberian hospitality for failing to report a suspected enemy of the State. Of course you weren't to know that the person had, in fact, been recruited or coerced into acting in this way to entrap others. So obviously the safest policy was to be as politically discreet as possible and to assume that if anyone were stupid enough to tell questionable jokes to any but their closest confidantes, they were probably doing it deliberately to set someone up.

In retrospect it is easy to see that our self-censorship helped strengthen and perpetuate Stalin's evil regime. But there was no getting around the fact that it seemed pointless to throw away one's life for the sake of a few laughs by way of a harmless crack at the Government, which would do nothing to improve things in any event. Unfortunately the world has learnt many times over how easily ordinary, good people can be corrupted and poisoned by a corrupt and poisonous system. Luckily for me Igor had decided not to put me in that position—which of course was not one I could have declined. Nowadays it would be understood immediately as 'an offer you couldn't refuse'.

'But you're mistaken,' I told him. 'I would never inform on my comrades.'

'Don't be so sure,' he replied. 'You could have been placed in a situation such that you couldn't have declined. I know better than you how to recruit collaborators. Never say anything risky to anyone at any time.'

I never forgot his warning and never trusted anyone. It was impossible for anyone to ever provoke me into a political discussion.

My eight-month stay in Kalinin meant that I saw little of Igor over that period, but whenever I went back home for a visit we would see each other as regularly as before. I still hadn't made any decision about marriage. I cared about him a great deal, but I was still getting over the disastrous affair with Tolya. Of course I took Ina to Kalinin with me. It was difficult at first because I knew no one there, but I soon found a woman to look after her while I was at school. She was the mother of one of my colleagues and still had a little one at home, and found looking after Ina no extra burden. I was constantly concerned about my baby, however, because she was often sickly. When

I took her to the local hospital, I was told not to worry, that she was just a little under-developed physically for her age and therefore more vulnerable to the usual childhood illnesses. She was now fourteen months old. Despite the doctor's attempt to assuage my anxiety, I wasn't satisfied with this diagnosis and decided to ask Uncle Vanya to examine her as soon as I could get back to Smolensk.

I returned to Smolensk to graduate with Honours from the Institute in the spring of 1938 and immediately got a posting to the Smolensk Regional Theatre in Honour of Lenin's Komsomol. The artistic director of this theatre was himself an actor and director, V. R. Gorich. The first play he chose was by the Spanish playwright Lope de Vega, the classic *Foolish for Others, Clever for Herself.* Gorich chose this brilliant comedy as a vehicle for his wife, a young actress he wanted to make into a star. He surrounded her with young, inexperienced actors so that she wouldn't be overshadowed or upstaged.

There are two main roles in this play. One is Diana—the fool—played by Gorich's wife; the other part—Duchess Theodora—was assigned to me. This was a huge coup, to get such a noticeable and important part so early in my career. The play was an enormous success, eventually running for over two years to capacity audiences. The costumes were sumptuous, but extremely heavy: several starched petticoats, heavy velvet and brocade dresses, capes, corset, wig, crown, a hooped skirt underneath all this, and a high, stand-up, starched collar. On the days when we were required to perform two shows I would be so tired I could barely finish the second performance.

My second role was in a play called *Youth*, in which I played a fishwife. This was also a tiring part, as I had to wear lots of padding, several layers of clothes—including a sheepskin coat—and carry two heavy sacks. I also wore a woollen scarf over my head and carried a heavy basket. This play was presented in the middle of summer, when the heat could be unbearable. Sweat ran in rivulets down my face and body, gathering under my fake rubber nose and once, weighed down with sweat, my nose fell off on stage. Instead of a bulbous red nose, I had a white spot on my face. I tried to resurrect the scene by grabbing the fallen nose and sticking it in my basket. Too late—the audience had seen what I was up to and roared with laughter.

I carried off six roles in my first season, not a bad effort. My career was doing better than I had ever hoped, earning me both respect and jealousy from my colleagues. My mother saw me in two of my roles, sitting in the front row and watching me with pride. In her eyes, I was the best. I was trying to do my best for her, to let her know that her help in sending me money was being rewarded.

Roslavl, where my parents still lived, is 104 kilometres from Smolensk. Often, after a performance, I would take the night train home, just to see Mother, occasionally leaving Ina with Igor or Uncle Vanya. The next morning I would have to turn around and go back for rehearsals. Leaving her and Father was always hard and I would often break down in tears. She would always ask, 'Darling, what's wrong? What happened?'

I would reply, 'Nothing's wrong, I just miss you both terribly.'

She was always so grateful for my visits and always tried to give me everything she could, whether it was a little bit of food or some money that she managed to put away for me and my baby.

My beautiful Ina was now almost eighteen months old, but she was still a sickly child due to the very poor conditions under which we lived. I tried my hardest to give her milk and any other nutritious food I could, even though it meant I often went hungry myself. Unfortunately, I had been unable to breastfeed her since she was a few months old. Uncle Vanya would always try and bring something extra for us to eat, but he didn't have much either. Such things as diet supplements, vitamins and tonics weren't to be found anywhere, so we had to rely only on the food we consumed.

Later that year, Uncle Vanya fell ill, suffering a stroke that paralysed his left side. He had to spend six months in the same hospital in which he worked as Assistant Professor of Medicine. When he was released, he was no longer able to work as a doctor—even though he could walk somehow, his left leg and arm remained paralysed. My darling mother was also constantly unwell due to high blood pressure. Existing medications just weren't effective in combating such a simple problem.

Uncle Vanya tried to help me look after Ina while I was at work at the theatre, but he was physically very frail and living in conditions as destitute as my own. Russia was suffering intensely under Stalin's purges of 1936–38. Hunger was rife throughout the country and countless innocent people starved to death. Ina became even more unwell. She suffered constantly from diarrhoea, which brought on bouts of severe dehydration. She needed medicine and nutritious food—neither of which was available. The hospitals had no medicine and there was almost no food to be had at the shops. You could stand in a queue all day and finally, when it was your turn at the counter, the shop assistant would say, more often than not, 'Sorry, nothing left.'

I watched my baby—my little girl—become weaker and weaker. In desperation, I tried everything, but there were just no medical supplies, even on the black market. It was a Friday night. I raced home to see Ina, who had been ill when I had to leave for the theatre. Uncle Vanya was with her.

'Lilya, I've been putting cold compresses on her all day. She has a high temperature, I'm afraid,' he told me. 'My darling girl, it's up to God now.'

Nooo! No! I screamed silently. This can't be happening. Not to Ina. She hasn't even lived yet. No. It's so unfair. I held her in my arms, praying to God, making all kinds of bargains with Him. Just let her live, please just let her live, I willed.

At 4 am, my little girl, my angel, quietly slipped away. Uncle Vanya, who had stayed the night with us, gently tried to take her, but I clung on fiercely. 'I can't let you go, I love you more than life itself,' I said to her over and over again, kissing her little face, her head, her tiny fingers. 'Sleep, little one, sleep.' I began singing to her, and rocking her tenderly, just as I had for so many nights, lulling her to sleep. My lullaby, soft at first, turned to a deranged scream as I blacked out.

Uncle Vanya arranged the funeral. The day was bitterly cold, the frost crackling under our feet. We couldn't find a priest because the clergy were being fiercely persecuted and church services were no longer being performed. He arranged everything through the registry of deaths. Mama, Papa, Alec, Uncle Vanya, Igor and I stood around my angel's tiny wooden casket. My father and Uncle Vanya said a few prayers quietly and lowered the casket into the ground. I lunged forward to try and delay it for just a little longer, but Alec and Igor grabbed me and held on tightly. 'Let me go. Let me go!' I screamed. 'I don't want to be here.'

Mama and Papa hugged me and our tears mingled in grief. As I threw the first handful of earth into the grave, my life went with it. I went about in a fog of unreality, as though the events of the past few days had happened to someone else. I stopped eating and took up smoking. When I got home at night, I would go straight to Ina's things, smelling their sweet baby smell and then sit, cradling her little doll, staring straight ahead for hours. Nothing and no one could console me.

This was the beginning of the most painful and traumatic part of my life. Mother's condition continued to deteriorate and towards the end of 1939 she too died, only four months after my Ina. When I heard that Mama was seriously ill, I raced home to see her, but I was too late. I was inconsolable. Then I realised there was not a trace of food in the house. She had obviously given everything to Alec and me. I didn't want to tell Uncle Vanya she was dead because he was still so ill, but he soon guessed for himself. Mother was only fifty when she died. A dreadful emptiness and despair now engulfed me—first the death of my precious Ina such a short time ago, and now my beloved mother. I lived from moment to moment and from day to day, mainly for the sake of the rest of my family. Life had to go on, I supposed. I didn't care one way or another. Igor tried his best to help me, but my depression was so deep that all I could do was go to the theatre, complete my performance robotically and go home. I don't know how I didn't lose my position in this period, as my performances could only be described as adequate at best.

I stopped seeing all my friends, including Igor. The dreams we'd shared of becoming a family were totally shattered. I couldn't even contemplate living with him as a huge part of that previous equation was now missing. I suppose that unintentionally I hurt Igor very much, but my own pain so overwhelmed me that I was oblivious to anyone else's feelings, other than those of my immediate family.

Alec had met a girl and married during his second year at the university. She came from a simple, poorly educated background, and they were totally unsuited to one another. Her name was Larissa. She was studying to become an engineer and lived in the students' dormitory where Alec also lived. They couldn't live together because there was no room available, and when Larissa became pregnant she went to live with her parents, who had been against the marriage from the beginning as Alec was still a student and not earning a living. Larissa gave birth to a little girl whom, with my blessing, they called Ina. Ina was to become a central character in my life many years later in a way I couldn't have imagined at the time. But when this Ina was born, their lives were difficult, filled with hunger and poverty. My own was little better—living in a tiny one-room apartment paid for from my meagre theatre salary. There was no way that I could take in my brother and his family, even though both Father and I gave him money when we could.

After Mother's death, my life turned upside down. Alec had a breakdown, stopped studying and began drinking even more heavily. He drank away all the money I gave him for food. I would look for him in all the drinking holes in town, sometimes until two or three in the morning. The university threatened him with expulsion because he failed to sit for his exams. I desperately tried to persuade them to allow him a postponement. They also stripped him of his stipend. Alec then began stealing from Father and me to support his drinking. Then he started to steal from his friends, his acquaintances, anyone. We didn't know what to do.

Larissa wanted to leave him and, anyway, they weren't living together as man and wife. I didn't have the time to keep looking for him every night to try to reason with him. Nor could I take him in with me and look after him to keep him from drinking. I had only the one tiny room. There were no facilities for cooking or washing. I washed my clothes in a tiny basin, which I rinsed out before using it to cook potatoes—my daily diet. To survive on my actor's salary alone was impossible. So I worked elsewhere, whenever I could, to earn an extra rouble: on radio, in amateur theatre as a paid assistant, teaching modern dance. But the money wasn't steady, as my students themselves often had no money.

From 11 am to 5 pm, I was in rehearsals. Then I had two hours of free time when I would go home, rest and eat. From 7 pm I would be in the theatre, often till midnight or 1 am, when the make-up came off. I would arrive home about 2 am. The next day, it would be the same routine. In such circumstances it would have been impossible to look after Alec. So Father and I made the fateful decision that Alec should go into the army. He would have needed to do army training for two years anyway, as it was compulsory, after which he could return and resume his studies. Hopefully the army had the discipline and resources to cure Alec of his alcoholism—he would have no choice but to be cured.

The regional theatre in Smolensk was relocated to Roslavl during 1939–40. The cast and personnel were cut back because Roslavl was such a small town. I decided to look for work in another theatre, but that meant that I had to go to Moscow. Actors wishing to join other theatres went to Moscow, once there applying to the relevant authorities to be sent elsewhere. The risk was ending up somewhere you didn't want to go. The only other avenue was to find a theatre yourself. In Moscow's Mayakovsky Square there is a small park called the Aquarium. During the summer, this became a meeting place for actors and directors from all over the Soviet Union who were looking for work—directors were looking for actors, who in turn, were looking for a theatre to join.

I found a job in a theatre right away. Unfortunately it was far from Moscow and from home: the theatre was in Udmurt, in the Udmurtskaya Republic, 1000 kilometres to the east. My wages would be higher than in Smolensk and I was offered more roles, so I accepted. Frustratingly, while still in Moscow I met an interesting young director from Onega, a town near the Arctic Circle, who offered me a terrific contract—but it was too late. I had already contracted myself to the theatre in Udmurt and couldn't get out of the contract. He and I wrote to each other for a year. I promised to visit him in Onega but once again, due to unforeseen circumstances, all my plans collapsed.

CHAPTER FIVE

I arrived in Udmurt at the beginning of September 1940. It was raining heavily. Everything was mud-laden and soggy. Udmurt's main industry was forestry and the timber was exported for ship-building. The wind howled through the enormous birch trees and created a sense of foreboding and gloom. Once the rains stopped, however, the onset of winter brought incredible beauty. The air was as clear as crystal. The temperature sometimes reached 35–40°C below zero, but what a healthy climate! Tuberculosis sufferers went there to recuperate, as in those days Udmurt had no heavy industry, so there was no pollution.

I was welcomed with open arms at the theatre. They already had me lined up for a whole series of roles and I got to work on them immediately. Despite an overwhelming feeling of homesickness and depression, I hoped that the year would pass quickly and Alec would soon be visiting. We had arranged that he would leave the army and continue his studies at university. I was always thinking about him— I was sure that army discipline could help him overcome his terrible problem and that he would return to us healthy and happy. I had so many plans for the future. I would earn some money, Alec would return and perhaps I would be able to get us both positions in a theatre in central Russia somewhere and then I could get Father and Uncle Vanya to join us and so the whole family, or what was left of it, would be reunited.

My first role with the theatre at Udmurt was that of Beatrice in Goldoni's *Servant of Two Masters*. The director was very pleased with me. I then began to rehearse the role of Betty in Shalom-Aleikim's *The Cruel Joke*. I finished up playing all the roles that had been scheduled for the theatre's leading actress, who fell ill with a serious infection of her mammary glands. She had first one, then a second, then a third operation—but to no avail. She remained in hospital in a desperately ill state. On the one hand, replacing her allowed me to gain lots of experience very quickly, but on the other, I was soon overloaded with the demands of fulfilling all the allocated roles. I worked day and night, preparing roles simultaneously, one on stage and the other in the foyer or dressing room between scenes. There wasn't a single day without a rehearsal or an evening without a performance. During that season I played twelve major roles.

At that time theatres in the Soviet Union were organised into four distinct ranks or classes. The first rank included the Russian Institute of Dramatic Art, the Bolshoi Theatre, the Maliy Theatre, the Mos-Sov (Moscow-Soviet) Theatre, the Theatre of Satire, and one or two other leading theatres in Moscow. It also included major theatres in other cities such as the Maryinsky and Alexandrinsky theatres in Leningrad. The second rank included a number of somewhat less established or less well equipped Moscow and Leningrad theatres. The third rank consisted of regional theatres. Finally, the fourth rank included the touring theatre companies and the smaller independent or cooperative theatre groups. The various ranks determined the rates of pay earned by the actors and other staff. A leading actor in a first rank theatre could earn about 1200 roubles a month, in the second rank 900 roubles, 750 in the third and 500 in the fourth. Additional wages could be earned by working in the far north, due to the isolation involved. The theatres also subsidised clothing costs, for although period costumes were provided, modern-day plays involved actors using their own clothes.

Since the entire economy of the Soviet Union was based on centralised planning, the business of each theatre was also directed from Moscow. A financial plan was drawn up for each one and it had to operate accordingly, otherwise it could be closed down. The government took the lion's share of theatre proceeds and the remainder was divided up between the needs of the theatre, including the wages of staff. This explained why staff were seldom paid on time, because otherwise the theatre might seem to be operating beyond its budget and this would mean serious trouble. Actors were usually forced to ask for at least some kind of advance and often had to sell off personal items not absolutely necessary for day-to-day living. All the actors had to moonlight at drama clubs, games groups, factories and so on, which usually had some funds available for cultural purposes. It all helped us get by. So although there were hard times, there were also good times. The hardships and joys balanced each other for the most part.

You could moonlight as much as you liked, but everyone had to be at the theatre by 7 pm even if you were only in the final act. An actor could be docked a month's pay for being twenty minutes late or being late for, say, four periods of five minutes each. In addition, they could be 'laid off' and not given any good roles. The offence would be recorded officially in their 'Work Record Log', which every worker in the Soviet Union had to produce upon request. In serious cases one could even be criminally prosecuted for breaching the code of standards of Soviet professionalism. As with all such matters the actual details often depended on the particular individuals involved. For example, if you were on good terms with the assistant director and you were late, but didn't have to go on stage until the third act, you might be lucky and be let off with a warning. If you were late and delayed or disrupted the performance, then nothing could save you.

There was one particular actor by the name of Samarin with whom I had a problem. Not only was he an alcoholic, but he had the extremely disagreeable habit of eating garlic before and even during a performance. Eating raw garlic is not uncommon in the Soviet Union and it is undoubtedly of considerable medicinal value. But playing a romantic scene with someone who has just eaten some is unbearable! Eventually I complained to the theatre's officials and he was ordered to discontinue the practice. Did he ever hate me for doing this to him!

But fate paid him back for having been so nasty to me. On Red Army Day, on 23 February, we were performing *Furman's Revolt*. I was Naya and Samarin took the role of Furman himself. The theatre was full of Government officials, the Regional Head of the Communist Party and all sorts of other party dignitaries. At 7 pm—no Samarin; at 7.30 pm—still no Samarin. The play had to begin at 8 pm. The cast and crew were in turmoil. Someone was sent to his home—he was not there. By now we were in total panic.

Runners were sent to every part of the town in search of him. He was found eventually, and not surprisingly, in the snow outside a hotel. He was dead drunk and had become frozen to the ground. They dragged him back to the theatre and defrosted him. He had lost his voice and was barely audible. The director, furious with rage, put on make-up; he was going to try to play the role himself out of total desperation. Samarin, however, somehow got through the entire play in a hoarse whisper, but the performance was completely ruined. He was prosecuted and sentenced to several months' gaol, but allowed to serve it after the completion of the theatrical season.

In the theatre there are major catastrophes from time to time that are virtually impossible to get around without seriously jeopardising the performance. I was personally involved in a number of them. I don't know why it is, but assistant directors are notorious for being heavy drinkers and are often to be found in the bar area during a performance. Consequently, a large number of theatrical effects for which they are responsible are not produced when required. We were performing Fedorov's *Sisters* and I was playing the role of Sasha, the older sister. She is a teacher and is in love with a man who is in love with her younger sister, who in turn is in love with another man, an itinerant no-hoper. The man Sasha is in love with makes an attempt at suicide but fails, and Sasha looks after him while he recuperates. She stays up with him all night and then as morning approaches goes to the window and draws back the curtains, saying, 'It looks like dawn is almost here and I will have to go now.'

At this point the assistant director was meant to slowly bring up the lights to signal the approach of day—but outside the window one night there was total darkness. So I repeated my cue, only much louder, hoping to attract his attention. Still total darkness. The young man tried to help me. He got out of bed and moved slowly to the window, giving us time to adlib some lines about staying in bed. He also tried to attract attention by loudly exclaiming things like, 'Look, I think the sun is already rising, but the clouds are blocking it.'

Still there was total darkness and of course by this time the audience knew something had gone wrong. The young man began to giggle and, as is common on stage, this became an uncontrollable laugh that infected me as well. Both of us were standing with our backs to the audience trying to suppress our spasms and adlib at the same time—and by now the audience had started to laugh, though intermittently and not too loudly. Just then there was the sound of something approximating an express train coming from behind the scenery as a frantic assistant director ran headlong over some metal sheets left backstage as he desperately tried to reach the lights. The slowly approaching dawn, having taken so long to get there, now wasted no time at all—and from total darkness there was a sudden transformation to full glaring sunlight as the two actors on stage and the entire audience broke into uncontrollable laughter. For this little episode the assistant director had his pay docked, received a severe reprimand and was lucky to avoid a gaol sentence.

During one scene of Goldoni's classic, *Servant of Two Masters*, playing the role of Beatrice, I was obliged to fight a duel with the character Silvio. As the duel commenced I said some dramatic line, reached for my foil and pulled it out of its scabbard with a great flourish. To my horror the hilt remained in my hand but the blade, somehow detached, went flying out towards the audience. For the few brief seconds of its flight, with the blade flashing reflections from the stage lights, cast and audience fell into a sort of petrified state, knowing full well the possible consequences but unable to do anything. There was a slow-motion gasp from the entire audience as the potentially deadly blade went somersaulting towards them—only to land point-first and embed itself in the only vacant seat of the twentieth row. Everyone on stage stood paralysed. It was immediately apparent no one had been hurt, as we could all see the blade wobbling drunkenly backwards and forwards where it had struck. Fortunately I regained my wits and adlibbed some nonsense that allowed me to go backstage and obtain a replacement. I was later congratulated for the quick thinking which had allowed the play to continue with only a minor pause, but the person in charge of the props had more than a little explaining to do. Was he a saboteur of some kind? Was he an enemy of the State seeking to undermine its culture? These were the sorts of questions that Party officials never failed to ask after an incident even when it was a simple, although potentially serious, accident.

There were several occasions, however, when the problems were of my own making. As the leading lady in a play whose title I have now forgotten, I was in the dressing room during one performance doing some sewing repairs. Suddenly a somewhat breathless assistant director burst into the room. 'Interesting that you're here…' he said in a constrained and dramatic tone. He paused, then yelled as loudly as he dared in view of our vicinity to the stage, '…since you have been on stage for the last five minutes or so!'.

I realised with horror that I was meant to be in a scene with the leading man, in the garden. I ran madly towards the stage and ascended the three steps leading up to it in a single bound—well, almost. The heel of my shoe caught the uppermost step and the leading lady made her entrance to a tender love scene in rather unconventional style, diving headfirst onto the stage some seven minutes late. I was really in trouble for that one!

I remember a very unusual incident when falling over actually benefited the performance, although I was severely reprimanded. I played the part of an empty-headed and jealous young woman who was spying on a young couple. They were seated on a bench next to a little picket fence by a river. A large tree, a real one, had been brought onto the stage and I was meant to hide behind it to conduct my spying. Ever alert to the possibility of adding some new and interesting element to my performance, I decided that as the tree seemed to be very securely attached to the stage I would climb it rather than just hide behind it. Upon reaching the first large branch, the tree, probably taking a cue from me in showing initiative and imagination, decided that it would be far more amusing if it didn't simply remain stationary but joined in the action. The tree and I tottered, slowly at first but ever more dramatically, as befitted our profession, directly towards the other, now rather alarmed inhabitants of the stage—the fence, the seat and the two actors seated thereon. There was an almighty crash and a tangle of actors, seat, fence, tree and unidentified debris sorted itself out very slowly, but the audience was laughing and applauding loudly, so impressed were they by this most remarkable mise-en-scène. At least they liked it—meaning it didn't spoil the play—but I was hauled over the coals for showing the sort of independence of judgement and wilful disregard of authority that was so unacceptable for a Soviet citizen of that time.

The 1940–41 season came to an end. My career had blossomed. I had gained considerable experience and had played many different roles. In addition, I had earned a great deal of money and now I headed back towards Moscow. There I would buy some things for myself and my family that I could never have afforded before and we would all be together again as I enjoyed a well-earned break. It was May 1941. Within a few short weeks, my life would change forever, in ways I could never have imagined.

CHAPTER SIX

Father was now working as principal of a school in Krapivenskaya, a tiny town eighteen kilometres from Roslavl on the main road to Smolensk. The house given to him was small, though comfortable. My intentions were to stay with him for a while, then go to Uncle Vanya's in Smolensk and while there visit the Council for the Arts to request a transfer to somewhere in central Russia and to move my family with me. I was also hoping to buy a holiday package to the Crimea, a popular health and holiday resort, before recommencing work.

On 22 June 1941, not expecting anything out of the ordinary, I got off the train in Smolensk. Surrounded by many other unsuspecting folk, I made my way towards the exit. It was a Sunday; midday. Suddenly there was a dreadful commotion, with people rushing in all directions, bewildered and confused. I attempted to find out what was going on but no one seemed to know. One man stopped and told me that an important radio announcement was about to be made. The voice of Molotov, Stalin's second-in-command, transfixed us all.

'Men and women, citizens of the Soviet Union, the Soviet Government and its head, Comrade Stalin, has instructed me to make the following announcement. At 4 am, without declaration of war and without any claims being made on the Soviet Union, German troops attacked our country, attacked our frontier in many places and bombed from the air Zhitomir, Kiev, Sevastopol, Kaunas and other cities…'

He spoke flatly and unemotionally, as was his usual way, but the effect was electric, as realisation sank in of the horrible catastrophe that had just occurred. The crowd was aghast, some screaming in fear: 'War! War! Dear God, please save our souls. What is going to happen now?'.

After some comments about Germany breaching the non-aggression pact, Molotov concluded with: 'The Government calls upon you, men and women, citizens of the Soviet Union, to rally even more closely around the glorious Bolshevik Party, around the Soviet Government and our great leader, Comrade Stalin. Our cause is just. The enemy will be crushed. Victory will be ours.'

Everywhere was chaos, people rushing about madly. My mind was spinning, unable to take in the momentousness of what I had just heard. I caught snippets of conversation as I automatically made my way towards my home at Uncle Vanya's. Some people headed straight for the banks to get out their savings. Others with currency on them headed to the stores and bought whatever they could, especially non-perishable foodstuffs, even though Russians generally distrusted canned goods. Who knew when or where they might get their next meal? My thoughts were with my family.

When I arrived home, Uncle Vanya was there with his two little girls, Vera and Lilya. He already knew the terrible news. Terrified, not knowing what to do, we wept together for a long time. A horrible thought hit me—Alec! By now he must have been caught up in this maelstrom. He was in the army, separated from us. Where was he?

We spent that first night in our clothes, unable to sleep, in total darkness in compliance with official orders. By early next morning, panic had broken out. People rushed the stores, buying everything in sight, and before long there was no produce to be seen. I decided to go to Krapivenskaya to be with Father and suggested that Uncle Vanya, Auntie Panya and the two girls come with me for their own safety. Krapivenskaya was about 100 kilometres from Smolensk and less likely to be bombed. Uncle Vanya agreed, but Auntie Panya decided to evacuate to central Russia. Rumours were rife that the Germans had already bombed Soviet border cities, including Minsk and Mogilov. On the second night after the announcement of the outbreak of war, crowds of people were making their way out of town any way they could—by foot, on horseback, by bicycle—all heading into villages and forests deeper and deeper into the countryside. We all understood that the major cities and towns would be the first targets for bombing.

By 24 June, Smolensk was being bombed mercilessly. I had arrived at Father's the day before to find him beside himself with worry about Alec. I tried to comfort him as best I could, but in my heart I shared his despair. I had already made up my mind to try to locate Alec, but I had no idea how to even begin this task.

A few days later I went to enlist. This might seem a strange thing to have done, but it had practical advantages. If I didn't enlist I was sure to be called up anyway. Once that happened I would have to report immediately to my posting. By enlisting voluntarily I had a much better chance of a later posting while authorities sorted out the most appropriate duties for me. When the officials realised what my profession was, they said they were happy to process my application, as there was a unit in Moscow for professional actors who would work as entertainers for the troops on the front line. I was to wait for an assignment. I didn't have the heart to tell Father just yet.

Uncle Vanya joined us on 29 June. His wife had taken their daughters and gone into the country. He was devastated, shattered at having lost his family, and feared he would never see his girls again. There were now three of us to face whatever was to come. In his state of depression, my darling uncle hadn't even brought a change of clothing with him.

Smolensk was under the fiercest bombing and was being systematically reduced to rubble. We had no idea of the whereabouts of the German army, as all radios had been confiscated, and listening to any form of radio transmission was at your own peril and under the threat of death. We were only allowed to listen to official public announcements over loudspeakers. These told us that the battles were still raging only in the outlying western region of the Soviet Union, but no one was told exactly where. Everything was shrouded in secrecy. So-called spies were being picked up daily and shot on the spot.

It was now July. Uncle Vanya asked if I could get back to Smolensk to pick up his belongings if they were still there. But how to get there? Trains were scarce and not for civilian travel. They were full of Jews from all over western Russia, escaping from the front line and from Hitler's troops. They were also heavily used by fleeing Government officials during the early days of the onslaught. Our house was on a main road, with heavy military traffic travelling non-stop in both directions. It was interesting to see high officials of the

Communist Party, the KGB, their wives, children, pets and furniture all being hastily evacuated. Ordinary soldiers would often stop at our house to ask for a cup of tea or a bite of food and this was how we gleaned any real information about the war. It gave me an idea of how to get to Smolensk. I would organise a lift there and back with some of the boys. It seemed simple enough. The danger of such a mission didn't even enter my head and before long an opportunity presented itself.

A small truck stopped by our house and a Red Army lieutenant and his driver got out. They asked me to put on the samovar and make them some tea. They had a wash, took out their provisions and began eating. We talked and they told me that the Germans were advancing from the south, north and west towards Moscow. The two soldiers had just come from a place called Karachev. They were going to Army headquarters and had to return to their post by the next night. This was the answer to my prayers.

'Boys, you've come here at just the right time,' I said, and explained what I wanted to do. They exchanged glances and replied that they had no right to carry civilians. I pleaded with them to take me and after much persuasion the lieutenant agreed, though reluctantly.

'Well, since it's an emergency, we'll do you this favour. We can actually take you to Smolensk and back, because we have to come back to camp. Just make sure you're ready by dawn, since we can't wait for you. We'll knock on your window when we arrive.'

I was waiting for them an hour or so before dawn. I wore my grey suit, a pair of flat shoes and, most important, was carrying all my documents. Thinking that I would be back home by evening, I felt it unnecessary to take anything else. During the trip the lieutenant talked about himself, telling me he would have to attend to his business first before taking me to my uncle's place.

Smolensk was deserted when we arrived. There was hardly any sign of life, only the smouldering ruins of a city heavily bombed. It was tragic to see the familiar and beloved streets in such a state. While the lieutenant went about his business I walked to the new Drama Theatre which was situated not far from Army headquarters. The theatre was closed but a few people were on duty to extinguish the fires from the night bombing attacks. These actors explained to me that several groups had already left for various destinations at the front to entertain our troops. I asked them to include me on the list of such groups willing to work at the front and gave Father's address for future notification. They told me that the Germans would probably be here shortly so we had little time for talking. They all appeared extremely downhearted. Some of the group were Jewish so it was easy to understand their feelings of fear and depression. Even in the heavily censored Russia of pre-war days, news had reached us via the grapevine of the terrible treatment of Jews under Hitler's Nazi regime.

When I got back to the truck, the lieutenant was already there.

'Have you completed all your business?' I asked him.

'No, I wasn't able to do anything,' he replied. 'Headquarters has been moved to Drogobuzh.'

'What do you mean, Drogobuzh?' I stammered, completely unprepared for such news. 'What do I do now?'

'What you're going to do I don't know,' the lieutenant responded, 'but we're going to Drogobuzh.'

'But I have to get back home,' I whimpered, almost in tears. 'They're waiting for me.'

His answer was blunt. 'You'll have to walk home then.'

'How do I do it on foot? It's 110 kilometres from here!'

The lieutenant grabbed my shoulders and shook me. 'Listen you, are you a child? There's a war going on, understand? This is not a theatre production. We're soldiers and we're under strict orders. So, get out of this truck and start walking home while it's still possible.'

I broke down in a flood of tears. 'Please, please don't leave me, Lieutenant. I'm scared that I won't make it. Please don't leave me here on my own.'

'Hell! Why did I agree to take you? Stop that bawling. All right, come to Drogobuzh with us while we sort out our business. We'll have to return to camp via Roslavl anyway. So you'll get home later than you expected, okay? We'll go to your uncle's place, pick up his things then drive on to Drogobuzh. After all, it's only another 80 kilometres from here,' the Lieutenant said with more than a hint of sarcasm.

When we arrived at Uncle Vanya's street, all I could see of his house was a chimney standing surrounded by rubble. Almost the whole street had been levelled. Uncle Vanya had lived near the bridge over the Dnepr River and the Germans had obviously concentrated on bombing this bridge. Suddenly air raid sirens began to wail.

'Quickly, the vultures will be here in a minute,' the lieutenant cried out to the driver. 'Let's get out of here while we're still in one piece—let's go.'

We began to drive towards Drogobuzh. Even though the driver stayed clear of the main roads, I was still extremely frightened at the prospect of the coming onslaught. The lieutenant told me that the Germans would invade Smolensk either today or tomorrow as they advanced towards Moscow.

'But don't worry. We will give them a mighty slap in the face,' he assured me. 'They will never take Moscow. Remember what I've just said.' He was quite emphatic.

I didn't want to respond to anything or to listen to what anyone had to say, for it was only now that I was beginning to realise the danger we were all facing. Where was Alec? What had happened to him? How on earth would I ever find him? What would happen to all of us?

'How beautiful it is around here in Smolensk. What forests and rivers,' the lieutenant was saying, taking in the surroundings and interrupting my anxious thoughts. 'And to think that we have to give this up to the enemy? Never!' The anger was obvious in his voice. 'Lilya, why do you look so glum? Don't be depressed. Tell us something about your life.'

I told them I was an actress and gave them a quick sketch of my career up until then, but I wasn't really up to talking very much. I had the strangest premonition that something was about to happen that would prevent my getting home—even tomorrow.

By the time we got to Drogobuzh it was almost evening. The lieutenant went to look for Army headquarters while I remained in the vehicle with the driver. I sat there motionless and depressed, waiting for the next piece of bad news. My premonition was right. Army headquarters were no longer in Drogobuzh, but had moved on to Vyazma—even further from Smolensk and closer to Moscow. No one spoke, our thoughts racing in all directions. After some time, the lieutenant broke the silence.

'Comrades. You know that we have no other choice but to go on to Army headquarters. I understand, Lilya, that you are now caught up in this mess with us, but what can I do? We have to follow orders. We should never have agreed to take you in the first place and now we're stuck with you. We still have to get back to camp in Smolensk, which means you'll still be able to go home. But your guess is as good as mine when that might be. So now let's have something to eat and try to get some sleep.'

We stopped on the outskirts of town. I found myself a bed for the night in one of the deserted houses. The two men slept in the car. I didn't sleep at all for fear they might drive away and leave me, but that didn't happen. When the sun started to break through the grey sky, we moved on towards Vyazma, speeding along a main road to a town called Moscow Negoreloe. I thought that if the Germans had been aware that this main road was not defended it was likely that they would have invaded Moscow already. The only sign of activity along the highway was an occasional Red Army patrol and the occasional civilian digging trenches. Hitler's tanks would have had a quick and unobstructed access to the capital.

'Lilya, I'm afraid that we're in for further trouble. This is an Army vehicle, in which civilians aren't allowed. You will be identified right away by your clothing. Sasha, do you have any Army gear in your haversack for Lilya?' the lieutenant worriedly asked his driver.

'The only clothing we could give her would be an Army shirt and beret. No pants or boots,' replied Sasha. The lieutenant told me to put on the shirt and to hide my long curly hair under the beret.

'Wear this bag of mine over your shoulder and sit close to the window so that your skirt and sandals aren't visible. Keep your mouth shut if we are stopped at a checkpoint but if you are asked any questions, say you're an Army doctor, 3rd rank, Division 191. Better still, cover your mouth under the pretext of a toothache and let me answer for you,' the lieutenant ordered.

I didn't say a word. My eyes were full of tears. I was scared and in total despair. I had lost all hope that I would ever see my family again, as we were travelling further and further away from home. The lieutenant tried to console me.

'Please, Lilya, don't panic so much. This disaster has struck our whole country, not just you and me. We may still be able to return. Army headquarters must be around somewhere.'

I had the strangest feeling that this wasn't happening to me, that I was watching a larger-than-life film. I was certain that the same thing would happen to us in Vyazma.

'Look, I'm convinced that we won't find headquarters even in Vyazma. What do we do then? And what if we don't find headquarters anywhere? What then?' I blurted.

'Well, when the time comes we'll think about it. For now, pull yourself together and don't forget that you're not on your own in this situation. How many others have been separated from their home and family? Be strong. And if you can't be strong, then simply act as though you are. You did say you were an actress, didn't you?' The lieutenant gave me a rueful smile and a reassuring hug.

When we reached Vyazma my worst fears were realised. The lieutenant went to find headquarters only to return angry and morose.

'We're going immediately to Gjadsk,' he told us, swearing belligerently. 'No one knows what's going on. The Germans are advancing rapidly and where is our bloody army? Where are our tanks? How do we stop the invasion? Sasha, can you understand any of this?' He was yelling, barely able to control himself.

'What's to understand? The bloody Germans took us by surprise. Nobody expected this to happen. No wonder everyone's in a state of panic,' replied Sasha grimly.

'Panic? Surprise?' The lieutenant was bitter and sarcastic. 'We've been working on developing our defence systems for years. We've been assured that our military resources are the best in the world. And what's happened? Complete chaos!'

The truth was that Russia was terribly under-prepared for war. The non-aggression pact between Russia and Germany did not represent any sort of ideological alignment of the two countries. Stalin had always had a profound distrust of Fascism and in 1936 had provided limited support to the Spanish Communist Government against the forces of Fascism there. The pact with Hitler was obviously to buy time to strengthen Russia's military capabilities, which had been seriously eroded due to the disastrous economic policies of the 1930s.

Similarly, Hitler did not wish to invade both western Europe and Russia as early as 1939, although nor did he want to wait until Russia had built up its strength. We all knew that Stalin's strategy would be simple and follow the traditional Muscovite pattern that had worked so well in the past. That is, any gaps in our defences would be plugged by the sacrifice of countless Russian bodies, while those in command waited for the impossibly difficult winters to sap away the strength and willpower of the invaders. This strategy had been used for hundreds of years. It had successfully defeated Napoleon and now it was hoped it would defeat Hitler the same way. But, as always, it would be at an enormous cost in terms of Russian lives. Would my brother Alec be one of these? Would I survive long enough to find out? These were questions to which I had no answers.

Gjadsk. It wasn't far from Moscow. Even if Army headquarters were to be found in Gjadsk, there was no telling when I would be able to get back home. I was devastated. What could Father and Uncle Vanya be thinking by now? They'd probably assume I'd been killed.

'Dear God, please help us,' I prayed fervently, bawling my eyes out. The closer we got to Gjadsk, the more obvious was the presence of Army patrols, checking everyone's credentials. My tear-swollen face, red eyes and nose all helped in my charade of a person suffering unbearable pain. I swayed from side to side and gave an occasional loud groan for better effect. At the next checkpoint, we were told to turn left into the forest where Army headquarters were to be found. This was right on the front line of battle.

'Thank God,' said the lieutenant. 'Even I began to have doubts that we would ever find headquarters. At last!'

Day had already turned to dusk when we entered a dark and forbidding forest. There were trucks and all kinds of military vehicles everywhere, including a few tanks camouflaged by tall branches. Above us German planes were circling in an attempt to find their prey. Sasha and I camouflaged our vehicle with leaves and branches too while the lieutenant went looking for headquarters. We got back into the truck and Sasha, covering his face with his beret and closing his eyes, said, 'Lilya, I'm going to grab a few minutes' sleep.'

I nodded, also wanting to snatch a bit of sleep, as I hadn't slept for two days. I felt a little more hopeful. Soon we could be returning home. I was awfully thirsty, but there was nothing to drink. Finding that I was too restless to sleep after all, I looked around me. All about were plump, juicy berries in abundance, hanging off the bushes. I tried to take my mind off my thirst, but I just couldn't resist the fruit, so I got out of the car, gathering and eating the berries. They were sweet and delicious and I couldn't stop.

'Hey Lilya! Don't go too far from the car. The lieutenant will be back soon,' Sasha yelled after me. He was obviously alert enough to notice that I was no longer in the truck.

'I'm just here,' I yelled back, but recoiled in shock as a severe voice sounded behind me.

'Citizen! Why are you dressed so ridiculously? Who are you?' I turned around nervously to see an officer in front of me, but I could not work out his military status. 'Who are you and what are you doing here?' he repeated. I was speechless. Was I an Army doctor, 3rd rank, as the lieutenant had ordered me to respond? Was I Lilya? I was so confused that I couldn't get a single word out.

'Show me your documents!' he barked at me. I took a timid look at him and saw a person of medium height, with a long thin face and small piercing eyes. 'Well, why don't you say something?' he persisted.

'I... you see, it's a long story... but I can explain. I'm not in the Army. I'm an actor with the Smolensk Theatre,' and I continued to tell him my story openly.

'Okay, okay,' he interrupted me. 'But how did you find out that Army headquarters were here?'

'Look, I've already told you that the lieutenant brought me here,' I pleaded, 'and he found out at the last checkpoint. You can ask him yourself.'

'Don't worry, I'll ask him all right. Where is your vehicle?'

'Just over there behind the bushes,' I stuttered. 'I only got out to pick some berries as I was tremendously thirsty.'

'Okay, let's go back to your car.'

He turned around without waiting for me to catch up. As we approached our camouflaged vehicle, so did the lieutenant. Seeing who accompanied me, he went white, as did Sasha, who quickly scrambled from the car. They both came to attention at once and saluted my interrogator. The stranger turned to the lieutenant and demanded to see his papers.

'Who is this girl and why is she travelling with you in an Army vehicle?' he demanded, his voice trembling with rage. The lieutenant, completely taken aback and glaring at me, tried to explain.

'Don't bother, Lieutenant. I learned the full story from the girl herself. What right did you have to transport a civilian in the first place and on top of that, tell her where frontline headquarters were located?' he roared.

'Sorry, Comrade Major of Government Security.'

Government Security? That meant the NKVD! What will happen to me now? I thought, panic stricken.

'Return to Gjadsk immediately. Leave the girl there and go back to your camp. I will ring them now. Lieutenant, you will answer for this. This little adventure will cost you dearly.' The lieutenant saluted and, turning sharply, returned to our vehicle and signalled to me to climb in the back. I was numb. The officer left us and disappeared into the darkness.

We drove out of the forest onto the main road in silence. The signs told us that 'left' would take us to Gjadsk and Moscow, and 'right' would lead to Vyazma and Smolensk. Sasha stopped the car while the lieutenant turned to me and said in a measured voice:

'Are you aware what you have done? Are you totally mad? Why did you tell him you knew where Army headquarters were located? God, I thought you were intelligent, but now I realise you're a total idiot. Well, now we have to pay for your stupidity. Because of you, I will probably be court-martialled. Why didn't I dump you in Smolensk? I had no right to tell you about the whereabouts of Army headquarters. That is a top military secret. I had no right to take you with us, but I felt sorry for you, and you said you were an actress, but you've simply blurted out everything and acted us right into a court-martial!'

He was absolutely right, of course. Acting on stage was one thing, but this was different. I had been no actress, I thought bitterly, merely a stage player. Fear had overcome me and I was disgusted with my own weakness. Well, I had suffered from stage fright before and overcome it. I determined that in future I would fully commit myself to a role, whatever it may be.

'I understand full well, Comrade Lieutenant,' I replied. 'I just didn't think. Please, please forgive me.'

'Sasha, turn in the direction of Gjadsk,' the lieutenant barked.

'Listen, Lieutenant,' Sasha began, 'the girl is a fool, that's obvious. A fool, but not an enemy. If we hand her over to the authorities in Gjadsk, she'll never get out. We're to blame for taking her in the first place. I suggest we go back to our own base while we still can.'

'And you! Why didn't you stop her? You let her out. Where were you looking?' he yelled at his driver.

Sasha took up the argument. 'Who knew that she was so stupid!' I glared back at both of them, but inwardly knew they were right to feel so angry.

'Well, all I can say is that it serves me right for being such a fool. What do we do with her now?' muttered the lieutenant.

'Comrade Lieutenant, let's just go home to our beds. We've been travelling for three days now and we still have no idea how to get back to our contingent. As for the girl, let's drop her off in Roslavl as we promised. We still have to pass by that area.' The driver was almost pleading. The lieutenant swore heatedly and waved his arms in disgust, unable to resolve the dilemma.

'I would like to say something,' I ventured meekly.

'You keep your mouth shut!' they both growled. 'You've caused enough trouble.'

I decided that this was no time to be meek, but the intensity of the outburst that followed took even me by surprise.

'Now you two listen to me!' I barked. 'I agree I was stupid, but that was before; this is now. You are not going to Gjadsk because you will probably be shot on the spot. And so will I. Just think about the total confusion we have experienced ever since we started out. That officer may call Gjadsk, but who has the time to sort out such things or look for us if we don't turn up? If we just turn ourselves in, your stupidity will be ten times greater than my stupidity. I don't want to die and I don't want to be responsible for your deaths either. Who knows whether we'll even survive all this. But let's not put our heads on the line so easily. Sasha, start the motor and please head for Vyazma.'

My speech had been delivered as though I myself were a major in the Secret Police. I was stunned by my audacity, but it was nothing compared to the looks the lieutenant and Sasha were exchanging. An enormous grin slowly spread across the lieutenant's face. After a long pause, he conceded, 'I have to admit that there's logic in what you've just said. Sasha, apparently you have your orders. Vyazma!' Sasha gave me a mock salute and a wink and again we set off.

My God, is it possible that I may yet see my family? I wondered, buoyed by my renewed determination. But when we finally neared the bridge near Vyazma, utter chaos met us. There were hundreds of vehicles—both trucks and cars—crawling along to a checkpoint where guards were demanding identification documents. Some vehicles were ordered to go ahead, others directed to turn around and head back to Moscow. When it came our turn at the checkpoint, the guard addressed the lieutenant.

'How do you intend to get to the next village?' he asked.

'Through Smolensk.'

'There's no way you can get to Smolensk directly. The Germans have invaded the city and bombed it heavily. German tanks are already on their way here and heading for Moscow,' the guard informed us, adding, 'you may be lucky enough to circle Smolensk travelling there by some of the back roads.' We thanked him, crossed the bridge and stopped.

'What do we do now, Sasha?' The lieutenant appeared lost in thought.

'I'm damned if I know,' admitted the driver. 'We may be lucky enough to get through the back roads. On the other hand, maybe we should head back to Moscow. Look at the number of vehicles turning back.'

At this point I piped up again. 'No, no, Lieutenant. I'm very familiar with Smolensk and its surroundings. I can lead you via the back roads, past Smolensk and on your way to Bryansk. I promise you.'

'Oh sure, you'll lead us back. You've proven how reliable you are,' he sneered at me. 'Maybe we should just head straight for the front and you can order the Germans to surrender.'

'Come on, Comrade Lieutenant,' Sasha said, laughing. 'A broad is a broad. What can you expect of her? She's been punished enough and it's really not a bad idea. So what do you say? Let's go on.'

The lieutenant thought for a moment then said, 'Okay, let's go. We'll try our luck and go the back way. It's faster that way, anyway. I just hope we don't end up actually bumping into the Germans. Sasha, hit the gas.'

And so we continued towards Smolensk. I was feeling frightened, stressed, hungry and tired, but I kept quiet and put up with my discomfort. Please let me get back home, I thought.

Just before Smolensk, we came to a hill covered with dense forest. The road divided at that point. The main road led to Smolensk; the other way led to a township called Yartsevo. There were vehicles just in front of the forest as well as dotted between the trees. On the road to Yartsevo were three Russian tanks. We stopped, Sasha saying he was going to look for petrol as we were down to our last litre. The lieutenant went to find out what was happening in Smolensk. I also got out to stretch my legs. Sasha returned shortly with a small supply of petrol, which he promptly emptied into the vehicle's tank. Just then the lieutenant came back, anxiety-ridden. He told us that we had arrived at what was an extension of the front line of the Russian Army and that at any moment they expected the Germans to attack.

'We've got to get out of here immediately and escape through the fields and head towards Roslavl,' he snapped. 'We've got to leave the truck behind or we'll end up within firing range of the German tanks!'

Suddenly we were deafened by the roar of planes overhead—German planes.

'Hide in the forest everyone,' was the cry all around us. 'Germans!'

'Come on!' yelled the lieutenant, running for his life. I followed as fast as I could, my heart pounding. I lost count of the times I fell, picked myself up and ran on again. Suddenly I fell headlong into a huge chasm, with something extremely heavy falling on top of me. The noise from the bombing was deafening. I had no idea whether I was dead or alive, or how long I had lain in the darkness with the weight still on top of me. I was frozen with fear.

What seemed like hours later, the noise stopped, as suddenly as it started. The silence was unnerving. I learned later that this was the first wave of the air attack on Moscow. The forest began to come alive, accompanied by the agonising sounds of the wounded. As I tried to get up, I realised that what had landed on top of me was a Red Army soldier, who was now shaking me vigorously to find out whether I was alive. We climbed out of what appeared to be a trench.

'Lieutenant! Sasha! Where are you?' I yelled. They too had landed in a trench and returned my call.

'Quickly, let's get back to our vehicle, before there's another attack!' the lieutenant bellowed in my direction.

All around us was sheer bedlam. Medical units carried scores of wounded soldiers to some form of safety. People were yelling; vehicles were burning. We ran towards our vehicle on the edge of the forest, hoping that it was in one piece. Three officers were now approaching us. The two on either side carried guns; the one in the middle was a tall and stately man with a holstered pistol strapped around his waist. My God, I recognised him immediately from portraits I had seen. It was Field Marshal Timoshenko himself—one of the highest-ranking officers in the Russian Army. The lieutenant, Sasha and my companion from the trench immediately saluted him. I also tried my best to salute, bringing my hand up to my beret.

He looked at us fleetingly, returned the salute, smiled and said, 'Well, Comrades, did you get a fright?' He grinned. 'Never mind, don't lose hope. We'll give them such a thrashing that they'll never forget it.'

Even under our current circumstances, his charismatic personality was apparent and we were all encouraged by his fierce spirit. The officers moved on. Sasha was awestruck.

'Do you realise who that was? It was Field Marshal Timoshenko, the Commander-in-Chief of the entire Western Front.'

The lieutenant picked up his pace. 'Come on, come on. We've got to get back to our vehicle as soon as possible. We've got to get out of here while we're still alive.'

Our truck was still standing where we had left it, in one piece and undamaged. Around us other vehicles were moving off in droves, heading towards Moscow by the main road. Two of the Red Army tanks were engulfed in flames. Within a few minutes, we became aware of approaching German fighter planes, strafing the road with machine-gun fire. Wounded soldiers were falling off the backs of the trucks like flies, but no one stopped to pick them up. I realised the unimaginable. The Russian Army was retreating in panic.

'Bastards! What are they doing?' cried the lieutenant helplessly. 'Where are our fighter planes? Why aren't we fighting back?'

Too late, Russians found out that their Army had little artillery, no fighter planes and only a few old tanks at the start of the war. Because of the non-aggression pact between Stalin and Hitler, Russia probably had bought some valuable time. But the Army's strength had been so depleted by the blunders of the past decade that it seemed too late to have made a difference. Stalin had proven himself to be Russia's own worst enemy. All the propaganda about the might of Communism and the glorious leadership of Comrade Stalin was being brutally exposed as the sham that it had always been, but at the expense of the lives of Russian people.

Our windscreen was suddenly shattered by a barrage of bullets. Sasha caught shards of glass directly in his eye and face and began to bleed profusely. He screamed and instinctively put his hands to his face, letting go of the wheel. The vehicle went out of control, overturned and skidded off the road into a ditch. As quickly as I could, I threw myself out of the truck into some bushes. Sore and bleeding, I got back on my feet only to fall heavily into a creek. Sasha and the lieutenant scrambled up from where they had fallen and, without saying a word, we ran like lunatics into the open fields.

A large piece of glass was sticking out of Sasha's cheek. We stopped and I pulled it out for him, the lieutenant somehow bandaging the wound with his ripped singlet. Then we ran on. All my documents, including my passport and work permit, were back in the vehicle in my handbag, I realised with horror, knowing the consequences of being caught without identification. Finally we arrived at a tiny village where we saw a group of trucks and other military vehicles. We washed our faces with water drawn from a well, sat down and began to wonder what we were going to do next. The lieutenant finally spoke.

'There's nothing to do but to steal another car. If we don't, we'll never get back to our base. But we'll have to keep to the back roads. Look, you two wait here until those soldiers go to sleep. I'll see what I can find out and keep my eyes open for a suitable vehicle.' About 2 am the lieutenant returned and whispered, 'I've found a vehicle. Come on, let's go quickly.'

We jumped up and ran to the vehicle—which turned out to be a small truck—and drove off. About half an hour later, we crossed the main road and continued towards Roslavl. The men shared the driving. We travelled the entire night and not until 7 pm next evening did we near our destination. We stopped in a small, quiet street in the town and began to make our farewells.

'Well, I guess this is goodbye, Lilya. Sorry we couldn't drop you right at your front door but there are only about 20 kilometres left for you to go. I think you can thank your lucky stars you weren't left behind earlier, even though at times I thought you deserved it. Frankly, you were a pain in the arse at first but we have grown rather fond of you, haven't we, Sasha?'

Sasha nodded quietly.

The lieutenant continued, 'Good-bye, Lilya. God help us all. I hope we all survive this hell.' He patted me on the back and Sasha gave me a big hug. I cried for all I was worth, wiping my eyes with my dirty hands.

'Thank you so much, Comrade Lieutenant. May God also be with you both and help keep you safe,' I spluttered.

'Well girl, run. Run! The Germans are almost overhead.' The lieutenant gave me my last orders.

He was right. The planes were circling the outskirts of town and machine-gun fire was beginning again. I took off my torn sandals and began running towards home barefoot. I have no idea where my strength came from, but about two hours later I finally reached home.

Dear God, how happy and relieved Father and Uncle Vanya were when I appeared. They had given up hope of ever seeing me alive again. But I barely had time for a wash and a cup of tea before three Red Army soldiers came to warn us to evacuate immediately. We threw a couple of things into a wheelbarrow and ran into the forest, sitting there all night. When there was no battle we returned, gathered as much as we could into a cart, borrowed a neighbour's horse and started our journey on foot to the tiny village of Makarovka where Father was born. It lay off the main road about 35 kilometres from Roslavl and we thought we'd be safer there.

In Makarovka we stayed with my cousin Nicolai, ten of us crammed into a tiny hut. It was dreadful to say the least, but what could we do? I worked by day in the fields, doing all the chores done by the others on the collective farm, picking and stripping crops. Our food consisted of black bread, potatoes and soup made from a prickly grass watered down with a bit of milk. This we ate daily. Mushrooms and berries were luxuries that we found occasionally; somehow, we managed to survive.

There was no sign of the Germans for over a month, until at the end of August they arrived in our village on motorcycles. Terrified by Soviet propaganda, we believed that the enemy raped women and children, cut off people's noses and carried out other unspeakable atrocities—this despite Russian soldiers coming back from the front who told us that, in fact, the rank and file German soldiers treated the general population far less harshly than they had been led to believe. I was so terrified of what the Germans might do to me that I ran into the fields, rubbed dirt on my face to look as awful as possible and hid amongst the potato crops.

I heard screaming and shouting behind me. When the commotion died down, I cautiously got up and approached the hut—running straight into three armed German soldiers. Oh my God, this is the end, I thought, and froze. But all they wanted was some milk, which I gladly brought for them, and they left without any trouble. Some time later, the same thing happened when a few more German soldiers stopped and asked for something to drink. They also left and as yet, not one of us had been killed. But these were only the ordinary young rank and file German soldiers. It wasn't until the Russian partisans began blowing up and derailing trains carrying German troops, and carrying out other forms of sabotage, that the SS stepped in and began the brutal reprisals against any village that harboured partisans. The real atrocities were yet to come.

Ordinary Russians, like me, were caught between two fires. On the one hand, the partisan groups were made up of our fathers, sons, brothers and friends and of course we had to help them in any way we could. On the other hand, German reprisal was fierce. They tortured and killed the women and children. There were many times I thought of joining either the partisans or the Army, but the idea of leaving Father and Uncle Vanya, who were both so helpless and dependent on me, was too much to bear. I stayed with them until events took their own course.

The winter of 1941 was now fast approaching. We realised that our accommodation couldn't withstand the oncoming cold. So we decided to move to Terrebin, the village where my mother and father had worked as teachers for many years. We found out that the school principal's house where we had lived was still intact and unoccupied. Father, Uncle Vanya and I moved in towards the end of September.

The little house consisted of a single room divided in two by a curtain. The half with a large oven served as the kitchen. In the other half were two beds with straw mattresses instead of normal mattresses. There was a table and several chairs. Father and Uncle Vanya slept on the beds and I slept in the kitchen on a bench. There were not many creature comforts but after living in a room with ten people this place was like a palace. In Terrebin everyone knew my family and looked after us. They brought us milk, potatoes and flour. I baked the bread myself in the large oven. Of course we had no meat or butter. Occasionally German troops stopped at the school, but they didn't ever bother us. Uncle Vanya knew a little German and, when they were told he was a doctor, they even gave him some medical supplies such as iodine, mercurochrome and bandages, advising him to keep them on hand in case wounded German soldiers needed assistance.

People from all around came to get treatment from Uncle Vanya. Word was spreading and his services were sought by ever-increasing numbers, including wounded Red Army soldiers who had become separated from their units. Most dangerous to us were the partisans who came for help. To have been caught giving them any assistance would have meant death at the hands of the Germans. Most of the time people needed their wounds rebandaged to avoid infection setting in. I helped as much as I could, since Uncle Vanya's left hand was still partially paralysed. On one occasion a cart pulled up at the house. In it lay two Red Army soldiers and a Red Army nurse. A shell fragment had sliced through her buttock down to the bone. The wound required stitching but we had no anaesthetic, no proper thread, no needles. She was running a high temperature and couldn't travel any further. We dressed the wound as well as we could and allowed her to stay, to see whether she would improve or indeed, even survive. Father gave her his bed and slept on the oven instead. The woman's youth and determination helped, and her wound improved considerably. She remained in the area and got a job milking cows for the collective farm. If the Germans had found out, we would have been shot, but God must have been on our side and we were never caught out helping our troops.

Unfortunately, the Germans decided to appropriate our house for their own lodgings, simply turning up one day and telling us to leave. We were forced to take our meagre belongings and move to the tiny shack that served as lodgings for the school caretaker. I was furious with the Germans for evicting us from our home and swore at them in Russian. Although they couldn't understand the words they knew I was being extremely disrespectful. Later that evening when I was returning home with some milk, two German soldiers passed me and gave me the Fascist salute. I was still very naive and tried to annoy them by replying 'Red Front' instead of 'Heil Hitler'. When I got home, I discovered that Father and Uncle Vanya had already been arrested and sent to one of the Nazi detention camps. Apparently the soldiers had immediately reported the incident to their superiors, who then sent them to pick up everyone where we lived. Now I was responsible for the arrest of my father and my uncle, merely for the sake of showing defiance. I felt wretched. The Germans ordered me to join them and we were all interned in a POW camp near Roslavl as punishment for being 'active Communists'.

We were there for four days, during which we were continually interrogated. I was honest with the Germans and told them I had indeed said 'Red Front', but only because I was so angry at being told to move out. As for being Communists, we all said that was ridiculous and we had never belonged to the Party, as anyone in the village could attest. We were released, but warned to be civil to the occupying forces and not to return to Terrebin. Despite this we hired a cart and returned to the caretaker's shack, deciding that if the Germans were still there we would say that we needed to get our things before moving elsewhere in accordance with their orders. When we got there we found that the Germans had completely trashed our place in the short time we had been away. It was obviously not suitable for them any longer, so we felt it would be safe to move back.

At the beginning of hostilities the Russian intelligentsia had been moderately sympathetic to the German cause, naively believing that the Germans had, in part, come to liberate Russia from the horrors of Stalinism. But the Germans had no such intentions. They had come to take over the entire country and invoke their own brand of terror. In general, they treated the Russian people with extreme contempt. We were their slaves and deserved no respect whatsoever as human beings. Of course there were individual Germans who were very fair and considerate but, on the whole, treatment at the hands of the Germans was appalling.

We set about restoring our tiny house to some semblance of reasonable living quarters. Everyone prayed that the harsh Russian winter would prove a stumbling block to the Germans, as it had to so many previous invaders. I hoped that we could somehow just wait out the war in remote little Terrebin. After all, what interest could anyone, busy invading a country like the Soviet Union, have in any of us? Unfortunately, I was entirely wrong about this, as later events would prove.

CHAPTER SEVEN

One wintry day in February 1942, an official German car pulled up outside our house. Two military police officers came into the house without so much as knocking. Most Germans didn't believe such niceties were necessary when dealing with us Russian 'pigs'. They asked whether Fraulein Makarova lived here. Uncle answered in German that she did. But what did they want? They had orders to take her immediately to Field Headquarters in Roslavl. Why? They didn't know, ordering me to be ready immediately. I tried to hide my fear, but Father and Uncle Vanya were beside themselves. I put on my coat, snatched a piece of bread for later, said goodbye and we were on our way. Sitting in the car, I wondered what this could mean, but I was certain something terrible was about to happen.

The car stopped in front of Field Headquarters in Roslavl and I was led inside and told to sit down. Shortly thereafter, a German officer appeared, an aristocratic-looking man with a neatly trimmed moustache. In one brief moment I had been transported from the relative obscurity of an out-of-the-way corner of a small village to the cold hard presence of the enemy. He addressed me in broken Russian.

'I am Captain Mueller. You Fraulein Makarova? We have work for you.'

'What work?' I asked.

'You are an entertainer—yes? We, the German Wehrmacht, want start theatre for our soldiers.'

'What sort of theatre?' I responded, completely puzzled.

'You have to put together shows for our German troops.'

'Oh my God,' I thought, immediately aware of the danger to both my family and myself. We would all be punished with death if I were caught working for the Germans. I tried to think of a way to wriggle out of the situation. A flat refusal was out of the question. The Germans did not take no for an answer.

'Captain Mueller,' I stammered. 'It...it is an impossible task for one person to accomplish. And...and anyway, there are no other actors around.' Unfortunately, my objections were easily countered.

'You can recruit people from the Russian POW camps,' said Captain Mueller in a matter-of-fact manner. 'In return we give you food—soup and bread. Also coffee. You will report directly to me. Understand?'

I told him I understood but wasn't confident that I could find anyone with artistic ability. Mueller insisted that we were bound to find people who could sing and dance, and that I was to start looking tomorrow. He added that Germans really liked Russian culture, especially music and dancing. You certainly have a strange way of showing it, I thought, but bit my lip lest I blurted out something stupid and dangerous. Well, at least this will give me an opportunity, perhaps, to save someone from a miserable death by starvation.

Mueller showed me where I was to stay; a little house where an old man called Nikiforevitch lived. The officer was about to evict him but I asked that he be allowed to stay, as I was afraid to be on my own. I asked if I could be permitted to go home so that I could explain what was happening and collect my things. Mueller agreed to this and said a car would be made available. He then turned around in his finest military style and left.

Oh God. To have to work for the Germans—those same Germans who were destroying our Motherland, killing our people, stealing from us and treating us with the utmost contempt. We weren't humans to them, more like animals. On the other hand, there was the chance to save some of my own people. And anyway, there was no negotiating with the Germans. We had witnessed the way in which they treated our prisoners of war. They beat not only the prisoners, but also any civilians who tried to give them scraps of food through the barbed wire. I knew that if I refused to work for them, not only I, but also Father and Uncle Vanya, would end up behind barbed wire to face the same hell as those other poor souls. Nor would I have the chance to save anybody. When I discussed all this with my father and uncle, they agreed with me entirely. I had no choice but to work for the Germans. Father begged me to be careful.

At the first POW camp I was surrounded by hundreds of sick and starving Russian prisoners. I knew I couldn't choose them all, but it was absolute agony deciding which of them to take. Anybody with any ability whatsoever was chosen. I selected forty people on the pretext that I needed every one of them to form a proper choir. The commanding officer told me in no uncertain terms that if I selected just one more person, I would find myself taking their place in the camp without further ado. It seemed that he realised what I was up to but, nevertheless, agreed to allow all forty into my troupe. For this I was very grateful.

The troupe members were allowed to reside in the local community and, inevitably, many used this as an opportunity to disappear. Some probably went back to their families; others may have joined the partisan movement or just gone into hiding. Luckily, it seemed the Germans hadn't kept track of the people I'd selected, and probably had even less idea of the numbers they had imprisoned.

Because I had to report regularly to the commanding officer, my own movements were far more restricted. As it turned out, I really required only eight people. The small group of finalists included an accordionist, two guitarists, a singer, a dancer, a juggler, an actor who claimed to have worked at the Moscow Arts Theatre, and a whistler. With these people, I had to produce a variety show. I had absolutely no idea how I was going to organise any sort of production without costumes, make-up or musical instruments.

The Germans gave us a house. It was cold and empty, so we dragged in some straw so that at least there was something on which the troupe could sleep. I was still living separately at Nikiforevitch's house. The Germans provided us with canteens and spoons which we took to their mess at headquarters to collect our rations. They found us a piano and a number of red flags to be cut up and used for costumes. We called ourselves the Red Devils as a kind of joke at the Germans, but they actually liked the name and so it became our stage name.

Struggling to work out a reasonable program, I was taking quite a while to organise the first show. Captain Mueller became more and more impatient and insistent, because he was reluctant to keep giving us full rations for no return. My task was made easier when two young women, Katya and Galya, joined us. They, together with our other dancer, Vasya, danced the gopak, an exciting Cossack dance, and a polka. Vasya and I danced to Monte's Czardas. I also choreographed a Gypsy Suite in which the girls danced solos while Vasya and I did a duet. The rest of the group sang to the accompaniment of the two guitarists. Both of them were good musicians, especially Kostya Zubov, a young man from Moscow. Another item was a sketch featuring the juggler, the whistler and myself. The MC for the show was none other than Captain Mueller, who also wrote our sketch, in German; the sort of bawdy farce the Germans seemed to like so much. We all struggled to learn it as none of us spoke the language.

Mueller was pleased with this part of the program, but kept pressing me about the Russian choir he had been promised. I stalled as long as I could until he finally acknowledged that he had long since suspected that the others had escaped. He added that, by rights, I should be arrested but because he valued what I had achieved so far, he would make an exception. After all, he was the one responsible for establishing ongoing entertainment for his soldiers. In other words, if he were to take serious action against me, the whole project would have to be abandoned as a failure. This would obviously not impress his superiors. So our small group practised some Russian patriotic songs: the famous 'Stenka Rasin' and 'Luchinskaya', a folk song.

Our first performance was to be at the airfield outside Roslavl. The show was received very enthusiastically by the Germans, who afterwards invited us to join them for supper. Even though we were all buoyed by our success we still felt depressed—after all, we had been entertaining our enemies. Mueller and the other Germans had been treating us reasonably well, but we reminded one another of the alternative—imprisonment, starvation, beatings and probably death. I went home rather earlier than the others, exhausted by all the work I had been doing to get the show ready. Had I remained, the events that followed might never have occurred.

Next morning I was woken by frantic knocking at the door. Nikiforevitch barely had time to open it before a German officer stormed into the room, followed by Captain Mueller, who had been the commanding officer at yesterday's performance. He began to abuse me, yelling, 'Get up, you damn Russian slut!'

Terrified, I put on a dressing gown and asked what was the matter.

Mueller grabbed me by the shoulders and shook me violently. 'You filthy Russian pigs, you'll all be thrown back into the camp.'

During the interrogation that followed, I was told that during last night's supper, some of the troupe members had stolen soap, shaving utensils, chocolate, a comb, gloves, a bottle of cognac and, worst of all, a revolver, together with its holster.

'If all these items aren't returned immediately, the lot of you will be sitting behind barbed wire!' Mueller shouted.

I pleaded with him to give me time to find all the troupe members so I could retrieve the stolen goods. Captain Mueller looked at me with barely disguised disdain and said curtly, 'You have three hours.' Then the two officers left.

Crying and in a state of panic, I dressed frantically and ran to my group's lodgings. Most were still asleep, obviously having polished off the bottle of cognac. I screamed at them, dragging sleeping bodies off the floor.

'Wake up! How could you be such idiots, putting all our lives in danger? The front's only twenty kilometres away. Being found with a revolver means we could all be shot like dogs.' They were silent, exchanging guilty glances.

'Who took the revolver?' I demanded angrily. Everyone remained silent. 'Don't you understand the consequences of this? You must know what the Germans are like by now. Either we return everything we can, especially the revolver, or we'll most certainly be shot,' I railed at them.

After about twenty minutes we agreed that I would leave my premises and they would return their stolen goods anonymously. They would go to my place, one at a time, whether they had taken anything or not, and replace whatever they could. Two hours later, I returned to find everything there except the cognac and chocolate. I didn't care about the other items; I was just so relieved the revolver had been handed in. I gathered up the bits and pieces and took them to headquarters, very apologetically explaining my comrades' behaviour as a consequence of drinking alcohol—we had all been without it for so long that it had affected our judgement and common sense. Mueller stared at me for what seemed an eternity. He then barked some orders to his immediate staff, turned on his heel and left without another glance.

We soon found out what was in store for us. Mueller forbade us to perform for the next three months. This meant we had to do without rations, but at least we weren't sent back to the camp. Nevertheless, the punishment was severe. For food we dug up whatever frozen potatoes we could find. For cooking we used machine oil, thawed out from the frozen soil around nearby factories. As the Germans approached, all Russian heavy industry had done whatever it could in the very short time available to sabotage its production capabilities. One of the best ways to do this was to drain off all fluids, especially lubricant, into the surrounding countryside and then run the machinery until it seized up. The Russian people would gather the oil by thawing out shovels of frozen dirt over a fire and straining any residual oil through a piece of cloth. Wood was so scarce that even lighting a fire was a luxury. During the worst days of the war, this salvaged oil was used not only as fuel—for cooking grass, old shoes, twigs, bark, bones and, if we were really lucky, berries—but also eaten.

Three months passed and Mueller put us back on rations. We were sent to perform at the front itself. The soldiers had orders to shoot immediately should any of us make an attempt to escape. This would include not only any attempt to get to our own lines, but even running away in panic during an attack. The Germans watched us extremely closely. Although the thought of returning to our own side was constantly on our minds, in reality we all understood that Stalin's regime would deal just as mercilessly with us for collaboration.

We often performed under heavy fire, in bunkers, sheds, trenches and barns. There were even occasions when we were told to perform as quietly as possible in order not to give away our position to Russian artillery. Every few weeks we were given a few days off at the base in Roslavl. We were trapped between two enemies. On one side were the Germans. On the other was Stalin and his boast to the world that there could be no such thing as a Russian prisoner of war.

Anyone who wasn't prepared to give their life in defence of their motherland was considered a traitor. My troupe, all prisoners of war, believed that they were not Russia's enemies but that Stalin's regime was certainly their enemy.

Nevertheless, despite considerable risk to ourselves, we helped as many of our fellow Russians as we could. We shared our rations with others who found themselves in desperate circumstances. On one occasion, a member of the local partisans who had been separated from his group came to the house and asked that we hide him temporarily. I didn't know where to put him—since there were no suitable places in such a small house—and decided the safest thing to do was to make him a member of our troupe. Fortunately, he was a good balalaika player. For several months everything went well. Then the Germans arrested him. I didn't know if it was because someone from the local community had informed on him or because the Germans received information about him from somewhere else. Captain Mueller told us that the man was a Russian spy and that in future no one was to be accepted into the group without the Germans being formally advised, so that they could run any security checks they required.

On another occasion, Katya came to me in tears, panicking because someone had told the Germans she was married to a Jew and had a daughter by him. We found out that the Russian police who worked for the Germans had informed on her. These people were far more dangerous to the local community than the Germans, because they knew so much about their own people and of course understood the language. This allowed them to follow up on any rumour they heard and to eavesdrop on community members. These were the real traitors. The extent of their collaboration made ours appear totally insignificant by comparison.

Katya was terrified that the Germans would take her daughter away from her and deal with them both as they did with all Jewish people. I told her to send her daughter immediately to the countryside, as far away as possible, and that I would go to German headquarters and tell them a story that would put Katya out of danger. We discussed the 'plot'—that I had known Katya for a long time and knew she'd had an affair with a Russian, who had left her when he found out she had become pregnant. Since she had not wanted her child to be illegitimate, she had married someone else who turned out to be Jewish. Most fortunately the Germans accepted my fabrication and didn't seem particularly interested in pursuing the matter further. They were far more concerned with the current progress of the war.

The head of the Russian police in Roslavl at that time was a person by the name of Aristov, a small man with hooded, dark, shifty-looking eyes, a convicted criminal who had served quite a lengthy term. The Germans had released him, and many other prisoners, who agreed to collaborate—not surprisingly, as they could gain their freedom in exchange for simply informing on the activities of their acquaintances. They had little regard in general for their country or the society that had imprisoned them, and were unscrupulous and treacherous. Their information was as often based on vague rumour or their imagination as it was on factual events. In this way they hoped to ingratiate themselves with the occupying regime. Moreover, they were given positions of greater authority and privilege in the community than ordinary people.

Aristov tried to inform on me on one occasion but things didn't turn out the way he intended. He had met me through his work with the Germans and asked me to go out with him several times. I took an immediate dislike to him and strongly rejected his every advance. Two of my friends who knew quite a lot about him advised me to be extremely careful, as he wouldn't hesitate to destroy someone's life. My cold response to his advances whenever we met meant that I was unwittingly putting myself in danger.

This became obvious during a concert we gave for the local Russian community. The Germans allowed this from time to time as a sort of pacifier, as they believed it would bring more cooperation and compliance from the population at large. I'd written a sketch which others thought funny, about a woman with a jealous husband who, suspecting her of infidelity, shoots her alleged suitors. Foolishly I named various characters in the sketch after some of the local officials—excluding the Germans, of course. Thus, one of the wife's lovers had the same name as the mayor, another was named after one of the other local officials and a third was called Aristov. The audience thought the sketch hilarious. Immediately after the concert, however, two German officers came up to me and told me I was under arrest. They took me by car to headquarters but refused to say anything about the matter on the way there. I was locked up and spent a sleepless night wondering about my fate. I was extremely frightened and thought that the Gestapo must have found out about my anti-German activities of one kind or another, probably in relation to the partisans.

In the morning I was told that I had been arrested on the recommendation of Aristov, who claimed that my concert had been staged as an open invitation to the local community to participate in resistance activities against the local Russian police and other officials. Thankfully, the Gestapo didn't agree that I should be sent to a detention camp but Aristov's constant badgering and accusations kept me under interrogation for three days. In fact the Germans seemed to have some knowledge of the fact that I had been in trouble with the Communist Party some time in the past. Finally, they told me that I was free to leave provided I apologise to Aristov and the others for using their names in a disrespectful manner, and to assure them that the sketch was indeed in poor taste and written in order to gain a few cheap laughs at their expense. In exchange for my freedom, I was more than happy to agree.

On this occasion things had turned out all right but it became increasingly apparent that Aristov was determined to cause further trouble for me and for the troupe. I was sure he would eventually sniff out something about the help we had given the partisans and wounded Red Army soldiers. My colleagues agreed with me and we decided we'd have to discontinue those activities or it would simply be a matter of time before we were caught and hanged. I started to look for a way out of our situation but it was difficult, as the link with the partisans was maintained through Father and Uncle Vanya.

As the war dragged on more and more Russians joined the partisans. Both the Germans and the partisans appropriated whatever supplies they needed from the locals but if either side found out that someone had provided supplies to the other, regardless of whether it was under threat of force or not, they would carry out reprisals—sometimes by shooting all the members of the family. Of course, it was hoped that helping the partisans would speed up the eventual outcome of the war and drive out the Germans, but this was little consolation to those poor Russians whom the partisans executed.

It was now the spring of 1943. Germany's plans for the conquest of Russia and the destruction of its people were failing. The partisans too were exacting a heavy toll, sabotaging supply lines, especially by rail, blowing up supply depots and killing German officers. Although the Germans exacted terrible retribution on the population nearest to where these acts took place, this did little for their war effort, since it had no effect whatsoever on discouraging partisan activities. In fact, the partisan movement became even stronger as a result, since more and more people believed that it would be safer fighting with them than being caught in the middle ground. Few women and children could join the partisans, so they suffered the most severe German reprisals. We heard that in Minsk, for example, after the partisans killed a high-ranking German officer by planting explosives in his bed, the Germans shot innocent women and children in retaliation. After the war, the world found out the full extent of German reprisals, such as the destruction of the entire village of Lidice in Bohemia in retaliation for the assassination of Gestapo leader Heydrich by Czech patriots.

Despite having advanced to within a few kilometres of Moscow, Leningrad and Stalingrad by late 1941, the Germans had been unable to take these major cities. The brutal Russian winter of 1941–42—the worst in living memory—had severely paralysed the Fascist war machine. Moreover, the Russian defence had been of a ferocity and determination that had taken the Germans completely by surprise. Another extremely harsh winter in 1942–43 had helped prevent the capture of Stalingrad, enabling the Red Army to surround and destroy General Paulus' 6th Army of almost 300 000 men in January 1943. Along a 1500-kilometre front from north to south, the German Army was forced to retreat. We were hopeful that in the not-too-distant future, perhaps a few months from now, Smolensk itself would be liberated.

At this time, a dreadful fate befell Father. The Germans forced him to become the 'designated official' of his village, a position they used to establish a first point of contact with the local populace. If, for example, the Germans wanted notices posted around a village this official would be given the task, and in addition would be expected to inform them of any unusual activity in the village which was not in the interests of the occupying forces. Consequently, appointment to this post was seen by the partisans as direct collaboration with the enemy. Much as Father protested and tried to avoid being delegated this dangerous task, he couldn't directly disobey German orders unless he was prepared to be shot. Father came to Roslavl to see me and we wept together over his terrible predicament. I couldn't do anything to help him. He feared that as soon as the partisans came to his village he would be shot, since one of the first things they did was to identify Russians occupying such positions, interrogate them to ascertain the nature of their collaboration and execute them. And that is exactly what happened.

Uncle Vanya came to see me and told me that the partisans had wanted to take him as well. Fortunately there was no evidence that he'd had anything to do with the Germans, so they left him alone on this occasion. Uncle Vanya stayed with me, but I never found out what actually happened to Father and I never saw him again.

My despair at this loss was unbearable and when, just a short time later, Uncle Vanya fell foul of the Germans I almost collapsed. My world was over, I was certain of that, but I had to maintain some semblance of sanity to help my uncle out of this serious situation. What he had foolishly done was to collect propaganda leaflets dropped by our air force, but he hadn't told me he had been doing this. Nor did he ever explain why he had done it. He actually brought them home and hid them under a cupboard. The Germans forbade us picking up or reading these leaflets under penalty of death. Some detestable swine, perhaps that same Aristov, found out and informed the Germans. So the inevitable occurred. Uncle Vanya was arrested and interned.

As soon as I found out I rushed to German headquarters. I knew one of the officers fairly well, a Captain Becker, who was a priest. He was a very religious and fair-minded person even though he was the enemy. Occasionally we chatted about religious topics and I often told him about the terrible repression and deprivation suffered by ordinary Russians under the Soviet regime. He had serious reservations about war, had some sympathy for the ideals though not the practices of Communism, and treated me very well and with a good deal of respect. I asked him to help obtain Uncle Vanya's release from the camp. I explained that he was a sick man, an invalid, who had not understood the nature of what he was doing. After all, he had simply hidden the leaflets, not kept them for distribution to the community. Captain Becker promised to do everything he could.

I was overjoyed when, after a week or so, Uncle Vanya returned. I begged him not to pick up any more leaflets and he promised me he wouldn't but he didn't keep his word. Not even a month had gone by when he was again arrested. This time Captain Becker told me he could do nothing and advised me not to intervene, as it was most probable that I too would then fall into the hands of the Gestapo. I went to the camp and asked to see Uncle Vanya, but in vain. I was forbidden to see him and never saw my beloved uncle again. I explored every possible avenue to discover the fates of Father and Uncle Vanya, but it was fruitless. My questions remained unanswered forever. I truly don't know how I survived these tragedies, so acute was my grief. I continued on in a kind of stupor, reacting to situations in a daze, feeling only numbness.

Shortly after this, in July 1943, my troupe and I were ordered to Smolensk and told that we would no longer perform more or less independently, but would join a newly arrived German group, with our base in Smolensk. I felt, quite rightly as it turned out, that we were viewed with some suspicion and were constantly under some surveillance. I stopped off in Roslavl to get my things before joining my colleagues—but there was no house to be seen, only a huge chimney standing amidst a pile of smouldering debris. Roslavl had been bombed and now neither Nikiferovitch nor his house existed.

My God, what else? How much grief could a person survive? I was deeply depressed and frightened. My daughter and mother had died, the partisans had taken my father, the Germans had probably killed my uncle, my brother was goodness knows where. I felt utterly alone. My artist friends tried to comfort me as best they could, but I was inconsolable. I buried myself in my work. I often wonder why I even bothered trying to stay alive but the answer is always the same: as far as I knew, Alec was still out there somewhere and I would do whatever I could to find him.

We continued our trips to the front to give concerts, but now we did so under complete and careful scrutiny and couldn't do anything without express permission. Several members of the troupe left and went back to Roslavl. Those remaining with me were two young women who were dancers and my dancing partner, Vasya. We now had no accordion but needed one to prepare additional items for the show, as the Germans had requested. We had no option but to work with what we had.

One evening during rehearsal, two Russian policemen came in and announced that Miss Makarova was requested to accompany them and report to their commandant for questioning. Well, this is finally it. My colleagues equally feared the worst. I went with the police to headquarters and was led in to see a man in Russian uniform with his back to me. When he turned around I couldn't believe who it was—Cverchkov, one of my teachers from Kalinin; he had taken our classes in Theatre History at the Drama Institute. I couldn't speak, I was so taken aback.

'Sorry if I frightened you,' he said. 'I guess it was rather childish to send for you in such a dramatic way but I couldn't resist it because I wanted to surprise you. Sit down and tell me all about how you come to be here.' He offered me some tea.

'Tea?' I said. 'A surprise, you call it? More like a near heart attack, I can tell you. How could you do such a thing?' He apologised once again and asked me why I was so frightened.

'Are the Russian police so terrifying?' he asked. I remembered Aristov.

'Yes, they are sufficiently frightening for my tastes,' I said. 'But you tell me how a teacher of fine arts becomes a commander of the Russian police which works hand in hand with the German Gestapo?'

'Don't be too quick to judge me, my dear,' he replied. 'I've always hated the Soviet regime, and with good reason. I bet you didn't know that my wife and I spent several years as guests in one of their labour camps. They killed my poor Alla, you know. The inhuman conditions under which we lived led to her getting tuberculosis, but they couldn't be bothered treating her. So why should I have any loyalty to that bastard Stalin and his thugs?' I muttered a question about why he was imprisoned and he became even more agitated.

'Oh, good question, Lilya. Big-time criminals like my wife and I should be locked up, shouldn't we? You know what we were guilty of? I told an anti-Soviet joke to some supposed friends at a party. Alla wasn't even there but paid the same penalty. Five years, Lilya. Can you believe that?'

'Yes, but being in the Russian police, and giving Russians up to the Germans…'

'Just a minute,' he said. 'On the contrary, I have been able to help many. The Germans give me quite a bit of authority amongst our own people, as you should know. This gives me a lot of opportunity to help them where otherwise they would fall foul of the Germans in no time at all. But in any case, I invited you here to find out about you, not tell you about me. I have heard that your troupe is very popular. Tell me how you came to start it up.'

We talked for several hours and I told him just about everything except certain classified information that I had overheard from indiscreet German officers about the strength and disposition of their troops. If the Germans found out that I knew such details, I would certainly be shot. I thought it would prove to be extremely useful for our troupe to have such a powerful ally, for I felt entirely sure that Cverchkov could not be an enemy like Aristov. I trusted him. When I returned to the others that night they were overjoyed to see me and to learn what had happened.

We finalised our program and awaited orders to go to the front, but before this happened we were directed to give a concert locally near

Smolensk. We were just about ready to go when all of a sudden I fell ill. My ulcers flared up. I had suffered from them for several years but this was a very serious attack. I was given a shot of morphine but was still unable to perform, so the Germans arranged for a different troupe to give the concert that night. On their way back they were attacked by partisans assuming that the occupants of a German car must be Germans. They threw grenades, killing the German driver and Regina, a young woman in the troupe. Then they opened fire with machine-guns, killing two more men and wounding three others. One of the group jumped from the car shouting that they were Russians. The partisans broke off the attack but it was already too late. Practically the whole troupe had been destroyed. Fate had dealt my group a very lucky hand, saving our lives in exchange for the lives of those poor unfortunate substitutes.

The Red Army was getting closer and closer by this time. The Germans were enraged by their own failure and becoming desperate. They were virtually seizing people straight off the streets, putting them into transports and sending them to Germany to provide forced labour. Katya, who had stayed behind in Roslavl, came to see me in Smolensk one day especially to convey some very important information. She told me something that filled my heart with hope. Returning home one evening she had struck up a conversation with a German soldier who asked her whether she knew a young woman in Roslavl by the name of Makarova. Yes she did, but how did he come to be asking that? He told her that he was returning from leave in Dortmund in Germany, where a young prisoner of war had asked him for a favour. Would he try to locate his family, and tell them what had happened to him? He had been held as a prisoner of war in a camp in Warsaw and then sent to Dortmund where he was working as a translator. Anyone in Roslavl would be able to tell the soldier where he could find the family, as the Makarovs were very well known there. Of course it could only be Alec! Katya told the soldier there was no one from the family left in Roslavl but she knew of a family member in Smolensk. And so she had come to see me. I asked Katya whether the German had told her the name or address of the place where Alec was translating, and whether she had obtained the German's name and address. Unfortunately she had asked for none of this information so I was unable to write to anyone to obtain more news.

Katya's news reignited my soul. From that moment on only one thought and one aim occupied my being—to go to Germany and find my brother, whatever it took and whatever the cost. He was all I had left.

One fateful day in early August 1943, our supervisor informed us our group had better get ready to go to Germany. I didn't hesitate for a moment, because this seemed to be the answer to my prayers. The others, however, were understandably filled with trepidation at the prospect of leaving their homeland. There were really only two alternatives: to accept the order and go, or escape to the forest and try to find the partisans. But knowing the fate that might be in store for us at the hands of the partisans, we all decided to go to Germany.

We were transported to the town of Mogilov, then to Minsk in Byelorussia, then to Baranovich. From there we were to be sent to Berlin within a few days. What we were to do in Berlin neither we nor the Germans knew. None of us wanted to leave Russia, but to remain behind was also a terrible prospect. The Red Army was by now only 100 kilometres or so from Smolensk and it was obvious the city would be recaptured shortly. Like the partisans, the Red Army and the Soviet regime dealt savagely and uncompromisingly with anyone who had cooperated in any way with the Germans. Those who managed to avoid reprisals at the time later told how the KGB dealt with so-called collaborators: they were executed. The KGB made no exceptions if they had any evidence whatsoever and under no circumstances took mitigating factors into account.

The evening before we left we got together, drank a glass of vodka, talked and cried, all feeling crushed by this latest turn of events. I noticed that they were all very kind and considerate towards me and thanked me for having saved them from the camp and probably from death. Nobody wanted to retire for the night. One or two would leave and then return and once again talk and hug one another and thank me for what I had done for them. This went on until the small hours of the morning. We all felt that the move to Germany was a pivotal point in our lives although no one knew what would happen to us once we got there.

Early the next morning we were awakened by a formal reveille. Our baggage, costumes and musical instruments were loaded and we were taken to the railway station. Accompanying us as our supervisor was a fairly high-ranking German officer. We took our things aboard the train, which stayed at the platform for some time. I took a seat by the window, ignoring what was going on around me. While deep inside I felt glad that I would have the opportunity to look for Alec, I was utterly miserable and couldn't stop crying. Where were my father and Uncle Vanya? Would I be able to find Alec? Would I ever be able to return to my home? With these thoughts going round and round in my mind I eventually fell into a tormented half-sleep, to be woken by shouting. The German officer was standing over me, his face contorted with rage.

'Where are your artists?' he screamed. I said they were probably in the next carriage.

'They are gone! You damned Russian bastards!' he squealed.

He delayed the departure of the train still further and German soldiers appeared everywhere, searching the entire station and its immediate surroundings, but my artists were nowhere to be found. It was only much later, in Berlin, that I found out what had happened. Apparently my troupe had planned everything in advance. They had got in touch with the partisans, who arrived at the station with a truck, looking as if they were engaged in some kind of work for the Germans. As soon as the artists had put their luggage, costumes and instruments on the train, they made their way to the truck and made their escape.

I was on my way to Berlin on my own. Overcome by loneliness and desperation, choking on my tears, I wanted only to fall asleep and never wake up. The uncertainty of my future lay like an oppressive darkness before me. I had thought I would have a better chance of finding Alec in Germany, but in truth I was probably deluding myself. I was heading straight into the heart of the enemy. There would be nobody to help me and I would have no freedom to do any proper search. I was not concerned about my own future. I didn't have one, in either Russia or Germany. I wasn't afraid—simply broken and in the depths of depression.

The German officer sat opposite me in silence, just watching. I could see by his expression that he understood what my thoughts were and how I was feeling, although he never once expressed any sympathy. I suppose he was too busy thinking about his own problems. The countryside rolled by, mile after mile, the monotonous clacking of the wheels and the train's gentle rocking from side to side gradually lulling me into intermittent bouts of restless, nightmarish sleep.

Heading deeper and deeper into enemy territory, with each passing hour it seemed more and more unlikely I would ever see my homeland again. I kept thinking, how could the Germans have come all this way with their war machine—and how will our poorly equipped and ill-prepared forces ever be able to drive them back? I tried to shut out these negative thoughts, but spent the remainder of the journey in a state of resigned hopelessness. The German beast had captured its prey and was now in the process of devouring it.

CHAPTER EIGHT

The train slowly pulled in to Berlin's Freidrich Street Station. It was some time in early September 1943. I don't recall the exact date because time had become meaningless at that point. I awoke from a disturbed sleep and collected my things. All around, inside the train and on the station platform, there was the frantic commotion of people hurrying about. Soldiers, young and old, were everywhere. Most were probably on their way to the front, a few returning on leave. They were all speaking in German. The sound of a foreign tongue, together with the realisation that I was in an alien land, overwhelmed me, emphasising my feelings of isolation and helplessness. The officer called for a porter to take our luggage. I had only two small suitcases of personal possessions.

'My orders are to take you to headquarters,' said the officer, 'and my responsibilities end there. You will have another officer as your superior.'

We got into a taxi and headed off. I asked where we were going—to a central place where all the artists and entertainers mustered from Russia and other German-occupied countries were to be found. I wanted to know what they did there but was told only that I, like all the others, would receive my working orders from there.

As we drove along the streets of Berlin there was already plenty of evidence of the effects of Allied bombing. Huge swathes of the city were almost completely devastated. My first reaction was a kind of subdued joy: I was glad to see the damage the Germans were sustaining. They were still my enemy and the enemy of my homeland. But I was conscious of not showing my true emotions, probably out of an innate sense of self-preservation. At that point it hadn't dawned on me that I too was now a resident of a city that the Allies were bent on destroying.

Headquarters were located in an old hotel called the Vinetta, an enormous but uninspiring building. Inside were throngs of people, with rehearsals under way in various rooms. Those who weren't rehearsing were wandering along the corridors, conversing with others or relaxing, smoking or reading. Hearing Russian voices all around me, my spirits began to lift. There was a familiar feel to the place—the feeling of being backstage at the theatre, which I knew so well. I tried to begin a conversation with one of the Russians, but the officer accompanying me quickly barked out some kind of order. I didn't understand what he'd said but his intention was very clear. The Germans ran things here and I should know my place.

Eventually, my superior brought over one of the German administrators, introduced him, said farewell and left. The administrator asked me to wait while he obtained ration cards, a work permit and accommodation details. Several artists from various theatres came up to me, introducing themselves and asking who I was, where I was from and other such details. I soon got to know a great many of these people. There were opera singers, ballet dancers, actors, writers, painters: in fact, the whole gamut of artistic talent was represented here. The Vinetta was known as the Berlin Actors' Club.

I told myself that things were really not as bad as I had feared. I learned that various mixed troupes were selected here, programs worked out, prepared and rehearsed, and the troupes then sent off to countries under German occupation such as France, Belgium and Holland. Indeed, the Germans even paid the performers a small but welcome salary for purchasing any personal items that they didn't provide directly. Well, if the others could put up with it I guess I could too. They all seemed to be getting by. In any event, I had no choice in the matter.

The administrator returned and took me to my new accommodation in Bleibtraustrasse. The house was small but very clean; other people from the Vinetta lived there as well. They were Maria; her daughter Lida, a pianist; and Susanna, who was from the Kiev movie studios. They introduced themselves and made me feel very welcome. With four of us together, I certainly should not feel lonely.

We shared our food and some of our possessions, but were far more circumspect about sharing background details and personal histories. Of course we all had a story to tell, but each of us respected each other's privacy in this regard. Coming from a Soviet background steeped in secrecy and paranoia, we all knew the possible consequences of talking too much and giving out information which might later be found not to be in one's best interests.

We had to give our ration cards to the landlady, who provided us with all our daily meals. Germany was in great difficulties with its food supplies, so our meals were spartan affairs, to say the least. But it was tasty, wholesome food and better than I had become used to in Russia. For breakfast we had coffee and a small roll with a tiny dab of butter. Dinner usually consisted of vegetable soup with potatoes. There was no meat to be had anywhere, as it was needed for the men at the front. We were always somewhat hungry but there was no fear of dying of starvation. In addition, my room was neat and comfortable. After all my misadventures at the front—the shooting, artillery barrages and machine-gun fire—this was the height of luxury. I could even have a bath.

'Don't get too carried away with how great it is here,' Susanna told me. 'Berlin is constantly being bombed at the moment and you'll soon realise what a threat we're under. I just take things one day at a time as you never know what a new day may have in store for you.'

'I already practise that philosophy,' I told her, 'since I have just come from the front and know all about fate. Tell me, where do you go for safety when the bombing starts?'

'Most times,' she replied, 'we just stay home and hide in the cellar. When we get sufficient warning we go to the Zoo. They have an enormous bomb shelter there which can accommodate 22000 people. So far we've been lucky, but you never know.'

Less than a week had passed before Susanna's words were dramatically realised. I had just returned from rehearsal at the Vinetta when the radio announced that an air raid was expected in fifteen minutes. The others were not yet home. I decided to go to the giant shelter at the Zoo, but I had not been en route for more than five minutes when bombs started raining down. In my panic I lost a shoe and staggered clumsily towards the bunker. Amidst the frightened cries of the crowd, the roars of the animals and the deafening explosions of nearby bombs, I heard the low rumble of the massive doors of the bunker being closed. With a last desperate effort I threw myself through the now almost closed doors and crashed heavily to the floor. The bunker had five floors, three of them above ground, two below. The reinforced walls, which were four metres thick, provided very good protection against bombs and shrapnel, but as there were anti-aircraft guns positioned on the roof the bunker was constantly the target of aerial bombardments. These caused the bunker to sway drunkenly, for it was supported by massive springs under the foundations.

This air raid was an extremely heavy one and seemed to go on forever. When we did eventually emerge into the daylight again the sight was unforgettable. Berlin was ablaze and there was rubble everywhere from the countless buildings destroyed. The zoo animals were mad with terror, for without suitable shelter they had endured the horror of the bombardment first hand. I wrapped my bare foot in a handkerchief as there was shrapnel and glass strewn everywhere and somehow managed to find my way home through the destruction.

The next day Lida, Susanna and I went to the Vinetta to find out what we should do next. I was placed with a theatrical troupe under the direction of Radlov. This troupe had been stationed at the front near Leningrad, their home city. I learnt that Smolensk had been liberated by the Red Army in September and it seemed inevitable that the horrific 900-day siege of Leningrad would be lifted soon, so the Germans were pulling back various units from there, including this entertainment one. The troupe was reassigned to go to France shortly.

Within the Radlov troupe I met Olga Pavlevna Gromov, an actress with whom I had worked in Smolensk. We were delighted to see each other again. At the Vinetta there were a great many artists from Smolensk, all hoping more than anything else to be able to return to their homeland. I was amazed that they could believe in some kind of major political change in the Soviet Union after the war but they were so convinced that Stalin would gladly take them all back and extend his kind forgiveness that it was impossible to argue with them. This blind faith proved to be their downfall. What happened to them following their return to the Soviet Union I found out only after the war, when I discovered many of their names in the pages of Solzhenitzyn's *Gulag Archipelago*. They were amongst the many unfortunates sent to Siberia to work in the labour camps as 'guests' of the Soviet Government. There they lived under the most appalling conditions and died from one or other of the many diseases to which one can so easily succumb when suffering from such bitter cold and chronic malnutrition.

No matter how much I questioned people from different parts of the Soviet Union I was unable to find out anything about Alec. Many of them suggested, however, that I turn for help to the commander of the ROA, the Russian Liberation Army, General Andrei Andreyevich Vlasov, who had been captured while defending Moscow. The ROA consisted of Soviet prisoners of war released from various German POW camps. Its aim was to free Russia not only from German occupation but from Stalinism as well. As far as the Germans knew, however, the ROA had only one objective—the overthrow of Stalin's regime—but still they distrusted Vlasov and kept him and his army under strict control. Nevertheless, Vlasov managed to free tens of thousands of Russian prisoners of war. He had access to all the camps and thus should be able to help me locate my brother. The ROA barracks were in a Berlin suburb called Dabendorf.

New Year 1944 was approaching. I was reassigned and no longer had to go to France with the Radlov group. I was relieved, as this would give me another chance to inquire about Alec. By now I was becoming desperate, as not one of the leads given to me had brought me any closer to Alec. But I couldn't yet give up hope of finding my brother alive. 'Please, please, dear God, let me find him alive,' I would pray, day and night. I wasn't ready to face the future without him.

I was able to join a group sent to give a concert for the ROA at Dabendorf, a stroke of luck that would give me an opportunity to speak with Vlasov himself. The large hall at the ROA barracks was lit up like a Christmas tree and packed full of military in ROA uniforms. The orchestra was playing Russian melodies. I approached an officer and asked if he would direct me to the commanding officer, telling him I had some unfinished business to discuss. He willingly agreed. Andrei Andreyevich Vlasov was quite tall and wore glasses. He had a plain but distinctively Russian face.

I asked him to forgive me for disturbing him with my problems, and he very obligingly agreed to hear me out. I briefly told him my life story and what I had last heard about Alec and he promised to do whatever he could to help. Then he invited me to join him at the officers' table. I was honoured to do so and to be introduced to General Trukhin, General Zhilenkov and General Zakutnov. By this time Vlasov had already had quite a deal to drink. Next to Vlasov, on the other side from me, sat a very pretty young German woman called Elsa. She spoke to Vlasov in broken Russian, telling him not to drink any more, but this annoyed him so he sent her packing. I was taken aback by his rudeness and very timidly asked why he was so severe with her.

'Because she's a whore,' said Andrei Andreyevich. 'She was introduced to me by the Gestapo, obviously to spy on me and report my every action to them. She is my mistress, but really I hate and despise her. She is trash, understand? She is the lowliest scum.'

He said all this very loudly, so Elsa must have heard him clearly. She simply smiled and pretended not to understand him. I felt very uncomfortable being witness to such a display of humiliation.

A constant stream of ROA soldiers approached Vlasov. They too had all been drinking heavily. They were obviously on very friendly terms with him and didn't follow any of the usual military protocols, because they jokingly addressed him as 'Your Eminence' or 'Your Almightiness'. He poured each of them a glass of vodka and kept refilling his own glass.

Elsa kept saying, 'Andrei, don't have any more. You've had too much already.' But Vlasov just swore at her in Russian and continued drinking, while apologising to me for being so rude towards Elsa. 'I know you must be shocked, Lilya,' he would say, 'but this witch is just driving me crazy.'

'Perhaps you really shouldn't have any more to drink,' I suggested.

'Lilya my dear, do you know I have a son in the Soviet Union? Do you know what Joey [Stalin] will do to him because of me? Why do you think I drink so much? Of course, it's no use. No amount of vodka can erase my despair and frustration, knowing what my family faces back home.'

As the evening wore on and Vlasov became increasingly intoxicated, he spoke more and more about Stalin and the early days of the war. 'That bastard put us all in this position, you know. You, me, everyone here.' He rambled on for ages, telling me how Stalin and his cohorts had led the Soviet Union to the brink of defeat. Stalin had obstinately refused to believe the mass of information made available to him prior to the war, which had made it crystal clear that Germany was about to invade. Even eight hours after the invasion had begun, Moscow was still issuing orders that Russian troops were not to return fire if fired upon.

'Many of our troop positions were overrun due to the incompetence of that madman and his cronies,' Vlasov said. 'And when they were fired upon, he would have the commanding officers shot as saboteurs and traitors. Someone should have shot him when they had the chance.'

'Perhaps no one has ever had the chance,' I suggested.

'Wrong, my dear,' he said. 'Do you remember that announcement that marked the start of the war?'

'Yes, as if it were yesterday.' I shuddered.

'Well, did you ever wonder why it was Molotov rather than Stalin who made that announcement? Do you think Stalin was too busy planning Russia's defence? Nothing of the kind. I'll tell you why,' he said, pouring himself another drink. 'He was so dumbfounded by his own stupidity in believing Russia was safe from attack that he just cracked, like this…' Vlasov threw his empty glass to the floor, smashing it into bits. 'He completely broke down and locked himself away. No one could communicate with him for days. So final orders could not be given to field commanders because they didn't have Stalin's approval. We were all just guessing, totally in the dark. That's when they should have put that son-of-a-bitch out of his misery. I hate to think how many officers and commanders he had removed or shot. But I can tell you it cost Russia dearly. Especially when he kept replacing good officers with Party bureaucrats who didn't know the first thing about commanding troops. Anyway, it's all too late for regrets now. We all do our best to fight for our country in the way we think is right, don't we?'

'I guess so,' I said vaguely.

'You guess so, do you?' he scowled. Then he broke into a broad laugh. 'Well, I'll tell you, my young one, there was nothing but guessing when the war broke out. No one knew anything and even if they did, they couldn't do anything because Russian snowballs don't count for much against German tanks. Do you know we were given express orders not to take one step backwards in retreat, no matter what the circumstances? I don't know whether you understand anything about military tactics, but usually it's necessary to move in several directions to secure an advantage.'

At this point Vlasov signalled to one of his officers to join us. 'Sasha, come over here.' Vlasov poured him a drink. 'Sasha, tell our young Lilya about the bear trap.'

I wasn't really interested, but Sacha launched into the account with such passion that I was forced to listen attentively.

'Things were so bad at the beginning, we had to resort to all kinds of ruses and tricks. Our illustrious leader here,' he said, slapping Vlasov on the back, 'was in charge of most of Moscow's defences, but had little in the way of military supplies to do it with. So he set up a number of bear traps, so to speak. The trap consists of a series of fortifications that are lightly defended, or so it seems. The Germans pour into this defended area once they see us give up our positions because we are hopelessly outnumbered. But then the trap is sprung because the real defence is flanking the invader from concealed positions and crushing him a bit at a time. Many soldiers have to be sacrificed to spring the trap but that's the only commodity we have a lot of, I'm afraid. The trick is,' continued Sasha, 'that various units must make what appears to be a withdrawal or retreat, in order to fool the enemy. Understand?'

'Yes, I think so,' I replied hesitantly.

'But that's just it!' snapped Vlasov at this point. 'Our fearless genius of a leader, Stalin, forbade a withdrawal of any kind. It made sheer mockery of military tactics.'

'So what did you and the others do?' I asked, now genuinely interested.

'I can't speak for all the others,' said Vlasov, 'but I'll tell you what I did.' There was a fierce gleam in his eye. 'When I gave the orders for the fake withdrawal to begin, the commissar whose job it was to shadow me and oversee everything I did, screamed, "You are not to fall back. That is against the express directive of Comrade Stalin!"'

'So what did you do?' asked Sasha in such a mock-serious way that it was immediately apparent he knew the answer. Vlasov had obviously told this story several times, because he acted out the rest of it, slowly and deliberately.

'I carefully weighed up my responsibility to the Party, to my country and to the leadership of our Comrade Stalin,' he said with mock gravity.

'And then what?' urged Sasha and one or two other officers who had joined in and had obviously heard the ending before.

'And then...I shot that son of a bitch right between the eyes,' said Vlasov, to the roar of laughter and approval of those who had gathered around.

'That's right, he did,' said Sasha, 'because I was there. Amazing isn't it, General Vlasov, how those stray German bullets seemed to find their mark on those Party bureaucrats who were always under our feet?' And they all roared with laughter again.

I had been listening to Vlasov for quite a while now and was very thankful when the orchestra started playing again. General Zhilenkov got up and asked me for a dance, a mazurka. We were the only ones who seemed to be able to dance this and so we performed to an enthusiastic audience amidst great applause. I had no idea that Zhilenkov would be such a good dancer. I had always loved dancing, often winning prizes in dancing competitions, and had taught dancing while a student at the Institute. During the break I started receiving lots of invitations from the officers to dance with them and so I spent the night dancing till I was ready to drop.

The evening concluded at Vlasov's quarters. He invited us all to supper—the three generals and a number of other high-ranking officers, the other artists and myself. Vlasov continued to drink during supper and rudely threw duck and goose bones onto Elsa's plate. But she merely giggled and said, 'Don't do that, Andrei dear, I don't want them.' After supper, cars were provided for us and we were chauffeured home.

That evening left me with a certain sense of disillusionment. Somehow I had expected more of the famous Vlasov, some kind of grand seriousness, I suppose. Instead I saw a drunken and embittered person, who swore at and abused the young woman with whom he was living. This didn't seem to befit the image of the commander-in-chief of the ROA.

I was involved in most of the performances at the Vinetta. I had a pleasant contralto voice, so I usually sang the German torch songs so loved by German audiences. I also performed dances, both Russian folk dances and modern ballroom dances, either solo or with a partner. One of the most popular songs in the show was the well-known 'Lili Marlene', which I sang at every performance. Most nights, the same groups of German officers and soldiers visited the Vinetta. After a few performances they would recognise my cue to go on stage to sing and would call out, 'Lily, Lily, sing "Lili Marlene" for us!' Before long, both the other actors in the troupe, and the audience, began calling me Lili Marlene. And so it became my stage name for the remainder of the war. Later I would realise how fortunate it was that I learnt some basic German through singing these songs and doing occasional comedy routines in the language.

There were a dozen or so other tenants in my boarding house, apart from those with whom I worked at the Vinetta. Many of them asked why I never invited any of my fellow artists home with me, because they would really appreciate some different company. At the time, there was little opportunity to go out anywhere in war-torn Berlin. I had recently become acquainted with a singer named Sergei, from Kharkov in the Ukraine, who asked if he could visit me at home sometime. So I invited him over one night and introduced him to Susanna, Lida and her mother, Maria. Sergei arrived with some black bread, a packet of cigarettes and a small bottle of brandy. This was such a treat when our daily menu consisted mostly of turnip soup and potatoes. We all enjoyed the visit immensely, particularly since there were no bomb alerts that night. Susanna recited a monologue, Sergei and I sang a cappella and we all generally reminisced about our lives before the war. As he was about to leave, Sergei asked whether we would mind if he brought along one of his friends next time, an actor and painter. 'Of course not,' we replied, almost in unison.

One evening in March, as I came home from rehearsal, Susanna burst into my room and told me that Sergei and one of his friends had dropped in and I had to come right over. I really didn't feel like it, as I had just lain down to rest, but was too polite to refuse. I dressed again, fixed my face and went to Susanna's room. Sergei got up, said hello and kissed my hand, but his friend just sat, smoking a pipe. I returned Sergei's greeting, but only nodded in the other man's direction, thinking what an ill-mannered type he was—although I couldn't help noticing he was extremely handsome. He was moderately tall, with a thick head of wavy brown hair, piercing blue eyes, a generous mouth and a quizzical expression. His demeanour was self-assured, even smug, and I was loath to admit that he disconcerted me.

A stilted conversation started up between Susanna, Sergei and me, made all the more uneasy by the stranger's sitting there, just watching me. Finally, I couldn't help myself and said to him, 'What's the matter? Why are you sitting there staring at me?'

'Nothing's the matter. I just like the look of your face,' he replied nonchalantly. 'Aren't I allowed to look?'

'Yes, I suppose you are. But you make me feel uncomfortable by staring so directly,' I replied. 'Anyway, what do they call you, since you haven't been polite enough to introduce yourself?'

'They call me all manner of things,' he replied, 'but my name is Boris.'

'Don't you want to know my name?' I responded with a certain amount of indignation.

'I already know that, Ludmila,' he replied in a matter-of-fact way. 'But I would like to know what you do and how you came to be here in Berlin.'

I took out a cigarette which Boris lit for me as I told him briefly about myself, about graduating from the Smolensk Institute of

Drama, being forced to work for the Germans in Russia as an actor and how I came to be in Germany.

'Now I'm sharing the same fate as other Russians here who come from German-occupied regions in our country. Is that all—any more questions?' I asked him, rather sarcastically.

'Not for the moment, but there'll be lots of questions in time.' He continued to look at me with those piercing eyes.

I blushed against my will and, trying to recover my composure, weakly shot back, 'And why are you so sure that I'll want to answer them?'

'I'm not at all sure. I just hope that I'll see you again. I'll give you my phone number and you can call me. I'd like to paint your portrait. I'm intrigued by you,' said Boris.

'What exactly are you intrigued by?' I asked, even more confused.

'I think you're smart. I always thought attractive women were only meant to be beautiful, not smart,' he replied.

'Is that so? In your opinion, only unattractive women are intelligent then?'

'I think that's generally true, but you are an obvious exception!' He smiled warmly and handed me a piece of notepaper. 'Here's my phone number.'

'Thank you. But I thought that it was you who wanted to paint my portrait. I hadn't mentioned anything of the kind. So you call me,' I told him, annoyed by his self-assurance. I folded his bit of paper and, smiling directly at him, popped it into his shirt pocket.

'All right, I will. You have quite a personality,' he said.

'And you have none,' I added tartly. There was a brief pause while Boris looked at me quizzically.

'Is that so?' he replied. 'Well, I'll just show you whether I have personality or not.'

'We'll see,' I said, not wanting him to have the last word.

At this point Sergei interrupted us. 'You know what, folks? I suggest we all go to dinner at Schlesinger's. What do you say? It's not far from the Zoo and if the bombing starts, we'll be close to the bunker.'

We all agreed, though I was half-hearted about the idea. Still, I did not want to be the spoilsport. We left the apartment, Sergei with

Susanna, Lida with her mother, and Boris walking with me, though he didn't offer me his arm even though the pavement was slippery and littered with debris. Once again I thought that he was short on manners.

'Why are you walking with me and not with Sergei?' Boris asked suddenly.

I stopped and turned to him. 'Listen. If you don't want to walk next to me, walk on ahead, or drag behind or even go and walk on the other side of the street.'

'It's not that, I just thought…'

'Oh, and you can think as well!' I wasn't about to let him get away with any assumption.

'I thought that you liked him,' finished Boris.

'And did I show that in any way?' I asked.

'No, but…'

'You know what?' I interrupted again, 'I'm getting tired of you and your assumptions. Can't you talk about anything more interesting?'

'It looks as if we're here,' he said somewhat gratefully, opening the door for me and taking my arm.

We began to take out our ration cards as we were led to a table. Our group was the only one there. It was obvious the waiter wasn't too happy with our arrival, as it was almost 9 pm and he appeared to have been on the verge of closing for the night. The decor was rather tatty, but in the dim light of the restaurant, the whole place seemed almost cosy. A scratchy recording of 'Lili Marlene' was playing in the background, which I found rather ironic. We were seated at the table nearest the door, Boris next to me. The meal was poor, a watery soup followed by some stale bread and dumplings, but considering this was wartime, we were lucky to be served even this. I ate my portion hungrily and asked for a second serve.

'You certainly have a good appetite,' remarked Boris, watching me intently as I finished eating.

'And does that bother you as well?' I asked, barely able to control my voice. 'Don't worry, I won't ask you to pay for me. I have enough ration cards to cover my share.'

'How prickly you are,' he replied good-naturedly. 'I'll be happy to pay for you. Just eat and enjoy.'

'And have you never heard of the word tactless?' I glared at him. 'If not, look it up.'

'Okay, okay, I give up,' sighed Boris, resigned to this exchange of bickering.

'It's about time.' Again, I couldn't let him have the last word.

After dinner, everyone decided to come back to our place and, fortunately, bombing didn't spoil the evening. We all felt like a cigarette, but cigarettes were extremely hard to come by during the war and I had finished my last one earlier that evening. Sergei had some tobacco and Boris produced some paper from his pocket so that we could roll our own cigarettes. I took the paper and realised it was a typewritten note. I took a closer look and saw that it was a love letter written in German from some woman to Boris.

'This is a note to you,' I told him, handing back the scrap of paper.

'So what? We'll use it as cigarette paper,' Boris replied. 'At least it has some use after all.'

'Really,' I said. 'That's very rude of you.'

'Perhaps. But the woman is a fool and I don't know how to get rid of her,' he answered, rolling the cigarette.

'Rid of her? Why can't you just be honest with her?'

'I've tried but it hasn't helped,' Boris shrugged.

'You're just a big braggart. An uncivilised, rude egoist,' I told him, looking at him with some distaste.

'All right, all right, stop criticising me. I am who I am. Let's have another cigarette, sit here for another half hour or so and then I'll go,' he said.

I ignored him for the rest of the night, while the others chatted amongst themselves. When Sergei and Boris took their leave, Boris just curtly nodded to me.

Well, that's the end of that, I thought. I'm sure I'll never see him again. But despite the prospect of early morning rehearsals, I found it difficult to sleep. My thoughts kept returning to the infuriating man with the piercing blue eyes.

The next day, I had just come in from rehearsals when the phone rang.

'Are you home?' asked a voice.
'It seems so. Who's speaking?'
'Me,' came the reply.
'Oh, it's you, Boris?'
'Who else would it be?'
'Well, what do you want?' I asked rather brusquely, even though I felt strangely flustered.
'You,' came the reply. There was a pause while I tried to make sense of what he was saying.
'What for?' I was nonplussed.
'To ask you out to dinner.'
'Aren't you worried that I'll use up all your rations?' I said. 'Today my appetite is even greater than it was last night.'
'Never mind. You can eat all my rations, little angry one,' he said, laughing.
'You're so generous,' I responded.
'Look, I told you, I am who I am. I'll pick you up at 7.30. Be ready, because I hate waiting.'
'And I hate being ordered about,' I told him flatly.
'I knew it. You're being difficult again. It's hard pleasing you.'
'Well then, why do you want to see me?'
'I'll tell you that this evening. Now, I can't remember how to get to your place. Is it the first or second turn right after the station?'
'It's the second turn. I live at the Ganzele Boarding House,' I replied.
'See you then, Lilya.'

After he'd hung up, I remembered that the turn into my street wasn't the second one but the third. Since I didn't have his phone number there was nothing I could do about it. He'll probably think I've given him the wrong information on purpose.

Still, I decided to get dressed. I put on a simple, fitted black velvet dress that had long sleeves and a rather low-cut neckline, and showed off my slim figure. I studied myself in the little mirror above my bed. Dark, curly hair to just below my shoulders; an oval face; generous red lips and large brown eyes. I had often been told that I was very attractive, even beautiful. 'I'll do,' I said, studying my reflection one last time.

I was ready by 7.30 pm. Boris hadn't arrived yet. It was a cold, wet and utterly miserable night, the wind howling outside; 8 pm, then 9 pm came and went and still no Boris. I resigned myself to never seeing him again. I admit that I was disappointed, but resolved that it was for the best. I'm sure he's a difficult person, I rationalised. I was just getting ready for bed—thankfully, there was no bombing that night—when about 10 pm my landlady knocked at the door telling me I had a visitor. It was Boris.

He didn't say anything, just came in, took off his coat and hat and sat down.

'Good evening, Boris,' I greeted him sheepishly.

'Why did you give me the wrong directions?' he exploded. 'It's stupid and impolite to say the least. I've been looking for your damn boarding house for the past two hours! You must have known that everything's blacked out outside so it's almost impossible to see anything. I was swearing at you and ready to give up and go home.'

'Well, why didn't you go home then?' I asked him meekly.

'Why? Why? You know perfectly well why!'

'Look, I truly didn't give you the wrong directions on purpose. Please forgive me.'

'All right then, I'll believe you. Get dressed and let's go.'

'Let's go where?'

'To dinner.'

'But it's ten o'clock. The restaurants are probably closed by now,' I said.

'We'll see. If they're closed, we'll just go for a walk,' he replied.

'But it's raining outside.' I didn't want to go out.

'Lilya, here's your coat. Don't argue with me.'

It was cold, dark and still wet outside. The wind added to the bitter conditions, cutting through my thin coat right to the bone so that walking was very unpleasant. Schlesinger's and two other restaurants we tried were closed.

'I can't ask you back to my place,' I told him. 'My landlady won't allow late night visits. As it is, she wasn't very pleased that you came when you did.'

'Never mind. I can ask you back to my place,' replied Boris, taking my arm. 'I don't have a landlady, but I do have a bottle of wine, some food and even something to go with a cup of tea. I hope you're not worried about coming back with me. I live nearby, in Hollendorf Place.'

'Why should I be worried? But I don't think it's a good idea. It's already so late and I have to be up early in the morning for work.'

'It's a great idea. I need to talk seriously to you.' He overrode my reservations.

'What about?' I asked, intrigued.

'You'll see.'

The apartment in which Boris lived consisted of one room plus a kitchenette. There was no bathroom or hot water. The kitchen lights didn't work. An unmade bed, a table and two chairs occupied the single room. The window, which had been destroyed by a bomb, was covered with a piece of broken fibro and a tatty old blanket. The room was dimly lit by an overhead bulb, showing a table scattered with books, papers and leaves of tobacco. In the middle stood an interesting centrepiece—a dirty old shoe and a plate with some leftover bacon and a half-eaten piece of cake. The floor was littered with bits of newspaper, cigarette butts, letters and general mess.

'Sit down, Lilya, over here on this chair. The other one's broken,' Boris offered. 'Now we'll have a drink and something to eat.'

'Do you really think I could eat in this pigsty?' I asked him. 'At least give me a piece of cloth and a broom.'

'Why do all women have this horrible habit of cleaning up? I don't have a broom or any cloth. Stop being so fussy.'

'Don't interfere. I can't stand looking at this pigsty,' I said. 'How can a civilised person live like this?'

'Perhaps I'm not civilised. Perhaps I'm just primitive. What then?' he laughed.

'Stop talking nonsense. Bring me that torn singlet and some water. And stay out of my way while I get this room into some sort of order. We'll talk later,' I told him firmly.

Within an hour, the table had been cleared, washed and covered with a piece of torn curtain that I found lying on the bed. The floor had been swept and wiped down with a wet rag. The bed had been made and covered with the remainder of the curtain. I found some glasses and cutlery with which I set the table and at last the room took on a look of respectability. Boris opened the bottle and poured us some wine.

'Well, what do we drink to, Lilya?' he asked me, raising his glass.

'Let's drink to the end of the war. Please let it come quickly.'

'That goes without saying. What else do we drink to?'

'Well, to our survival, and to my finding Alec again,' I replied.

'That also goes without saying,' he repeated. 'What else?'

'I don't know. You suggest something,' I said in exasperation.

'I'll tell you what, Lilya, let's drink to our engagement.'

'Engagement? What engagement? What are you babbling about?'

'I'm not babbling. I'm proposing to you. I've decided to marry you.'

'Boris, stop fooling around or I'll go home,' I told him.

'You're not going anywhere. You're saying yes and you're going to be my wife. So stop arguing,' he replied quietly.

I looked at him, thinking that either he or I must be out of our minds. Surely this isn't happening, I thought, shaking my head. A normal person wouldn't propose after meeting someone twice. I became angry at such a stupid and tactless joke. He was obviously playing some kind of game with me.

'All right, that's enough. I don't like your jokes or your manners. Take me home if you can. If not, I'll go on my own,' I told him, getting up from the table.

'Lilya, sit down and listen. I'm not joking. You must understand me. You're beautiful, intelligent and I fell in love with you at first sight. Please believe me. I'm not lying to you. Why should I lie? I'm not asking anything of you except to be with me. I'd like to look after you. And if I'm not repulsive to you, that's all I want. Lilya, say yes.'

Boris began to speak at length and I found myself listening to his impassioned arguments, thinking that perhaps he was right and that my scepticism was a product of my past hurtful relationships. I also believed in love at first sight, remembering how I fell in love with my little angel Ina's father the moment I met him. Who knew what would happen to each of us tomorrow? We were surrounded by death and the destruction of everything that we knew and loved. And it was true

I was very attracted to Boris, though God knows he was like no one else I had ever known. I had met many attractive and intelligent men in my life, but not one of them had affected me the way Boris did. Is this what they call a soulmate? I wondered, looking at him. While from the very moment I met him Boris had seemed to make all the decisions, in a strange way, even though I hated to be dominated, being with him gave me a feeling of warmth and belonging, of being protected. I hadn't experienced this feeling since the days when my parents and Uncle Vanya had been there for a younger me.

'Lilya, darling, what are you thinking?' Boris put his arms around me, softly stroking my hair. He began to caress me, gently at first, and then with a passionate ferocity that I reciprocated. He began to tear at my dress, revealing my full breasts, which he kissed. One at a time, his mouth nuzzled my nipples until I could barely stand it.

'Wait, my darling, my dearest,' I murmured, standing up. And, with our eyes locked in mutual passion, I began to take off my dress, slowly. I felt his breath on my cheeks as his hands began to lovingly explore my whole body. Usually I would feel shy, standing naked in front of a man, but this time was so different. Boris looked at me for a long time and then, whispering hoarsely, he entered me. 'Lilya...' He was a passionate but gentle lover, seeming aware of both my needs and my inhibitions. As his body penetrated mine, he kissed me wildly, stifling my moans of pleasure. We made love, again and again, till, exhausted, we both lay back on the bed. Despite the cold, I was flushed with happiness and warmth.

I stayed the rest of the night and we talked until morning. Boris had come to Germany as a prisoner of war. Conscripted into the Red Army in May 1941, he was wounded in the arm six months later and taken to Germany as forced labour. He left behind two children, a mother and two brothers, all in the Ukraine facing who knows what fate. Currently he was working as a radio announcer for Radio Berlin—a German propaganda radio station transmitting to all points of the front. He told me that one of the other announcers at the station was Lord Haw Haw—Winston Churchill's nephew, who would be tried and executed at the end of the war for collaboration with the Germans. Like me, Boris hated working for the enemy but, like all of us, he had little choice. We didn't believe that our work was of any significant value to the German war effort. Perhaps we were wrong about this but at the time it seemed we were justified in trying to survive like anyone else.

Boris had been married and divorced twice. He left his first wife as he hadn't ever really loved her and his second wife left him. She was a pianist, and this divorce hurt him badly, as he had been very much in love with her. He had a daughter, Julia, from his first marriage and a son, Serioja, from his second. He had no idea where they were or even whether they were alive. I knew only too well how that felt and realised there was a sort of tragic bond between us. Neither of us had anything certain to look forward to except the immediate moment. We made love again, just as the city was starting to wake. It was gentle and sweet and I luxuriated in waking with him in the soft light of morning. For the first time in so long, I felt as if I had come home.

The next day we handed in our application for a marriage licence and we were married within six weeks, on 12 May 1944. It was a simple wedding ceremony, conducted by a German Government official at the local registry. I wore a grey fitted dress with a small collar and three-quarter cuffed sleeves and a white orchid at the waist. My hair was swept up in the fashion of the day. Boris looked admiringly at me as I came into the registry office. He looked so handsome in a suit, with a collarless white shirt, the top button undone. Despite the bleak surroundings and the uninspiring service that lasted only ten minutes or so, nothing could mar my happiness that day. I looked at my new husband and kissed him lightly on the cheek. I was happier than I had been in a long time. Who was it that said you need to experience despair to be able to experience joy? Well, I had certainly experienced more than my fair share of despair. Even though Boris had told me of his previous two marriages, I didn't feel threatened or worried. I felt really secure and loved by this man.

As I got to know him better, I found my husband to be an extremely intelligent, interesting, well-educated and well-read man. Boris was also an excellent actor and wonderful painter, preferring to paint portraits than to be involved in the theatre. He was very compassionate but had an edge of sarcasm to his make-up and there was no matching his wit if one took him on. He was an exceptional human being and extremely talented.

But, as is often the case with such people, living with him was not easy even though it was interesting. Boris could become very moody and withdrawn. At these times he might disappear for entire days. Upon his return, he would tell me that he had been playing chess. I had no reason to disbelieve him, but I missed him terribly, especially if I was alone when there was a bombing raid. He had really far too much talent for just one person. Besides being a good actor, an artist, a chess master, Boris was also a brilliant journalist and theatre critic. All this meant he could never settle for just one profession. He didn't have the concentration required to stay with any one of them. I suppose if he had had to choose, he would have chosen portraiture as his most beloved interest. Unfortunately fate didn't allow him to concentrate on this talent alone.

At first we moved into an uncomfortable little apartment in Hollendorf Place until it was destroyed by the bombing. We moved several more times, each time having our home bombed to rubble while, thankfully, we happened to be away. We finally settled into an apartment close to one of Berlin's largest bunkers so that we could escape from the bombing quickly. It was mid 1944. Germany was being defeated on all fronts and Berlin was being bombed mercilessly. We went to bed fully dressed every night as the air raid sirens wailed almost incessantly. We kept two small cases packed with our most important possessions, and Boris would often have a supply of food on standby as well. It was rather embarrassing at times. When the air raid warnings sounded, we grabbed our cases and ran to the bunker for safety, but Boris would lag behind because he didn't want to spill the soup that he had snatched directly from the stove! People around us would stare at him in amazement, saying he must be incredibly hungry to risk his life for some soup. Boris would as often as not offer them the soup, saying he wasn't hungry at all. 'It's just that you may not be able to stop a bomb from taking your life but you can stop it from taking your soup,' he would joke. Boris's ability to retain a sense of humour in the most desperate situations was just one of the things about him that I came to love dearly.

Throughout 1944 to the beginning of 1945, Berlin was reduced to rubble. The air was thick with the stench of decaying bodies trapped under the burnt-out shells of buildings. It was by now patently obvious that Germany was very close to losing the war. The Red Army was closing in on Berlin. However paradoxical it might seem, the imminent end of the war made our future even bleaker. Returning home was impossible. Stalin would never forgive us for staying alive, let alone for working for the Germans. We would have been dealt with as enemies of the people, even though it was the regime, not the people, who considered us the enemy. But it was only I who thought this way. Boris disagreed. He and many others firmly believed that our motherland would welcome us back with open arms. It wasn't long before events proved me right, however.

Berlin became unbearable. The bombing was relentless. I began to think I would rather be dead and get it over with than have to put up with this way of life. I met up again with General Vlasov on New Year's Eve of 1944. I took Boris with me. Vlasov told us that he was on his way to Czechoslovakia to launch a Russian radio broadcast centre and asked me to work for him. In fact, he rang me not long after our meeting asking to see me again, but Boris became jealous and asked me not to go. He rang Vlasov himself and told him not to ring me again. In the meantime, I managed to find out from Vlasov that there was no news of Alec. I felt the connection with my brother was severed. I had absolutely no idea where he might be, or even whether he was still alive. Would I ever see him again?

There was no way of getting out of Berlin without the assistance of someone with political connections. Vlasov could have helped us get out of Germany by taking us on as radio announcers in his set-up in Czechoslovakia, but Boris had ruined that prospect. There was no way out other than to go to the headquarters of the Russian Liberation Army. There we found that the director of the radio station in Czechoslovakia was none other than General Zhilenkov, with whom I had danced that New Year's Eve. He told us he would get us both a job in the radio station, but we would have to audition like everyone else. Boris and I passed the audition with flying colours, both having worked in radio previously, and at the beginning of February 1945 we were off to Czechoslovakia to a new, but still completely uncertain future.

CHAPTER NINE

Just before we left for Czechoslovakia an unexpected reunion occurred. I was called into the Vinetta theatre by its director, Dr Knumper.

'I have a surprise for you,' he said, looking pleased. I thought that he was planning another trip for me. He had recently asked me to go to France to work, but Boris talked me out of it. However, it turned out to be something else.

'Would you like to meet up again with those actors you worked with on the Front in Russia?' Knumper asked me.

'Of course, but they went off to join the partisans,' I replied, thinking that the old man must be out of his mind.

'Yes, they did go off to the partisans, but now they're here. And, what's more, you can see them.'

The next few moments unfolded before me as though I were seeing them in a film. The door opened and in they came—Peter, Nadia and my old guitarist friend, Kostya. I was so overcome I couldn't speak for a few minutes while the tears coursed down my face. When we had all hugged and kissed each other and cried uncontrollably, they began telling me their news. After they left me at the station in Baranovich, they had decided to turn back and join the Russian partisans, while I went on to Berlin alone.

'Lilya, even though you told us that the Russians would treat us harshly because we worked for the Germans, we didn't believe you. None of us worked for the enemy voluntarily; we were all forced to do so. You know how it was. Because of that we thought that the partisans at least, would understand and welcome us into their ranks. Well, I can't tell you how wrong we were and how right you were.'

They went on to describe how they had contacted the partisans who promised to send them back to Moscow. At that time the group had included another friend of mine, Ivan. Instead of being sent to

Moscow, they were locked up, mercilessly beaten, called traitors, and starved for over a week. It was only when the partisans needed to retreat because of the German advance that they let the group out of their small lock-up and ordered them to follow. Ivan was wounded and left behind to die and the other three, weakened by starvation and harsh treatment, were also left behind. The Germans found them and sent them on to Berlin as prisoners of war.

'Once we got here, we asked about you and were told to start looking at the Vinetta. And so we're here. It's now very clear to us what awaits us back home if we ever try to return.'

Deep down I had known this long since, but it broke my heart to hear it. It was now certain that whatever my future held for me, it would never include returning to my homeland. Sadly, the reunion with my three friends proved short-lived as Boris and I were departing for Czechoslovakia within a day or two. Again, farewells and tears. When would all this end?

If we thought that in Czechoslovakia we would escape the incessant bombing that we experienced in Berlin, we were wrong. All Europe seemed to be in flames. Czechoslovakia was as much under siege from Allied bombing as Berlin. This time the attacks came from the Russians, who were daily gaining the advantage. The Red Army was advancing on all fronts as the war drew to an end. The Nazis were completely defeated on the Eastern Front but preferred to keep sacrificing human lives rather than capitulate. They kept on spouting propaganda and in order to do this they tried to locate their remaining facilities as far away from the front lines as possible. Czechoslovakia was one of the meeting points between the American forces to the south and west and the Red Army advancing from the east. It became clear that Czechoslovakia would soon be just as dangerous for us as Berlin had been. Boris and I knew we had to escape, but where could we go?

We had one thing in our favour. Upon accepting the jobs as radio presenters in Czechoslovakia we had been given passports and documents that allowed us some freedom to travel. These would prove to be crucial to our survival. For now, however, we would have to take things one day at a time.

Prague was a magnificent city. It was a pity we had so little time to enjoy its cultural richness. We arrived there at the beginning of March and immediately started work at the radio station doing routine announcing. After only two days we were given an assignment to travel to Bratislava, about 400 kilometres southeast of Prague, in Slovakia. From there, it is less than 50 kilometres to Vienna in Austria. We were very apprehensive about taking this assignment, as it seemed to be taking us closer to the Red Army. However, it was only temporary and, in any event, we were in no position to be arguing with the Germans as to where they should send us.

We moved to Bratislava and began work. One afternoon I began feeling particularly unwell and asked to be allowed to go home. I left a message for Boris telling him not to worry. By the time he arrived home my condition had worsened considerably. He came home to find me deathly pale, with a temperature of 106 degrees. I was suffering from an acute infection and inflammation of the kidneys.

Boris immediately rushed me to hospital in a critical condition. The doctors did all they could for me but for days I lay delirious, unable to eat or even recognise anyone. Boris was told that he had better send for a priest to administer the last rites. It was a terrible time for me but it must have been awful for my poor Boris as well. He stayed with me day and night, applying damp compresses to my face and talking to me to try to keep up my spirits. I made it even more difficult for him by telling him that if I died I wanted him to find someone else and go on living. I also asked him to keep trying to find Alec. Boris would have none of it, saying there could never be anyone else for him and that I must not even contemplate the possibility of dying. My condition remained critical and I grew progressively weaker and weaker. Then a truly extraordinary thing happened.

I awoke from a bout of delirium to see an old woman standing over my bed next to Boris. Boris said she was someone visiting sick patients throughout the hospital out of goodwill. Expecting her to be German, I was surprised to hear her say to me in perfect Russian, 'You're from Smolensk, aren't you?'

I answered that I was, assuming that Boris had told her, but he was startled to say the least.

'I didn't tell her anything about you,' he spluttered. Then, turning to the woman he asked, 'How did you know that?'

'Never mind,' she replied. 'What's important now is for your wife to get well, so let's not waste any time.' With that, she took out a parcel wrapped in brown paper and slowly removed a variety of pressed flowers and aromatic herbs, placing them in an elaborate array on my bedside table, on my bed, and around my pillow. As she placed each article in position, she whispered some sort of incantation or prayer in a language neither Boris nor I could understand.

'These will help,' she said, 'but your recovery depends primarily on you, my dear. You must will yourself to get better and then you will.'

'But of course I want to get better,' I protested weakly.

'Yes, I know,' she replied, 'but you must think to yourself why you want to live, and focus only on that. Obviously, there is your husband Boris, but that may not be enough. You don't have children, do you?'

Again I was startled and meekly replied, 'No. There hasn't been time because of this horrid war, but I would dearly love to have children...'

'Then let that be your reason to live,' she interrupted. 'You must live for them and for Boris. Think only about that and all will be well. I will return in a few days to see you again and I expect to find you well on the way to recovery.' She gave me her blessing and left. At the time I simply thought of her as a very kindly Good Samaritan, but over the next few days I made a wonderful recovery. I didn't understand what had happened. All I knew was that something miraculous had taken place. Even the doctors were amazed at the speed and extent of my recovery.

During my illness I had been worried about how it was possible for Boris to take so much leave from work, but he assured me that it was not a problem. His superiors were civilians who were extremely sympathetic and concerned for me. Notwithstanding the fact that we were Russians against whom Germany was fighting a desperate, losing war, ordinary Germans treated us kindly and humanely most of the time, so that despite the horrors of war I never lost my faith in human nature. Those not infected by the poisonous ideological rantings of Nazism or Communism seemed to be like Boris and me, just ordinary human beings.

By now we had been in Bratislava for a month. The Red Army was closer and our thoughts were preoccupied with getting right out of Czechoslovakia. One of Boris's colleagues told him that a war correspondent was needed urgently at a radio station in Karlsbad in far western Czechoslovakia, very close to the Swiss border. This could well be our last and best opportunity to get out of the war zone completely. Boris immediately applied for the position and was given leave by the German authorities to go there when he was accepted.

I was still weak, but at the beginning of April Boris took me to Karlsbad by train. It was almost 1000 kilometres from Bratislava and took two days. The trip was horrific. The carriages had no glass in the windows and were bitterly cold. My body became racked with pain as I again ran a dangerously high fever. Poor Boris suffered constant hunger and was sick with worry about my condition while I was still unable to hold down any food—even the meagre ration of bread we allowed ourselves daily. Boris's anxious face disclosed his fear and he would often put it close to mine, whispering, 'Darling Lilya, don't die, just please don't die.'

We arrived at Karlsbad station desperate to find our contact from the radio station, which was to have arranged our lodgings. After waiting for hours it was obvious that something had gone wrong. We phoned the radio station but there was no reply. We had no idea where we were or where we could go. We had no possessions and knew no one. We walked some distance from the station and came to an old building, which might once have been a school, where even at that hour of night there were people milling about. They were all in the same situation as we were: escapees on the run from their regimes, refugees of one sort or another. There were Latvians, Russians, Ukrainians, Poles and other Eastern Europeans, of all ages including children. Some were wounded, some were ill, and all were starving.

Somehow we managed to get a few hours' sleep huddled in a dry corner of the building. The next morning Boris left early to try to sort out the situation with the radio station. He came back with the worst possible news—the person who was to have met us at the railway station had been killed during an air raid several days earlier, which had also destroyed most of the radio station. There was no longer any position available and Boris had been advised to get in touch with the authorities in Berlin or Prague to find out what we should do next. Luckily, he decided to discuss the situation with me first. Because we might be ordered back to Berlin or some other place that would put us directly in the path of the approaching Red Army, we felt our best option would be to avoid making contact with the German authorities altogether, stay in Karlsbad until my health improved and then try to make our way towards Switzerland.

The old building in which we had spent the night was being used as a temporary shelter. There was no food, so we either begged for it from the Czechs or simply stole it. Those who had any possessions at all, however meagre, traded them for something to eat. The rest of us watched in silence. Surprisingly there was no envy, no animosity between anyone, even though we were all from different countries and walks of life. Our hunger and the dangerous conditions of everyday life seemed to act as a bond. As if things weren't bad enough, bombing raids over the next few days destroyed our shelter.

Those who weren't killed fled to other parts of the city. Boris and I went with one group which found shelter in an old bombed-out hotel, the Sans Souci. It had no doors or windows, but at least there was a roof over our heads. I was still extremely ill, with a constant high temperature, and one day Boris found a German doctor willing to come and examine me. He was horrified at my state and told me what I already suspected—that I should be hospitalised immediately. But that was not all. His diagnosis had shown that one of my kidneys was damaged irreparably and I would need to have it removed. The infection had also spread to my ovaries, which he said should also be removed—a full hysterectomy was my only hope. But how could I go to hospital at this point in time? Not only that, I was totally unwilling to even contemplate a hysterectomy as I had always wanted children badly. I would rather die than go through life without having children. My grief over losing my precious little girl had never abated and now that we were married, I dearly looked forward to having children with Boris—a girl, then a boy. I knew that no other child could replace my darling little Ina, but having a girl first would, in a way, make the experience of having another child a little easier emotionally. The doctor gave me some pills and, with great misgiving, left me.

Rumours abounded about the direction the war was taking. Some said that the Red Army was close by. Others assured us that the American troops had arrived and would allow us to stay in Karlsbad if we wanted to or help us get back home. But nobody really knew what was going on. There was factionalism everywhere. The Poles argued with the Ukrainians, the Czechs with the Russians and so on. Each nationality blamed the others for the catastrophe in Europe. People believed that after the war their individual countries would become independent. Even my own husband, who was certainly no fool, was naive enough to believe that the end of the war would bring about the end of Stalin's tyranny. He wasn't alone in thinking that it was possible Russia and its republics would experience the beginning of a new age of democracy and individual freedom.

Our fellow refugees at the Sans Souci had plenty of time on their hands to think about such things. In fact they thought about the nature of postwar Europe in great detail and even began to undertake some preliminary economic and diplomatic planning of their own. A major question that they felt needed to be resolved very early on was that of political boundaries. What started as reasonable discussions between competing views soon turned into all-out shouting matches that continued into the early hours of the morning. The less political amongst us—who also happened to be those who prized their sleep above arguing about the importance of non-existent borders—banished these 'new world' reformers to the remotest possible part of the hotel, an unpleasantly dank but fairly large hall.

So it was that in the midst of war, with no certain prospect of surviving even one more night, a band of political reformers set up camp in a bombed-out hotel to discuss and plan the future of Europe. They found the energy to assemble every conceivable piece of unused luggage and broken-down furniture into a large-scale map. Each country had its own 'government representatives' who conducted their business in their own language until such time as joint sessions were held, in which as many languages were used as was necessary to communicate. The scene was surreal. Groups of gaunt and dishevelled refugees seated themselves, very business-like, on top of old boxes and piles of musty magazines and newspapers, separating themselves from other such 'governments' with political boundaries composed of old shoes and bits of string or loose floorboards. Foreign affairs were conducted by shouting louder than the neighbouring government and demanding such things as freedom from trade sanctions and either full recognition or full abolition of pre-war boundaries, depending on where your interests lay. If it weren't all so pitiable, it would have been laughable.

These inhabitants of the new Europe were soon to be brought back to grim reality. Towards the end of April one of the refugees ran in, shouting that two American tanks had been sighted nearby. We began to think frantically about what information we wanted to pass on to the Americans. The problem as we saw it was that since the Americans didn't know any of us or where we were from, how would they know how to deal with us? We could end up being sent anywhere because none of us believed that the Americans understood our individual nationalities or our home countries. We would soon realise, however, how mistaken was our assumption that the Americans had any interest in dealing with us and sorting out our problems.

In the meantime, the different national groups amongst us each elected a nominal leader and a secretary who immediately started compiling lists of names. These lists included personal details including, in many cases, a person's movements during the war, as well as specifying whether they wanted to be returned to their homeland or allowed to remain in Karlsbad to decide their future homeland for themselves. Many people kept changing their minds and were moved from one list to another, often several times over. There were only a very few who, like me, were adamant that they didn't want their name to appear on any list and certainly did not wish to document any movements and actions over the past four years.

Finally, the entire group chose a number of delegates who would present the lists and explanatory memoranda to the Americans. Mind you, not a single delegate spoke more than one or two words of English, but this didn't seem to worry them and off they went to present everything to the American liberators who would solve all their problems. Neither Boris's name nor mine appeared on any list.

Soon the delegates returned, in high spirits, obviously very pleased with how their documents seem to have been received. I assumed I must have been overly suspicious about providing names and that the Americans did indeed represent the first really positive hope that eventually our lives would be returned to normal. Then I learned the details of their response and almost had a seizure: not only were the Americans totally uninterested in our situation, but refugees represented a problem that they would rather not have to handle. After all, they were a military force. They had placated the delegates by telling them that a combined Allied command was established expressly for this purpose and would take care of all refugee problems. At the first opportunity, they would pass on all the lists and memoranda to this appropriate authority. They thanked the delegation and motioned them to be on their way.

'What?' I exclaimed in horror, together with the other two or three 'paranoids'. 'And just who do you think is the appropriate Allied authority that will deal with us? Do you think it is the French or the English or the Americans?'

The rest of the group suddenly looked very much less high spirited than a few moments ago.

'No, it's the Red Army, you idiots, the same Red Army that doesn't recognise citizens of Latvia or Lithuania or Ukraine—only Soviet citizens. And what's more, I bet you it doesn't recognise the term forced labour either!' I hissed. 'But "traitor to the Soviet Union"—that is a phrase they will be familiar with, have no doubt of that. Then they'll deal with you just as they wish and you can kiss your precious nationality lists and memoranda goodbye. Except of course that you've given them all the details they could possibly have wanted to know, about just who you are and what you have done. You idiots, you unbelievable idiots!'

'Come on,' someone said. 'The Americans won't allow the Russians to do with us as they please.'

'Do you seriously believe that?' we gasped in astonishment. 'The Americans have been fighting a war for four years and, like us, they want an end to all the problems and difficulties. They simply want to go home. Believe it,' we said, 'they won't lift a finger to help us in preference over their new Red allies. They'll just pass on all this information and leave it to the Reds to sort out the less than pleasant problem of dealing with refugees from all over Europe.' All the different national groups dispersed, many people with worried faces. Others animatedly denounced our foolish suspicions about the unreliability of depending on the American saviours.

On 7 May 1945, the end of the war was announced, although it was not made official until the next day. The national groups at the Sans Souci suspended their petty bickering and awaited further developments with uncertainty and great concern. Early on the morning of 9 May we heard more news—the Red Army was almost here. Gunfire was heard in the distance, sections of the city were alight and all the residents of our hotel ran out into the streets to see what was going on.

Karlsbad had a canal running through the middle of it, into which the River Eger flowed. There were several bridges connecting the city centre to its outskirts and these were already swarming with Red Army patrols. There was certainly no way of getting past these soldiers without documents and since many people had had their documents confiscated by the Germans or had lost or destroyed them to escape identification, full panic broke out. In any case, our current documents were useless, since they had been issued by the newly overthrown Nazi regime. People began gathering their few remaining possessions and loading wheelbarrows and any other mode of transport they could find. Word was quickly spreading that the Russian soldiers were hostile and suspicious of everyone with whom they came into contact, so people were beginning to flee in all directions.

Some ran into the surrounding forests; others fled to the neighbouring city of Marienbad; others decided to stay and face whatever happened.

People began pinning red ribbons onto their clothes and loudly proclaiming that, with the arrival of our glorious Red Army, we could now return to our homeland and all would be well. Inwardly, everyone was trembling with fear and uncertainty. Those who didn't want to go back home soon found it was wiser to keep quiet and not say anything. It seemed that the good old Soviet habit of spying and reporting on each other was still alive and well. There were those in our group who would have done anything to ingratiate themselves with the Russian soldiers, even if that meant reporting on the so-called anti-Communist sentiments of their wartime friends and colleagues.

The next day Boris found a bicycle and told me that he was going to get closer to the Russian patrols to see if he could find out anything. I tried to talk him out of this plan, but he told me not to worry and simply to wait for him to return. One hour went by, then another, and still no Boris. Then a man whom I knew only slightly, but who disliked me because of my suspicions concerning Soviet intentions, informed me that Boris had been seen talking to some of the Russian soldiers on patrol. They had exchanged a few words and suddenly Boris had been placed under arrest and taken away.

'Don't bother waiting for your husband. You'll never see him again,' he stated with chilling finality.

CHAPTER TEN

The news of Boris's arrest was such a tremendous blow I couldn't think clearly. Word spread quickly and people suddenly began shunning me as though I were a leper. The Communist sympathisers with the red ribbons were the worst. They avoided me whenever they could. Only Tolya and Katya—two Russian refugees whom we had met at the Sans Souci and who became our close friends—remained close by my side, supporting me through the next few harrowing hours. Both had served a lengthy period of imprisonment in Russia for 'anti-Soviet' activities, so they were as distrusting of the Red Army as I was. They tried to persuade me to leave with the many others who began to flee once they heard that the Red Army was approaching.

'Run? Where to?' I retorted, angry and miserable. 'I'm not going anywhere without Boris. Anyway, you can't just leave me like this. I know that if he can, he will come back and get me.' I wept bitterly, hoping that my pleas weren't falling on deaf ears.

'Lilya, I just don't know what to say,' Tolya replied. 'We told you we should get the hell out of here before the Soviets arrived. Now they have probably got Boris and if we hang around here we'll all be joining him.'

'I'm not leaving here until I find out exactly what has happened to my Boris. Anyway, where could anyone run to from here?'

Finally Tolya and Katya agreed to wait another two hours or so. We had just hidden in the bushes opposite the hotel when a Red Army vehicle drove up and stopped across the road from us. Two soldiers with automatic weapons got out and approached the crowd milling in front of the hotel.

'Who's in charge here and who are you?' one of them asked the crowd.

People surged towards the soldiers, calling out, 'Brothers, comrades, thank God you're here.' But despite these exclamations of apparent joy and support, their faces expressed fear and uncertainty. 'At last you're here,' people shouted. 'Now we can go home.'

'Not so fast,' said one of the soldiers. 'We have to check you out first. Some of you may have been working for the Germans.'

The crowd froze. 'We're Russians. We're all on the same side!' people yelled.

The soldiers, who appeared to be under the influence of alcohol, asked whether anyone had anything to drink. Out of nowhere, alcohol and food was produced—obviously looted from the houses evacuated by the fleeing Germans and Czechs. The Russian soldiers became increasingly drunk, and aggressively called everyone traitors, particularly those who had worked for the Germans. The people in the crowd began protesting that they weren't here voluntarily, that they were taken to Germany forcibly, that they had done nothing that could be classed as traitorous to the Soviet Union.

'You're still all bastards who ought to be shot,' the drunken soldiers yelled back—but they drove away.

The crowd was in panic, dreading what the next visitation would bring. As Tolya, Katya and I began to scramble out of the bushes, we saw another Red Army vehicle draw near. And who was sitting at the wheel but Boris himself! I ran up to him but even though I wanted to hug him I couldn't help thinking he must have made some sort of deal with the Red Army.

'So, you've now betrayed us. Have you sold me out as well?' I cried, tears stinging my eyes.

Boris grabbed me and, pulling me aside, said under his breath, 'Be quiet, stupid, or you'll destroy us all. I came back for you. It's not what you think.'

He turned to the two soldiers accompanying him and said loudly, 'Boys, this is my wife. We'll get our stuff together quickly. Okay with you?'

'Yes, okay,' replied one of the soldiers gruffly. 'But be quick. We have no time to waste.'

'Look, you two can get moving. We'll follow behind as soon as we get our things into a wheelbarrow,' Boris assured them.

Boris and family, circa 1910. Left to right: Father Tikhon, Mother Ludmila, Boris, Uncle, younger brother Sergei and Aunt.

Boris and family, 1913. Left to right: Mother, youngest brother Grigoriy, Sergei, Father, Boris aged five.

Boris (second from right), his brothers, and other relatives, Ukraine 1928.

Boris, Ukraine, circa 1935.

Lilya's brother Alec, aged approximately 20, circa 1939.

Smolensk Drama Theatre

Lilya, wearing pearls, Germany, circa 1944.

The family with whom Lilya, Boris, Ksana and Bohdan lived in Missenberg, Germany, circa 1948. Bottom row: Oma and Opa. Top row: Daughters Babette, Rosette and Frenzel.

Lilya and Ksana, 1947.

Boris, circa 1950.

Boris and Bob in Thirroul, New South Wales, where they lived with the Williams family, who took Lilya, Boris and family in off the street. 1950.

Lilya in Bonegilla camp, circa 1950.

Bob at Thirroul, circa 1951.

Bob leaning on a chair, Thirroul, 1951.

Bob, Lilya and Ksana, Thirroul, 1951.

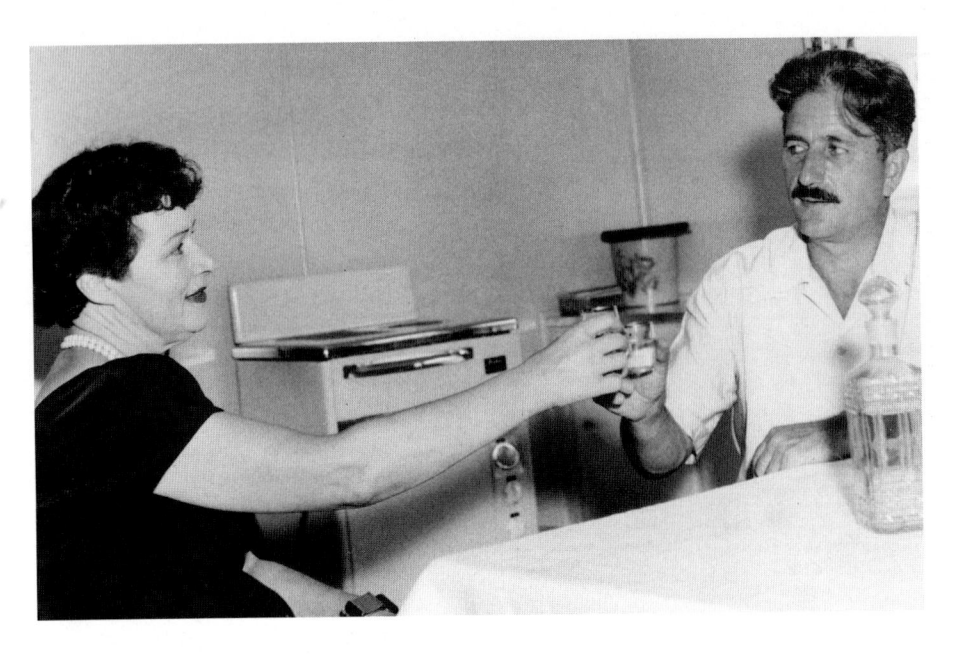

Lilya and Boris raising a toast, Corrimal, New South Wales, 1959.

Boris and Lilya at home, playing chess, Corrimal, 1959.

Bob, Boris and Ksana, Corrimal, 1960.

Boris and Lilya in the garden at Corrimal, 1962.

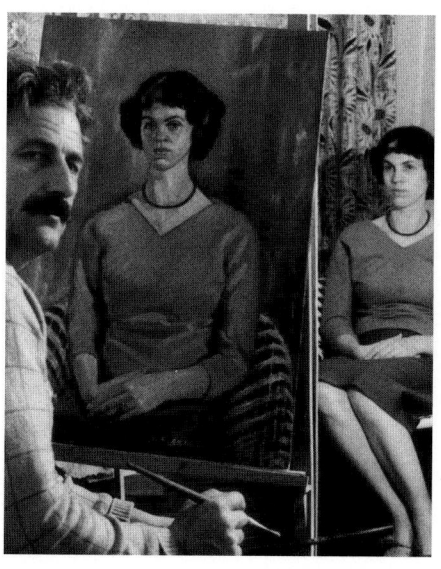

Boris, painting a portrait, 1960.

Lilya in 1990, aged 76.

Alec's daughter Ina, in Russia, 1990, receiving news of the family in Australia.

Bob and Ksana, 1992, at Ksana's 45th birthday.

'But can you manage all your belongings without our help?' he was asked.

'Sure we can. We have hardly anything to pack. You boys go on. We'll be fine.' Boris slapped one of the 'boys' on the back as they drove off, then quickly turned to me and hurriedly explained what had happened.

Boris had ridden the bicycle right up to the Soviet patrol at the bridge on the outskirts of town. He asked one of the guards what the prevailing attitude was towards actors who had been forced to work for the Germans. The guard, who didn't know what to make of this question, took him to his superior to sort things out. Boris, sensing that his opening gambit had been foolish, to say the least, changed his story.

When he was presented to the lieutenant, himself a young man, the soldier said, 'Here is one of the actors who worked for the Germans.'

'Thank you, Private. You may go,' the lieutenant said. Turning to Boris, he asked, 'Now, what's your story and who are you?'

'I'm afraid the private has misunderstood me, Lieutenant. I was telling him that I was an actor before I joined the Red Army. I was wounded at Sebastopol and taken prisoner by the Germans, and now I'm getting ready to return home,' Boris replied unflinchingly.

While this conversation was going on, more civilians were being brought in. The lieutenant was obviously inundated with civilian and refugee matters and not coping very well. He turned to Boris and asked, 'Can you drive?'

'Yes, I can. Just tell me where you want me to go,' Boris replied confidently.

'For starters, do you know where the hospital is?' the lieutenant asked.

'Of course.'

'Okay, I'll send two soldiers with you to the hospital and when you get back, I'll talk to you further.' The lieutenant walked away hurriedly.

Boris drove to the local hospital accompanied by two soldiers, where they picked up food and medical supplies. On the return trip, they took a detour via the Sans Souci, Boris having told his companions he had to pick up his wife before returning to Russia. This charade could only have occurred in the early days of the Red Army's advance into Eastern Europe, when everything was utterly disorganised. The KGB, who were not far behind, would not have allowed Boris to get away so easily, if at all.

When the other residents of our hotel saw Boris chatting amiably with the two Red Army soldiers, they began to swarm around us, pretending that we were all close friends and asking Boris what he thought we should do in our present circumstances.

What absolute hypocrites, I thought, remembering how they had shunned me for the last few hours. Boris assured them that all would be well, that we would be back home soon. Taking Tolya and Katya and me aside, however, he told us to pack immediately, that we had to get away as quickly as possible.

After loading our possessions into a wheelbarrow, we set off—not forgetting to pin on our red ribbons in case we met up with any Red Army soldiers. We wanted to cross the river, as we knew that the Americans were somewhere on the other side. We believed that once we found them our situation would improve. It simply could not be as bad as being held by the Red Army. While we had little confidence in the protection that the Americans might give us, we felt it would surely be easier to talk our way around them. Moreover, they weren't likely to actually detain us in a camp, we thought.

Moving through the side streets, we neared one of the bridges over the River Eger. The city was a mess; fires, shooting and rubble were everywhere. There was a Red Army patrol on the bridge, so we huddled in one of the burnt-out buildings and waited, not knowing what to do next. Towards evening, to our amazement, the soldiers on patrol left the post and headed towards the city, leaving the bridge unattended. We carefully moved towards the deserted bridge and crossed to the other side.

Feeling elated now that we were on the American side, we stopped by the river, washed our faces and ate a few slices of bread. Then we saw that the Red Army patrol had returned to its post. We cautiously moved through the darkness, further and further away from the Soviet-occupied part of the city.

We walked for a few kilometres and saw two black soldiers.

'Americans,' we said to each other happily. We waved to them and tried to continue on our way, only to be stopped. Although we could not understand English, we gathered that they wanted to know who we were and where we were going. This was our first encounter with the Americans, and only ordinary soldiers at that, yet they were immediately interested in our nationality and intended movements. Obviously they were under orders to restrict the movements of all civilians. Our prospects were bleak indeed if we couldn't even get past this first hurdle.

Boris whispered to me, 'Should I tell them we are Russian?' but I stopped him instantly and said, 'Let me do the talking.'

Our friends stood in silence, waiting for what would happen next. Some sort of instinct welled up inside me, because without any conscious intention whatsoever I found myself concocting a reply composed of bits of German, Russian and the few English words I knew from various plays. My reply came as much of a surprise to me as to Boris and our friends.

'Baby,' I blurted out, holding my arms out in cradle fashion. 'Baby not good.' I hit my chest with my clenched fist and coughed as hoarsely as I could. 'Baby—hospital,' I said, pointing in the direction we had wanted to go. By this time my acting instincts were starting to take over and I managed to produce what I thought was a very convincing flood of tears.

Boris whispered in my ear, 'Well done, girl, but don't overdo it.'

The two soldiers conferred. 'Documents,' said one of them, suddenly thrusting out his hand. I was about to go into another 'baby' routine because I couldn't think how to get out of this one. Boris came to the rescue.

'Documents—hospital,' he said, pointing to the fictitious hospital. He went into a simple but effective little miming routine, which explained that when we took the baby to the hospital we also had to hand over our documents. When we picked up the baby we would get our documents back. I kept on crying, repeating, 'My baby, my baby. Two kilometres. Please, Comrade.'

The soldiers looked puzzled, shrugged, said something to each other, threw us a packet of cigarettes and let us go. The four of us cried out in broken English, 'Thank you, thank you,' and went on our way, hardly believing our good fortune.

We realised that we had been very lucky to get by on this occasion. It was obvious that our story would have to be far more carefully prepared and thoroughly rehearsed if we hoped to get away with it again. So we spent several hours tightening up our account and trying to predict the sort of questions we could be asked in future.

We spent the rest of the night in an open field, huddled together on the single old blanket we had managed to bring with us, Katya and I covered by our husbands' jackets. I had the most peaceful night's sleep in many months, snuggled against my husband and believing that the trauma of the war years was coming to an end. What I didn't realise was that not only had we not escaped from danger, we were in fact surrounded by it.

We woke as dawn crept over the horizon and feasted on cold potatoes and salted cucumbers which we had appropriated from an empty cottage—obviously belonging to Germans fleeing the Red Army occupation. After deep consideration, we agreed that we should head away from the army and back into Germany to await news of Stalin's reaction towards Russian prisoners of war like ourselves. We also had no idea whether the Allies would grant us political asylum or hunt us down like animals and pack us off to the Soviet Union. Would the Allies believe we were not traitors, that we had had no choice in working for the Germans? Until all these things were made clear, we had no option but to push our tired, starved and greatly weakened bodies as far as we could. We trudged on and, after some 30 kilometres or so, came to a forest. It was so quiet and peaceful amongst the lush grass and pine trees that we could almost imagine the dreadful years of war had never occurred. We planned to stay here for some time, surviving on our remaining rations of potatoes. All four of us fell into a deep sleep.

Loud shouting woke us and as we scrambled to our feet we saw two soldiers with machine-guns aimed in our direction, motioning for us to raise our hands above our heads. We recognised them as Americans. Again the questions began: Who were we? What were we doing here? I repeated my revised and embellished story. We were trying to get to our babies who were somewhere in this vicinity and anyway, we were America's friends. Furthermore, I added, tears streaming down my face—a combination of genuine fear and long practice—as soon as we found our babies we were heading to America where we all had relatives waiting for us.

'We only need to pick up our babies and we'll be on our way,' I somehow managed to communicate. The soldiers looked at each other and to our amazement replied in Polish.

'Where are your passports and documents?' These American soldiers were of Polish descent. 'You can't walk around without any documents,' they told us, 'and you certainly can't get to America without them.'

We didn't understand that they were simply making fun of our naivety.

'Look, we'll tell you what. Go to the field commander who will look after you. He'll give you replacement documents and you will be able to get your babies and go to America,' they told us good-naturedly.

We asked for directions, which they gave us, along with what seemed to be the obligatory packet of cigarettes. After walking a few more kilometres and feeling suspicious about the ease with which we had been allowed to go, I stopped and said to my companions, 'Look everyone. This has all been too easy. Why should we go to field headquarters and face goodness knows what? I don't believe the Americans will hand over four passes, just like that. Why don't we continue away from the main roads as we have done up until now? I feel uneasy about this whole thing.'

The other three turned on me, telling me that my suspicions were ill-founded and only complicated everything.

'Lilya, Lilya, we're in American territory, the Americans won't let anything happen to us. And anyway, the Soviets are way back in Karlsbad,' Tolya and Katya tried to reassure me.

'Don't panic,' Boris told me, putting his arm around my shoulders.

'Okay, okay. Let's do it your way,' I told them resignedly and rather curtly.

We walked on another few kilometres and came to a small village on a hillside, called Johannesdorf. It was occupied by American troops. We approached a soldier walking in our direction.

'Comrade, we're Russian. Where is your commander?' we asked in our usual mix of broken English and German.

The soldier looked at us and our wheelbarrow in some astonishment, then turned and pointed to the right. 'There.'

We wheeled our barrow up to a hut and repeated that we wanted to see the commander and that we were Russian. The soldier on guard looked at us in even greater astonishment, before turning and yelling through the door something in English that we didn't understand. He turned back to us and in respectable German asked, 'What do you want? Are you Russian?'

When we replied in German that we wished to speak to the commander we were told to wait and the soldier went inside.

Several minutes later, he returned with an officer. Since I was the only one of our group who spoke German more or less respectably, I told him about our meeting with the patrol in the forest who had suggested that we should go to Field Command and ask for the passes we required. The soldier translated all this to the officer, who listened to me patiently and then replied, 'Look, there's nothing I can do. You'll have to wait for the Soviet troops from Karlsbad to arrive who will advise us what to do.' I quickly realised that we had made a big mistake in coming here, but before I could say anything else, Katya began to create a scene.

'No, no, just not the Russian Army,' she cried in her broken German. 'They will kill us.'

'Why would they want to kill you?' asked the officer. 'You're Russian, aren't you? Why would the Russian Army harm its own people?'

'Shut up, Katya,' I told her in Russian, but she went on regardless.

'Stalin is no good,' Katya pleaded. 'He will murder us. We don't want to go back.'

'Ah, so that's it, is it?' the officer said, after the soldier translated for him. 'So you want to escape from the Russian Army? I'm afraid I can't allow that. The Russian troops will be here tomorrow and you can sort it all out with them.' With this, the officer turned to the soldier, said something to him in English, got into a jeep and drove away.

'Well, did you get your passes?' I yelled at my husband and friends furiously. 'It serves you right.'

We walked away from the hut to some nearby bushes to consider what to do next. Surprisingly, the soldier standing by the hut didn't seem to take any notice and walked back inside.

'Let's get out of here while we're still able to,' said Tolya.

'Yes, let's get out of here fast,' agreed Boris, so we picked up our wheelbarrow and hastened away from the hut.

Within half an hour or so we saw another patrol on the road ahead. As they had also seen us, we were compelled to continue and bluff our way past them, calling out our usual, 'Comrades, we Russian allies,' to which they replied by throwing us a bar of chocolate and waving us on our way.

Evening was falling and we were now several kilometres from Johannesdorf. Not far ahead was a tiny village, so we decided to bed down for the night near its outskirts. Early next morning, we moved on again. Boris and Tolya began singing Ukrainian Cossack songs and energetically continued to wheel our barrow along the road. Katya and I dragged behind them, feeling tired and depressed. After another fifteen kilometres or so, I became very thirsty and decided to ask for a drink of water in one of the huts not far from the main road. I gratefully drank my water and was running down the hill to catch up to the others when, out of nowhere, I saw a jeep bearing down on me. It came from the American camp we had visited yesterday and the officer in the back was the one who'd ordered us to wait for the Red Army. The jeep stopped close to me and the officer gestured for me to get in. I shook my head, saying, 'No thank you,' thinking that he was offering me a lift.

The officer nodded to his driver, who ran over to me, took hold of my arms and pushed me into the vehicle. I still didn't understand what they wanted of me, but I sensed trouble and grew more and more frightened. We caught up to my travelling companions and stopped. Pointing to the road, the officer began addressing them angrily in English. We could only make out: 'Stay put! Stay put!' What this meant we didn't know. I wanted to get out of the jeep, but was restrained by the driver, and so we drove off. I had absolutely no idea where they were taking me and began to panic. I started to cry, rambling incoherently in a mixture of Russian, German and a word or two of English that I didn't want to be separated from my husband, that I was a Russian ally and that they should take me back to my group. During my tirade and in between wiping my eyes with my dirty hands, I grabbed the officer's arm to emphasise my plight. At this point, he shook me violently by the shoulders, yelling, 'Stop!' I promptly froze.

Believing that they were going to shoot me and I would never see Boris again, I nevertheless tried to take in where we were going so that if an opportunity to escape did present itself I would be able to find my husband and two friends again.

We drove for a long time, perhaps an hour or more, and finally came to a stop in front of a small building, guarded by two black American soldiers. The officer got out of the jeep and entered the building, leaving the driver and me outside. It wasn't long before he returned and gestured to me to get out. He hopped back in and they drove off. I stood there in the middle of nowhere, with no idea of why I had been brought here and fighting an overwhelming sense of panic. It was some minutes before another officer, a lieutenant, came out of the building and in broken German asked what my name was and whether I was German. I hurriedly replied that I wasn't German, I was Russian and therefore an American ally.

'Why are you here?' the lieutenant continued in German and led me into the building. We entered a small room with one chair on which I sat while he continued his interrogation. His German was extremely basic, but he understood the language better than he could speak it. I gave him a brief account of what had occurred the previous day in Johannesdorf, carefully avoiding any mention that we were fleeing from the approaching Soviet forces. In turn, he explained that according to the newly signed Yalta Agreement, any Russians captured on territories occupied by the Western allies were to be given over to the Soviet Army—without exception. I started to cry, realising that there was little possibility of escape this time.

'Don't cry, Miss,' he said to me, not unkindly. 'The captain is only following his orders in keeping you here.'

'And what then?' I replied. 'He separated me from my husband and friends. How will I ever find them now?' Again the tears coursed uncontrollably down my cheeks.

Taking pity on my distress, the lieutenant took me by the arm and led me into a canteen of some sort. He offered me chicken and rice, some of which I wolfed down; the rest I hid in my napkin for Boris, in case I ever found him again. My companion seemed a bit surprised by the speed with which the chicken—complete with bones—had disappeared, and offered me coffee and a doughnut. I drank the coffee gratefully but managed to hide the doughnut as well.

'When do you expect the captain to return for me?' I asked.

'Oh, he's gone to attend to some business. In the meanwhile, my instructions are to look after you and make sure that you don't leave.'

Some time later, I heard the sound of an approaching vehicle. It was the jeep with the captain in the back. After a brief exchange between the captain and the lieutenant, they took hold of me, seated me in the jeep and drove off. I had absolutely no idea in which direction we were heading and looked out for familiar signs on the road. Was I imagining it or was the church we were passing the same one we'd passed earlier? If so, we were heading back in the direction where the Americans had found us. Before long, I noticed a figure in the distance, waving to us. As we drew closer, I couldn't believe my eyes—it was my darling husband standing by the side of the road. The jeep stopped, Boris jumped in and, without a word, we embraced warmly, much to the amusement of the soldiers.

There was no sign of Tolya and Katya. I asked Boris what had happened to them and he told me that they had fled, attempting to persuade him to go with them. 'But I couldn't go and leave you here,' he told me, hugging me fiercely. 'Don't worry, we'll think of something.'

Before long we were back in Johannesdorf and, to our horror, being off-loaded into a refugee camp surrounded by barbed wire. There was a mass of people pushing up against the fence: Russians, Ukrainians, Poles, Italians, Hungarians, and even German prisoners of war, all desperate to get back home again.

With mounting despair, Boris and I found an area which wasn't quite as crowded and sat down on the ground. I pulled out the piece of chicken and the doughnut I had saved and we ate, deep in thought. We didn't know when or where our next meal was coming from. We had even lost the wheelbarrow with our few belongings when we were bundled into the jeep. I was desperate for a wash but there was no water, let alone soap or towels. Everything had been left in the wheelbarrow.

'I'll have a look around,' Boris said to me.

'Please don't leave me on my own,' I begged him. 'I'm afraid to stay here without you.'

'Lilya, you know I'll never leave you.' Boris kissed me and went off towards a group of men. I tried to remain calm, lay down by a nearby tree and waited for his return. As I lay there I couldn't help wondering what fate had in store for us now. We had survived the worst of the war, so it would be ironic if we now came to grief at the hands of some Stalinist KGB thug. I begged God to have mercy on us, closed my eyes and drifted into a troubled sleep.

Someone was gently shaking my shoulders. I opened my eyes and jumped up like a terrified animal. Boris was standing in front of me, speaking very quietly. 'Lilya darling, if you want to have a wash, we can go behind those trees. I found a small spring.'

Still only half awake, I was having trouble understanding where Boris was leading me. We were approaching a guard patrol. Black American soldiers were sitting on our side of the barbed-wire fence, which stretched endlessly, separating us from the main road. They were talking and laughing animatedly, oblivious, it seemed, to the groups of people wandering around the camp. Boris suddenly pushed me hard to the ground. We were close to the trees to which he was leading me.

'Quick, Lilya, lie flat and slide on your stomach this way,' he whispered. We crawled our way through the mud and thickets of shrubs before we reached another barbed-wire fence. It was criss-crossed with row upon row of wire, but there was a small space between the bottom row and the ground. I had no idea why we were going through these bizarre actions but there was simply no time to ask for an explanation. Boris lifted the bottom of the wire just high enough for us to crawl underneath to the other side.

'Lilya, we have to run for our lives. We have to get away from here if we want to survive,' he whispered, taking me by the arm and making sure we stayed low to the ground, out of sight of the American patrol. We crouched that way until all my limbs ached and our hands and legs were scratched and bleeding. It wasn't until we were a safe distance from the camp that we stood up and ran for all we were worth, falling, running again, not knowing in what direction we were heading. My heart was bursting, my body ached unbearably, I was completely out of breath and still we ran on and on, Boris leading the way, dragging me along, encouraging me to continue.

We came to a small hill and somehow, I still don't know how, I found the strength to climb it. As we reached the top we could see the camp as a speck in the distance behind us and a river in front of us. Not having the energy to stay on our legs any longer, we rolled down the hill to the water's edge. It was cool and clear and we drank like thirsty cattle before washing ourselves, unable to get enough of the fresh water and air. At last we stretched out on the grass, arms above our head and fell into a deep, contented silence.

Just as we were beginning to revive, feeling more relaxed than we had been for a long time, we heard the barking of dogs. At first the barking was distant, but to our alarm it got closer.

'Get up, sweetheart,' Boris said. 'That bloody captain has set the dogs after us. We'll have to cross this river to get them off our scent.'

Apprehensively we waded into the water, to find that it was no more than shoulder deep for some distance. Without warning, however, I lost my footing and went under; the water became too deep for wading and we had to swim. Luckily we could both swim, though Boris was by far the stronger swimmer and helped me as I clung to his neck. In that haphazard way we somehow made it to the other side. Almost unable to stand upright from weariness, we staggered blindly for several more kilometres. Finally I could go on no longer. We stopped to rest and fell into a deep sleep, huddling behind some undergrowth well away from the small road that ran nearby. When I awoke, Boris was nowhere to be seen and I immediately experienced a sense of panic. I couldn't call to him in case my voice drew unwanted attention—we had learned the importance of being as inconspicuous as possible—so I waited impatiently.

Boris soon returned; he had been scouting the area to try to determine in which direction we should continue. But I was still too exhausted to go on. I was curious about our recent escape from the camp so I asked, 'Why did you suddenly decide to make a break for it? I was hoping we could stay for a couple of days at least. The food wasn't too bad and we could have recovered our strength. Perhaps we could have found out what was happening.'

'That's just it,' replied Boris. 'I found out exactly what was happening when I went nosing around and it's lucky for us that I did. I don't think anyone else will be getting out of the camp quite so easily.' I waited impatiently for him to continue.

'I was wandering around trying to glean any information I could, but the people I spoke to were just as much in the dark as we were. Then I saw a Red Army jeep drive into the camp and pull up outside the administration block.'

'But what does the Red Army want here?' I interrupted.

'Just listen, and I'll tell you,' continued Boris. 'These two officers got out and went inside. Luckily the driver also got out and went towards a couple of Americans working on a jeep some distance away. This gave me a chance to get closer. I strolled casually around to the back of the hut and saw that it was a portable building, like most of the others. You know, supported by piles of bricks with a space underneath. I guess there was about 40 centimetres of clearance above the ground. No, on second thoughts, it was probably closer to 30 centimetres…'

'Boris,' I interrupted impatiently, 'it doesn't matter how many centimetres. Go on with the story, will you?'

'Oh, but it does matter, my dear,' said Boris with a rueful grin, 'because then you can appreciate the tightness of the squeeze I was in.'

'What if you had been caught?' I shuddered at the thought, giving him a hug.

'Well, I wasn't. Anyhow, here I was wedged under the floor of this hut. I could clearly make out the voice of one of the officers speaking in Russian, followed by what must have been a translation and then a reply from the American officer. And you know what? It appears that our beloved Stalin has made a deal with all the Allies—not just the Americans—that all former citizens of the Soviet Union are to be handed over to the Soviet authorities. Lilya, this includes not only the Russians, but also Poles, Ukrainians, Latvians, Lithuanians—everyone.'

'But that's just what I've been telling you all along,' I said gently.

'Yes, I know,' said Boris. 'But even you weren't sure of what would happen to these people. Now I know.'

'Well…' I prompted, as Boris paused and looked very gravely at me.

'They're finished,' he said. 'There's absolutely no hope for them. Stalin has decreed them all traitors and that's how they will be dealt with. So we certainly can't afford to be caught and handed over. I heard the American ask a question which the second officer translated as: "What steps are we permitted to take if the refugees don't co-operate or try to escape? After all, they are not our citizens and we wouldn't want to offend the Soviet Government by treating them inappropriately." The first officer laughed and replied in Russian, "Offended? Inappropriate treatment? Hell, just tell him that as far as we're concerned, they can shoot all those traitorous bastards on the spot if they want to. It will simply save us the job once we get them back in our hands. On second thoughts, you'd better tell him that Comrade Stalin would be most grateful if they can be returned in whatever condition they can be delivered." Then he laughed again and the conversation sort of petered out as they moved to another room in the hut. Anyway, I had heard the worst part and although I was anxious to hear when they planned to hand over the inmates in this camp, I decided it was too dangerous to stay any longer. It was clear we needed to get away immediately, so I looked for a way to escape as soon as possible.'

I couldn't speak. All my previous fears about being captured by the Red Army had become a certainty. A dreadful thought crossed my mind as I pondered our fate. Finally, I raised enough courage to broach the subject.

'Darling,' I began slowly, tears welling in my eyes, 'if it ever happens that…' Boris lovingly put his finger on my lips and hugged me tightly.

'I know,' he said. 'I was thinking the same thing. And I agree. We will never be sent back alive. We've been prepared for the worst for years now, living from day to day. I don't think either of us is scared of dying. But I, for one, don't want to die on Stalin's terms. If it has to happen, then it will be on my own terms.'

I nodded in silent agreement and, in a flood of tears, we sealed our terrible pact with a kiss. We agreed that from now on we would avoid going anywhere near a main road. We would only take back roads and keep to the forests. We were in a no-win situation. First we had feared the Germans, then the Russians, and now it was obvious we weren't safe with the Americans either. If we were to run into them again, we were finished, we knew that. The Allies had become our new enemy. All they wanted to do was to wash their hands of us and return us to our original enemy—Comrade Stalin. They neither understood nor cared what he would do to Russian prisoners of war. I continually prayed that all this would end, but I had no idea how it could.

'Don't worry, Lilya my love, everything will turn out fine,' Boris would say to me repeatedly when he saw the now permanent dejection in my eyes. 'We've escaped everybody so far and we'll keep on doing so until we're safe.' For the hundredth time I thanked God that he had sent Boris into my life.

We walked on, not sure where we were headed. About three or four days after our daring escape, we again came to a main road. It looked different to the one that ran past the refugee camp.

'Damn it, what a pity that map was in that wheelbarrow,' Boris said thoughtfully. 'But what's the difference where we head? No one is waiting for us anywhere,' he added bitterly.

'Yes, but we still need to know which direction we're going in,' I said to him. 'Where are we going and what are we going to do once we get there?' I looked at him helplessly.

'Well, we've been heading west and must be well inside Germany by now. I have an idea.' Boris looked at me. 'If we can get to Bavaria, across the *Bodensee* and into Switzerland, we would be safe for sure.'

There was only one problem with that: I remembered from my schooldays that the *Bodensee* (Lake Constance), a lake that divided Bavaria from Switzerland, was over 30 kilometres wide.

'But Boris, how on earth are we going to swim that distance?' I was dumbfounded that he could even think this was a solution.

'I know, I know, Lilya, but it's not quite as bad as that. See, the border runs down the middle of the lake and then starts again at the shoreline. We would only need to get past any guards on one side and swim a short distance around to the Swiss shore. It's a matter of avoiding border guards rather than swimming some impossible distance. The odds are still a hundred to one; I know that. But I also know this is a deadly game in which we've found ourselves. Either way our chances are slim.' Now his previous confidence seemed to desert him for a moment. 'But darling,' he continued, 'if we don't believe in miracles, then we're finished. We have to try anything to get out of here, no matter how impossible the odds.' With this, Boris began singing an old Russian folk song. I joined in and we went on our way to God knows where.

The road began curving downwards, and in the distance we could see it branching off in two directions. We could also see a figure standing in the fork of the road. As we cautiously approached, we saw it was actually a woman and a little girl of about four or five, both weeping hysterically. We came up to them and asked the woman what the matter was. She was Russian, and told us that she, her husband, two sons and little girl had been living and working in Germany for a German landowner as prisoners of war. After the war ended, they decided to stay in Germany. The woman and her daughter had been loaded onto a truck with other refugees, while her husband and sons managed to get hold of some bicycles and set out for unoccupied Germany. They had arranged to meet at a town not far from here, but when she arrived there was no sign of either husband or sons, so she and her little girl walked on hoping to meet up with them. It was now two days later and there was still no sign of the rest of her family. She was in despair, not knowing whether to continue waiting or go on. That was all that we could get out of her. When we tried to explain that Germany was a large country, all she came up with was, 'My husband asked me to wait for him.'

'All right,' said Boris, wanting to help but frustrated at not knowing what to advise, 'there's a valley just in front of us. Let's all go down there and wait. Perhaps your husband will still come.'

Boris picked up the little girl and carried her on his shoulders as we trudged down to a clearing. We built a small fire and baked some potatoes that we had picked from fields along the way. I felt ill again. I had a raging temperature and the soles of my feet were covered with blisters because of the holes in my shoes. Boris looked worried.

'Don't you dare die on me,' he chided good-naturedly. 'I have enough problems. You have to go on, we both have to.' He held me close and placed my head on his shoulders, wiping my red-hot forehead with his threadbare shirtsleeves. 'Look, we can't be the only ones not wanting to go back home,' he continued, pointing to our new companions. 'While we're still alive we have to go on.'

I knew that he was trying to be brave for my sake, but no matter how much I wanted to believe that everything would be all right, I just couldn't control my fear and lack of hope in the future. My legs and head ached dreadfully and all I wanted was to lie down and sleep.

Night fell. When I woke up, I saw the little girl sleeping with her head on her mother's lap, the mother sitting there disconsolately. Boris was trying to comfort her.

'Listen, Varya. What are you going to do? Your husband and sons must have missed you somehow. Are you going to stay here and wait or go on with us?' he asked her kindly. 'If you decide to come with us, we'll have to find a wheelbarrow somewhere. Your little girl can't walk long distances and she's too heavy for me to carry. What do you say?'

'Yes, I'll come with you. You seem to be going in the same direction as my husband told me to go,' Varya replied.

'Fine. Let's hope we find your family. We'll travel by night. It will be safer. And who knows, we might come across a farmhouse where we might be able to get something to eat. Surely the world isn't all evil?' Boris said to us both.

And so we went on. I could hardly walk and the little girl soon began whimpering with exhaustion. It was clear that we weren't going to get far like this. We had walked for another few kilometres, Boris alternately carrying the little girl and helping me, when we noticed lights flickering in the distance. As we got closer, we saw a well, so we drew some water to drink. We were in a tiny village of some five or six houses. Throwing caution to the wind, we went up to the first house and knocked on the door. An elderly woman opened it. She seemed friendly enough, asking who we were and where we were going. Our brief explanation seemed to satisfy her and she invited us in, bringing us some bread and milk. I continued to explain our situation.

'But you see, we have the little girl with us. We can't get far without some form of transport for her. Do you have a wheelbarrow you could let us have? We'll pay you something. We have a few German marks with us.'

'Who wants German marks?' the woman responded bitterly. 'You can't get anything for them. Look, I'll tell you what. Yes, I do have a wheelbarrow that I can give you. But can your husband fix my fence in exchange?'

'Of course I can fix your fence,' Boris said enthusiastically.

'Fine, then that's settled. You must be tired. You can stay the night but I can't put you all up in the house. You and your husband can sleep in the shed and the little girl and her mother can stay in this room,' the woman offered kindly. 'It doesn't matter to me who you are. Neither you nor I started this war. I have a husband and son somewhere on the front. Like you, they may be starving, lost and homeless. I only hope that some kind stranger will help them too,' she added, tears beginning to fall down her ruddy cheeks. Boris and I sat in silence thanking God that fate had led us to such a kindly soul. The woman bustled out, returning a few moments later with a blanket. 'Here, take this and have a good sleep.'

Boris and I slept without stirring. When we opened our eyes, it was daylight. The woman fed us breakfast and gave me a clean skirt and blouse to wear. I washed my own filthy clothes and hung them up to dry. Boris not only fixed her fence, but also did many other repairs around the house and within a day or so had completed all the jobs that needed doing. The woman went to the back of the shed and showed us the wheelbarrow. She filled it with bread, potatoes, onions and a change of clothes, and then it was time to say goodbye. We put the little girl into the barrow and began the next phase of our desperate journey.

CHAPTER ELEVEN

At least we now knew where we were and where to go. We had reached the southern border of Bavaria in Germany. Two weeks or so had gone by since we escaped from the Americans. We frequently came across camps holding people who were probably to be returned to the Soviet Union. These were mainly Russian prisoners of war and those whom the Germans referred to as 'workers from the East'; that is, civilians who, like us, had been used as forced labour by the Germans. We avoided these camps because we now fully understood that the Americans didn't understand or care why so many Soviet citizens didn't want to go home. For them it was just a matter of carrying out orders and holding all refugees until their own governments took care of them one way or another. Varya, with her little girl, chose to stay in one of the camps, hoping to be reunited eventually with her family. She was just too exhausted, emotionally and physically, to keep running.

Boris and I kept our mouths shut and completely stopped any talk of our attempts to avoid being caught and handed over to the Reds. Stalin had already officially declared that there were no Russian prisoners of war, only traitors who needed to be returned and punished accordingly. He had set up a special unit called SMERSH ('Death to Traitors and/or Spies'). For years after the war people all over Europe were flushed out and sent back to the Soviet Union. Many others committed suicide in preference to forced return, but the Allies just kept handing over refugees like cattle to the slaughter. It must be admitted, of course, that at that time in the West it wasn't generally known what fate awaited them.

Without Varya and her little girl, Boris and I were able to travel more quickly and we decided to move on as soon as possible. One of Boris's most endearing traits was the way in which he tried to keep our spirits up by singing his favourite Ukrainian folk songs, although it was obvious he was just as worried and uncertain of our fate as I was. We marched on, hungry, thirsty and exhausted, keeping away from main roads and large towns. We stole what little food we could from around farmhouses and ate forest foods like berries and green fruits. Occasionally we would stop in a small isolated village if it appeared to be unoccupied by soldiers. At one point, about a month after we had left Varya at one of the holding camps, we came upon one such village. I couldn't go on, either physically or mentally. My exhaustion had depleted all my reserves. I told Boris that I intended to stay put for a while—to find a bed where I could sleep for a few days. A bed? I had forgotten what it felt like to lie in one. Boris agreed, so we walked along a narrow track until we came to a house. It had a small wooden verandah in front. An old German man was sitting on a wooden stool smoking a pipe.

'Guten Abend, mein Herr,' I called to him. 'Do you have a small room where you could put me and my husband up for a few days?'

'Where are you from?' he asked me. 'From Prussia?' It was strange, but many Germans had asked me this. It must have had something to do with my accent.

'No,' I answered. 'My husband and I are Russian. We're waiting to go back home, and we're looking for somewhere to stay in the meantime.'

'Why don't you go to the Russian holding camp? There's one close by. You will meet your own people there,' the old man offered.

'Sir, I know. But I'm very tired and those places are so crowded and noisy. I'm ill and I just want somewhere quiet and peaceful for a few days.' I began to cry. I refrained from saying that neither Boris nor I had any intention of ever being held in one of those camps again.

'Well, perhaps I can help you. I have a small attic upstairs which is empty. You can stay there if you wish,' the man told us. 'But I will ask my wife first.'

He called out to his wife. Her name was Marta, a grey-haired, stocky woman who seemed pleasant enough. The old man repeated my story while she watched me, her eyes never leaving my face. Without a word, Frau Marta went back inside the shack and emerged a few minutes later, carrying sheets and blankets.

'Perhaps you would both like to have a wash?' she asked us. 'I'll boil some water for you.'

'Thank you so much,' Boris and I replied together. We couldn't believe her generosity. 'We won't have a wash just now. But we'd be happy to pay you while we stay here.' We still carried a few German marks with us, even though the currency seemed to have no practical value at that time.

'No, no, that's not necessary,' Frau Marta replied. 'You can stay here as long as you wish. Just get well again.' She showed us up to the attic. It was tiny, with two small windows, but it was clean and welcoming.

Despite our protests, her husband brought us two buckets of hot water, some soap and a towel. It seemed like a miracle. We washed and lay down to rest. Within minutes, there was a knock on the door. It was the old man carrying some bread, milk and *sala* (pork fat). We thanked him, ate, and fell into a contented and blissful sleep. It was well into the next day when we awoke. Dressing, we found our clothes had been washed, obviously by Frau Marta, and went downstairs.

The old man greeted us warmly and invited us to eat. 'You should go into the village and register for food rations,' he said. We continued to eat, saying nothing.

'The Americans are giving out food and some supplies. What is your story? Did you work for a German farmer?' he continued.

'No,' I replied guardedly. 'We're actors. We lived and worked in Berlin. We were brought into Germany by your army and now we're here.' I didn't want to lie to this kind-hearted man, so I told him the whole story.

'My God, what the war has done to people,' he said quietly. 'Look, I heard there are some actors in the camp,' he continued. 'Why don't you go and look for them?'

Boris and I thought about this for some time. We certainly didn't want to give ourselves up to the Americans, whom we had gone to so much effort to avoid. At the same time we needed to procure documents, if possible, and organise a reliable source of reasonable food. Being constantly on the run had taken a heavy toll on our health, especially mine. Moreover, we desperately needed to have better information on the state of affairs concerning refugees. How close were the Soviets? Were there any Allied camps which afforded any measure of safety? Most importantly, we thought that by having some contact with the camp we would get some warning, at least, of the possible arrival of Soviet authorities so that we could make sure we were long gone when they arrived.

So Boris decided to find the camp and meet some of the inmates if he could. He returned an hour or so later, telling me cheerfully that he had been introduced to some actors—six in fact—and that the camp authorities seemed happy to feed all comers. This camp didn't enforce imprisonment on the refugees and they were able to come and go at will. So he had invited the six actors to our new quarters that evening provided, of course, that Frau Marta and her husband didn't object—which they didn't.

I worked hard to make myself presentable. Frau Marta had washed our clothes, but they were extremely tattered. I asked whether I could borrow some of her old clothing for the occasion and she, also caught up in the excitement of receiving guests, took me by the arm and led me to a cupboard. She pulled out a white ruffled blouse, a full skirt and a black bodice, resembling the German national dress. I was overcome by such generosity.

'No, no, please take it, Lilya,' she said. 'I can't get into it any longer and I know it will look good on you.' I thanked this wonderful woman and ran up to the attic to try on my new attire. A few minutes later, I looked at myself in the piece of broken glass I carried as a mirror. My freshly washed hair was shining. My face was clean and the outfit did justice to my thin frame. I waited for Boris, hoping he'd approve of my new look.

Boris opened the door and stood motionless. He looked at me slowly and said softly, 'My God, you are even more beautiful than when I first met you.' He walked over and kissed me passionately.

'Darling, your new friends will be here shortly,' I laughed, gently disentangling myself from his arms.

Sure enough, within half an hour or so, Boris's new friends arrived. The house was too small to accommodate us all, so we went outside. We introduced ourselves and to my delight, they told me that they had also worked at the Vinetta in Berlin. One of the men was a dancer; another played the saxophone, the other two played the accordion and violin respectively. The two women, wives of the accordionist and violinist, were neither actors nor musicians.

'What are your plans?' I asked them. 'Where are you heading?'

'Well, at the moment we have no firm plans,' one of the men answered. 'We have been told that we are shortly going home.' Boris and I immediately froze with apprehension. We were only too familiar with this scenario.

During the ensuing conversation we ascertained that our new friends were, like us, terrified of going back, but had decided that there was little alternative. Boris spoke up.

'Well, listen everyone. Why don't we stay together and keep going west as Lilya and I have been doing for the past month or so? We don't intend going back either.'

'But we can't stay in the camp then,' said George the accordionist. 'Every day, a new group of us is transported back to Russia. It could be our turn at any time. In fact most of the people in the camp don't want to go back,' George continued, 'but since there are so many women and children, they wouldn't get far if they tried to run. The men don't want to leave their families behind, so they have resigned themselves to whatever fate our beloved Stalin has in store for them.'

We all understood that our situation was dire. The Americans were sending back all the Russian refugees they came across. The Germans were not willing to keep us as Russians were still regarded as 'the enemy'. Of course there were exceptions. Frau Marta and her husband, for example, couldn't have been more generous. We would never forget their kindness. But the reality was that we were in a hostile country which had just lost the war to our forces. We certainly weren't welcome here.

'What's the answer then?' asked George finally. We had, by then, agreed that whatever happened, none of us would go back to the Soviet Union.

'I have an idea,' yelled Ivan, the dancer. 'What if we offer to entertain the American troops? After all, that's what we did for the Germans. Why can't we work for the Americans? We only need food and accommodation in return and there's an American club of sorts here in the village.'

We took some time to think through this proposal. On the face of it, the idea seemed ridiculous. Boris and I had now been on the run for many months, avoiding the Allies as well as the Soviets. To turn ourselves over to the Americans would surely be the height of folly. On the other hand, we desperately needed a better plan than simply running away again each time the situation appeared to be getting dangerous. If we were ever handed over to the Soviets, no improvisations about sick babies or hospitals would get us out of trouble. Working for the Americans, it might be possible to obtain documents, since we would need these to enable us to move around the American zone. It could also buy us valuable time to make an escape should we be designated for return to Russia. Finally, we would be able to collect regular rations instead of living from day to day. So eventually we agreed that it was a good idea.

Amongst us we included singers, actors, a dancer and musicians. Surely we could organise a repertoire to offer to the Americans. Valya and Gina and I decided to go to the American field command to speak to the authorities. We were received politely and when we finished explaining our ideas, they were very willing to go along with our plan. The field commander rang the mayor of the tiny village and ordered that our group be accommodated in the local hotel. We couldn't believe our luck. When we got back to the hut the men rejoiced with us. We thanked our elderly hosts graciously, promising to keep in touch, and reported to our new quarters.

The comfort was heavenly. I had never seen sheets as white as those on our bed. We were given a change of clothes, and assured that the Americans could supply us with costumes from a theatre in Munich, which wasn't far away. Boris and I looked at one another, startled. If we were somewhere close to Munich, we must have travelled some 500–600 kilometres on foot over the past few months: from Karlsbad in Czechoslovakia, circling back through Germany and on down through Bavaria. We must be close to the Swiss border, I reasoned. Close to Switzerland and freedom, as Switzerland had held on to its neutrality during the war and remained a free zone.

We began rehearsing in the American Club. Everything was wonderful. We had comfortable accommodation, were well fed and being treated with respect. So why did I have a sense of foreboding? I couldn't understand it—but experience had already shown me that my intuition was usually correct. I tried to ignore my doubts and continue as though nothing were wrong. I didn't want to worry Boris and the others. We worked hard and tried to learn a little English so that at least we could speak a few lines, though all our songs were in Russian. Our 90-minute repertoire consisted of songs, dances, including the popular czardas, and a few musical numbers. Our violinist could also juggle, so we threw in a few comedy routines. Within a month, we felt ready to announce our first performance.

The Americans, true to their word, had tried to get costumes for us, but had only managed some for the three women. We made costumes for the men from curtains and any other bric-a-brac we could get our hands on. The day of our first concert arrived. The auditorium was packed full of American soldiers sitting at tables, smoking, drinking, in a rowdy but cheerful mood. Some had brought German girlfriends with them. Each item was received with whistles and thunderous applause, especially the Russian dance performed by the entire troupe with Ivan and myself as soloists. Some of the soldiers without girls tried to grab me and Valya and Gina, but we managed to escape their advances and, after many encores, hurried back to our quarters.

The day afterwards, two American officers turned up at our hotel, asking for me. I came down to see them, wondering what they wanted. They thanked me profusely for the performance and invited me and the other women in the group to the club as their guests. The men were definitely not invited.

'We'll pick you up at 7.30 sharp tomorrow night. Please be ready,' they said, and left. I understood immediately what they really wanted. Well, that's the end of paradise, I thought grimly and hurried to tell the others. The married men agreed that we couldn't go to the club on our own but George and Ivan argued that there could be no harm in our joining the Americans for the evening.

'Over our dead bodies,' Boris declared, with the other husbands nodding in unison. Boris and I went back upstairs and discussed our next move. We decided to escape that night and agreed to tell the others about our plan. The other two couples were in favour of escape but George and Ivan only grudgingly agreed to join us.

When night fell we left the hotel in groups of two and three to avert suspicion, leaving behind all the clothes and costumes provided by the Americans. Soon we met up with one another at the point we'd designated just outside the village. Boris and I led the group into the forest, away from the main road. There was no difficulty hiding, as the terrain was mountainous with lots of tree cover. Spruce trees, beeches, pines and firs grew around us in beautiful abundance. The air was crisp and clean. Fallen cones littered the ground.

We didn't get very far before major disagreements broke out. The two bachelors were disdainful and angry about leaving behind such comfortable conditions. The other two couples, obviously inexperienced at living on the run, felt that they couldn't continue.

'We're going to find the nearest camp and ask to stay there,' said Igor, one of the married men. The other couple agreed with him.

'But you'll be sent back to Russia!' I exclaimed.

'We'll leave the camp before they send us anywhere,' he continued. 'I know I can't go on carrying my musical instruments. Even if we do get to Switzerland, as you two believe, do you really think that they will accept us and jeopardise their neutrality? Be realistic and come with us.'

'I won't go back to any camp,' I declared. 'I would rather die here in the forest than find myself behind barbed wire again. And I certainly don't want to face the risk of being sent back to Russia.' Boris and I bade the others farewell and went on our way. We were disappointed, because we knew it would have been easier for all of us if we had remained in a group.

We worked out that it had been almost four months since we left Karlsbad. Autumn was upon us and we knew we couldn't go on sleeping outdoors or even in barns for much longer at this time of year. We would freeze to death. Something had to be done, but neither of us knew the answer. We travelled through the woods and occasionally wandered onto the main road, running off into the forest as soon as any vehicle approached, but always moving west in the general direction of Switzerland. During this time we learned of a new threat facing people such as ourselves—the danger of being caught by bounty hunters.

Although we tried to avoid contact with other people as much as possible, we still had to find food and shelter. So it was unavoidable that occasionally we took great risks and talked to strangers, hoping that they could help us out. One morning we decided to approach a middle-aged man collecting firewood at the edge of the forest. I spoke to him in German, but it soon became obvious to him that I wasn't a native German speaker. To our surprise, he suddenly spoke in Russian, giving us both quite a fright.

'You are Russian, aren't you?' he quizzed. We were so taken aback we didn't answer.

'It's all right,' he said. 'This is your lucky day. You may consider me a friend, but I understand your reluctance to trust me. My name is Volodya, but please call me Eric—that's my German name.'

He explained that he, too, was Russian, but had been posing as a German since the end of the war. He was, like us, a refugee. He had been captured in the early days of the war and sent to Germany for forced labour as an engineer. After the war Eric, the German citizen with whom he had been boarding, had died of natural causes. He had no immediate family, so Volodya buried the body and took on his identity, fortunately having found all his papers.

'I could have no reason for telling you this other than to convince you that I can be trusted. After all,' he continued, 'if you two aren't who I think you are, I would only be putting myself in jeopardy by volunteering all this information.'

'So who do you think we are?' asked Boris.

'Well, I'd say you are refugees, judging by your dishevelled clothes and nervous disposition. Am I right?' We nodded in affirmation.

'Furthermore,' he continued, 'I'd say you are just like me in the sense that you are trying to stay clear of the Allies, the Germans and, above all, the Reds.' Again, we nodded.

'Well then,' he said, 'the first thing we need to do is get you some decent clothes and I'll take a wild guess and say you wouldn't object to a hot meal. What do you say?'

On hearing this, I became quite tearful and Boris gave Volodya a great big bear-hug. On the way to Volodya's place we asked why he was doing this for us.

'I am just like you,' he said. 'So let me just ask one question. Would you do the same for me if the circumstances were reversed?'

'Of course,' we replied in unison. Volodya smiled broadly and gave us a friendly wink.

The next few days were like being in heaven. His place was small but very comfortable. We washed ourselves and changed into the new clothes Volodya provided. We ate as we had not eaten for years and told him our story and about having been on the run since the end of the war. He could not do much about getting identification papers, but he did manage to provide us with two travel passes which he got on the black market. He also filled us in on current news.

'Do you know about the refugee deal the Soviets have struck with the Allies?' he asked. We replied that unfortunately we did.

'Things have slightly improved in that regard,' Volodya went on. 'There are fewer Soviets in Allied-occupied Germany these days, so it's taking them longer and longer to process refugees back to the Soviet Union. That means if you get caught again by the Americans you would probably have weeks—possibly months—rather than days to escape before being sent back. If you can stay free for long enough you might even manage to get on a list for assisted passage to an Allied country.'

'But we thought all Soviet refugees were sent back home,' we said. 'How do we get on this list without the Soviets getting hold of us?'

'Well, the deal between the Soviets and the Allies is still in effect,' explained Volodya, 'but there are signs that the West is becoming increasingly suspicious of good old Uncle Joe and beginning to understand what he's really like. With any luck it shouldn't be too long before these terrible deportations come to an end. It's a case of surviving long enough and staying out of their clutches until that happens, I guess.'

Boris and I looked at each other. Could this be the truth? If it was, then at last there was some hope for us and we could begin making plans beyond the next day or even the next meal. Volodya had been unbelievably generous and lifted our spirits enormously. But there was one thing he couldn't do, as he explained. 'I'm sorry that I cannot put you up here any longer. In fact it is fortunate that you've had these few days here without interruption, because I get many officials calling in. They believe I am German, but because they know I can speak Russian I get called on to do a lot of liaison work—you know, translating documents and so on. They are due back tomorrow and then they'll be coming again fairly regularly, so it certainly wouldn't be wise to stay here. But before you leave, I'll get you a map to help you move around. There's also one last thing that I must warn you about.'

He lit up a cigarette, offering us each one, and explained. The manner in which the Soviets had gone about rounding up the refugees was extremely dangerous for people like us. While most Eastern European refugees had sooner or later finished up in holding camps, there were still a few who had managed to evade all the nets. So the Soviets used field agents, made up of their own military personnel, or recruited German or Allied personnel, to act as bounty hunters.

'Unfortunately this has created a very dangerous situation,' said Volodya. 'These bounty hunters stand to collect only a very modest amount for handing people over. It is often far more rewarding to rob them. Some refugees have managed to retain personal valuables, and in those cases they are simply disposed of.'

'Well, we certainly have no valuables,' we pointed out.

'I haven't finished yet,' he continued. 'You see, the Reds don't care how they get back their citizens. We are all traitors in their eyes, so we mean the same to them dead or alive. That means if you give these bounty hunters the slightest provocation, or act suspiciously or uncooperatively in any way, they won't hesitate to kill you.'

'What a pity that Boris and I can't speak better German so we could at least pretend to be German,' I said. Volodya replied that while it would have been generally useful, speaking the language would not have made us any safer against bounty hunters.

'They hunt Germans as well. Remember, these renegades have absolutely no love for their recent enemies. Look, I fear for my own safety with them far more than I do with the regular Reds or the Americans. Maybe I've simply been lucky so far. Who knows? I strongly suggest you work out some believable story about who you are that might buy you some time—and if you are caught by bounty hunters take whatever chance you get to escape. All that remains is to wish you the best of luck. I really hope you make it.'

'Well, if we do, it will be in no small measure thanks to you,' said Boris. We left at first light the next morning, after a tearful farewell, with renewed hope tempered by anxiety concerning the danger of encountering renegades.

With our new clothes we no longer looked like refugees, and over the next two days Boris and I worked out what we hoped was a plausible account of ourselves that would not give away our real identities. We decided we should base our cover story on things familiar to us. We both had extensive backgrounds in journalism, so we felt it would be fairly safe to pretend to be Russian journalists. We could handle any questions in this field in an entirely convincing manner. Further, we thought, if we included the idea that we were on assignment, covering aspects of postwar life in Germany, we could explain our presence in whatever area we happened to be, should we be caught. After many hours spent refining and revising this story, we began to feel more confident of our prospects. The only aspect we couldn't cover satisfactorily was why we were on foot. The best we could do about this was to say that although we did have a jeep at our disposal, it had broken down on the way to our next destination. The most reassuring part of it all was that we both felt confident that if we were to be questioned separately, our stories would match up. It made us realise how ill prepared we had been up to now and just how lucky we had been.

We had now been on the run for about nine months. It was March 1946. For about a week Boris and I made our way across country, heading southwest in the general direction of Switzerland. We figured we were about twenty kilometres from the town of Kaufbeuren. Frosty pines looked down on us as we trudged through a mixture of slush and snow. The country would be beautiful and lush again in the coming spring and summer months. Early one evening, the weather was particularly miserable with the prospect of a bitterly cold night ahead. It was the kind of weather which made us look for proper shelter, although we always hated having to approach any place that was likely to have people around.

I had noticed a small hut about a kilometre back, so we retraced our steps. As we approached it cautiously, we were taken completely by surprise by two men who jumped out of the bushes beside the hut. They were brandishing guns and bombarding us with questions, in both Russian and German. Before we could even start to answer, they yelled at us to go into the hut. We were pushed towards a table and two chairs, where we sat with our hands in front of us while they sat in the far corner of the room pointing their guns at us. Our hearts were racing, but as we exchanged a glance, we remembered how important those long hours of working out our cover story could now be to our survival. We tried to act as calmly as possible, just as genuine journalists who had every right to be there might do, and it wasn't long before the two men relaxed and stopped pointing their guns at us.

'Okay comrades,' said the older of the two in Russian, 'you can relax. We didn't mean to alarm you. It's just that there are so many questionable types roaming around the countryside that we can't afford to take any chances.'

'And just what are you guys doing out here anyway?' Boris asked, assuming the calm and authoritative manner of a journalist going about his business. He added a little theatrical gesture, offering the two men some of our very limited supply of cigarettes. I hoped he wouldn't compromise us by over-acting his part, but I needn't have worried. The offer of cigarettes really put them at ease and they volunteered much more information than I could possibly have expected. They introduced themselves as Ilya and Kiril. Ilya looked like a thug, coarse and swarthy, while Kiril was young and rather delicate. I wondered how he came to be mixed up in this dangerous business.

'Like you, we work for the Soviet Government,' said Ilya, evidently the one in charge. 'There are still many Soviet traitors inside Germany who haven't been apprehended, as you would be aware.' We nodded knowingly, but I felt a familiar cold shiver run down my spine. 'So it's our job to round them up and hand them over to the Americans, who then hand them over to our authorities, so it's all legal and neat. There are two more of us besides myself and young Kiril here. Stefan and Oleg are in Kaufbeuren at the moment stocking up on supplies. They are due back tomorrow, so you will meet them then. You explained about your broken-down jeep so I know you'll be anxious to get back to your base to repair it.'

'Yes, that's right,' said Boris, puffing on his cigarette.

'Hey, you know what comrades? We'll accompany you tomorrow to make sure you get back safely. One can't be too careful out here away from any towns as you can imagine.' Ilya roared with laughter, satisfied with his brilliant idea.

I tried not to look over at Boris for fear of showing my rising panic. But all he said was, 'Thank you very much for your offer. We would really appreciate your help in getting back. We have a map, of course, but it's pretty hard to find your way around unfamiliar territory.'

I was surprised that Boris had not made some effort to convince them we didn't need any help and would be quite happy to make our own way back. But when we had a moment together as the men went outside to relieve themselves, Boris whispered that we would make our escape that same night.

'Lilya, I just didn't want to arouse their suspicions. But I certainly don't want to meet their two friends who might be harder to fool than these two idiots.'

We continued our charade when Ilya and Kiril came back, taking out our rations of cold potatoes and black bread and offering to share theirs. They got out their rucksacks and we could see that they were much better stocked than we were, putting out *sala*, cucumbers and bread.

'Come on comrades, eat up,' Ilya urged, his mouth full. All of a sudden shots rang out close by. Ilya and Kiril grabbed their guns and motioned for us to get down, when a voice outside bellowed, 'Where's your lookout, you idiots? You're all dead now!'

Boris and I had no idea what was going on and looked at Ilya to see his reaction. To our surprise, he leapt up and shouted, 'You stupid oaf, Stefan, I'll shoot you one of these days because of your idiotic pranks!'

Stefan! That meant the others had returned earlier than expected. How could we escape from four of them? Boris looked at me and shrugged his shoulders, as if to say, 'I know what you're thinking and I have no idea what we'll do either.'

Stefan came into the hut first, roaring with laughter. 'I bet that put the wind up you two. Hey, who's this?' He stopped in his tracks upon seeing Boris and me get up off the floor.

'They're okay,' said Ilya. 'I'll explain in a minute.'

Once the fourth man, Oleg, had joined us, Ilya went over the details of our circumstances, while we chipped in from time to time to elaborate on some point or other. Boris and I looked at Stefan and his partner surreptitiously. Stefan was a raucous giant of a man, and extremely suspicious of our story. Oleg seemed similar in personality to Kiril, rather quiet and unobtrusive. Stefan asked many more questions than Ilya had done. It had been relatively easy to get away with our cover earlier on, but now Boris and I were both sweating profusely despite the cold. I silently thanked God that we had gone over and over our story so that we knew it backwards.

After grilling us for almost an hour, Stefan seemed to grudgingly accept our story, but added that it didn't really matter what he thought since the authorities in Kaufbeuren would check us out thoroughly. We had bought some time, though I realised our chances of escape were now even more remote. But escape we must.

While Stefan was interrogating us, the other three were bringing in rucksack after rucksack of supplies, not only masses of food, but also a seemingly endless supply of vodka. They filled tin mugs to the brim and downed them within minutes. Stefan especially was gulping his like water. I noticed Ilya watching him closely, before he said through clenched teeth, 'Hey Stefan, take it easy with that, will you? These supplies have to last us for quite a while.' Stefan, already a little drunk, became more aggressive.

'What's the matter with you?' he shouted. 'We've got guests here and you're acting like some sort of nanny.' With that, he grabbed another bottle, drank a few mouthfuls, and offered it to Boris. To my horror, Boris also drank a few mouthfuls. *What is he doing?* I thought. *He doesn't drink. If he gets drunk, we'll never get out of here tonight.*

Just then Boris winked at me and looked pointedly at the bottle. I caught his gaze and saw that the level had barely changed. It suddenly occurred to me what he had in mind. If the others had enough to drink, perhaps that would give us an opportunity to escape. I needn't have worried about him, I thought. He's only taking minute sips. I hope no one notices. The only one drinking in moderation was Ilya. He was obviously still worried about how long the supplies would last. I had an idea.

'You have all been so generous with us,' I said looking at each of them and smiling. 'All this food and then all this vodka my Boris is drinking. You know, he literally drinks like a fish once you get him started and I haven't seen anybody keep up with him yet. But it's all right, because we can make it up to you once we get back to our lodgings in Kaufbeuren.'

'How so?' asked Ilya immediately. My idea seemed to be working. I thanked God silently and continued.

'Well, we've been given lodgings at a place that obviously belonged to a very well-off family. You should see the supplies they have in their cellar.' At this, all four became keenly interested.

'What sort of supplies?' asked the usually silent Oleg.

Now Boris jumped in. 'Vodka, schnapps, brandy—you name it,' he said. 'And you're more than welcome to anything you want, since there's more than Lilya and I can ever use.'

Ilya changed his attitude completely. 'Well, let's not just sit here,' he said, pouring himself another glass, 'let's drink to that!' The bottle was quickly passed around.

'So, Boris, your Ludmila there says you drink like a fish, hey? Nobody can keep up with you, she says. Well, we'll see, shall we? We'd better drink to that!' With that, Stefan poured Boris a full mug of vodka too, obviously challenging him to a drinking duel.

This is terrible. This wasn't supposed to happen. Sure, they might get drunk, but so will Boris. I tried to get his attention with looks and subtle gestures, but he was joking and laughing as uproariously as the others and didn't seem to notice me at all. Another hour or so went by and I was becoming increasingly anxious. Except for Oleg, the other men were by now very drunk and I feared Boris was too, judging by his actions. Boris turned to me and gave me another wink and I knew that somehow he was merely pretending to be drunk. I noticed that Oleg was watching us and was about to say something, then thought better of it.

'I'm just going outside to check on things,' Oleg muttered to no one in particular. As soon as he left, Boris whispered that he had managed to pour most of his vodka down the cracks between the rotting wooden floorboards. I don't know how he did this without the others noticing, as even I, who was watching him closely and sitting nearest to him, hadn't noticed.

Oleg was away for only a few minutes. Shortly after he came back into the hut, Boris and I were startled by what sounded like gunfire. None of the others seemed in the slightest bit perturbed.

'Sounds like they're at it again,' said Stefan drunkenly.

'What do you mean?' asked Boris, alarmed. 'Who are "they"?'

'Our boys, of course,' laughed Stefan. 'Taking care of those bloody Fritzes and our own traitors. Who do you think?'

'I don't understand,' I said. 'Why do you need to take care of the Fritzes, I mean the Germans? I thought you were only interested in catching Soviet traitors?'

'Well, my innocent little journalist,' said Stefan, with heavy sarcasm, 'it shows how little you really know. You don't realise how many of those Fritzes avoided capture at the end of the war by trying to blend into the general civilian population. You know, to avoid the consequences of attacking us and ravaging our country. They knew what would be in store for them.'

'But how can you really tell who the true Fascists are and who are ordinary Germans? Or even who the refugees are? What if you're mistaken?' I persisted.

'Who really cares?' said Kiril, with an evil grin on his face. My God, so much for this delicate-looking boy! 'As far as we're concerned, they are all guilty of one thing or another, so we give them all the same treatment. Don't we, boys?'

'That's right,' said Stefan. 'Get rid of the whole bloody lot of them, we reckon. I can tell you we've certainly got rid of our fair share of the rats. Even young Oleg there, who you wouldn't think could kick a miserable dog, has done his share.'

Boris and I realised that this was not just a group of bounty hunters rounding up Soviet refugees, but an evil gang of murderous thugs, disposing of anyone they wanted to and collecting whatever booty they could get their hands on. Volodya's chill warning came to mind vividly. The sooner we could get away from them the better—that was patently obvious.

By midnight, a considerable amount of the vodka was gone and all but Oleg were lying around in a drunken stupor. Boris and I thought it would be safer to pretend to be asleep. At one point Oleg came over and kicked me hard on the shins. I stifled a cry of pain as I realised he was testing to see whether I was indeed asleep. I mumbled something drowsily and he went off. I heard him leave the hut, apparently satisfied that we were asleep. Suddenly I felt a hand on my shoulder and Boris whispered, 'Stay here until I get back. If you hear a shot, get out of here and run till you drop. Don't wait for me. I'll find you if I'm still alive.' I started to protest, but Boris put his hand over my mouth. 'Don't argue. Just do as I say.'

I was terrified. I lay there in silence, listening with disgust to the drunken sounds of the three men on the other side of the room. It seemed as though an eternity went by. Then the door of the hut opened slowly and someone came in. I hardly dared to look, but was overjoyed when I saw Boris.

'Where's Oleg?' I whispered.

'Don't worry about him, I've taken care of it,' he answered calmly. Then he quietly went over to where the drunken trio had put their guns on the table and took them, one by one.

'Grab our things,' he whispered. There was only one rucksack to worry about so we made a dash for it without delay.

Outside the air smelt fresh and wonderful. Several hundred metres from the hut we came to a ravine. Boris took out the guns and disposed of them one by one. He took the rucksack from me, which had seemed to get heavier by the minute. We pushed forward rapidly for several hours before stopping for a rest. We had been following a forest trail in the dark, but as first light approached, we decided to take to the trees again after resting briefly.

Boris finally told me what he'd done with Oleg. 'I couldn't take any chances, so I waited for him to come past where I was hiding near the hut and knocked him out. It was relatively easy because he didn't expect it. Then I tied him up with that cord from our bag. I thought about killing him, and then shooting the other three sons of bitches, but I just couldn't do it in cold blood. Let's hope we have enough of a head start. We certainly wouldn't stand a chance if they caught up with us.' I shivered at the thought of what might happen should they find us.

We still had an hour or so before full daylight. We continued on even though I was sick and completely exhausted. Not only was walking becoming difficult, but my back ached terribly and I had begun to bleed profusely. Only adrenaline had got me through the past few hours. I tore strips off my skirt to stem the flow of blood. Dawn was creeping over the tops of trees ahead of us, but I hardly noticed, I was feeling so feverish. We stopped to rest in the undergrowth, though we could hear the unmistakable sound of gunshots some way off. Boris wiped my face, now bathed in sweat and misery, while we waited for daybreak to unfold. The welcome respite was short-lived, as we had to keep on the move. So it went on for many days.

Very soon the pain in my back was almost unbearable. We eventually came across a small farm where Boris asked for some food and shelter for a day or two. The owners, thank heavens, understood our situation and hid us in a small hut, giving us milk and bread. We were in a village called Obersdorf, about fifty kilometres from the *Bodensee*—the border between Bavaria and Switzerland. We were told that Obersdorf was occupied by American troops, and there was a combined Ukrainian and Russian refugee camp nearby.

I waited in the hut while Boris went to see what was happening in the village. He returned a few hours later with a piece of bread and a tomato, begged from one of the locals. I hungrily ate what he had brought me and we lay down on the floor to sleep, deciding to go down to the village together in the morning.

But I couldn't sleep. The floor was very hard and I was in great pain. Despondency and severe depression overcame me. I didn't care any more whether we lived or died, since this was no way to exist. I just hoped that whatever our fate was, it would come soon. The episode with the renegades had shaken me more than I had realised.

Boris could do little to help me. Again he left me to see what food he could find. By now I was running a high temperature and was half-delirious, shivering and crying. When I came to, Boris was holding me. He proudly showed me what he had brought back with him—an American doughnut and an orange!

'Where did you get this?' I asked him. 'I haven't seen an orange for five years.'

'Darling, just eat and try to get stronger. I'll tell you everything that happened.' Boris peeled the fruit for me and related his latest adventure. He had wandered into the village to scrounge what food he could, when he came across a club for American servicemen.

'As I came up to the entrance, I found a pencil on the ground. Then I had an idea, Lilya. If I could get some paper I could sketch some portraits of the Americans in return for cigarettes and chocolates.' At the time, these commodities were common currency and could be traded for just about anything, including food and clothes. 'I waited for a while, and at last a couple of American soldiers came out. I somehow made them understand that I would do a portrait of them.'

One of the soldiers understood Boris's mixture of English and mime and beckoned him into the club, where he offered him coffee, a doughnut and an orange. 'I'm sorry darling, I drank the coffee, but I brought back the rest of the food for you.' He hugged me warmly. 'I'll go back there tomorrow. How do you feel?'

I told him I was still feeling dreadful. Boris held me and kept talking.

'I also met some Ukrainian refugees, near the hotel. They aren't going back either. They told me there's a Ukrainian refugee camp close by and asked me to visit them. I said I would see if you were well enough to come with me. If you're up to it we'll go there tonight. I told them you were Ukrainian too, so don't say too much.' While Boris was talking, I tried to eat. I felt awful but I had to eat something to get a bit of energy back. I really didn't want to go anywhere, especially to another camp, but the prospect of a bit of warmth overrode my long-held resistance to the idea.

Somehow Boris got me to the camp. When his new acquaintances saw how ill I was, they immediately organised a cubicle with a bed in it. I must have passed out because when I came to, Boris told me worriedly that I had been delirious and feverish for two days. He had begged the camp authorities not to move us until I was well enough to walk and thankfully we were given permission to stay.

My condition got worse. The bleeding wouldn't stop and I was losing weight fast. My skin was a dark grey and the pain in my lower back unbearable. The camp medical officer examined me and took Boris aside. A few minutes later they came back. Boris held my hand while the doctor gave me the same diagnosis I'd been given in Karlsbad.

'You must have an operation immediately, Frau Natalenko. One of your kidneys has been irreparably damaged and we must remove it before the infection spreads to the other. You will also have to have a complete hysterectomy as your ovaries have been infected as well. I'm sorry, but you have no choice.' I looked at Boris aghast. Again my dreams of having children were being taken away from me

'No, no!' I cried wildly. 'I'm not going to have any operation!'

'Lilya, Lilya darling, what are you saying? If you don't agree to this operation, you won't recover and I couldn't bear to lose you.' Tears in his eyes, Boris looked at me forlornly.

'I can't! I won't! If I can't have children I'd rather die!'

'Well, Frau Natalenko, of course it's your decision, but I must warn you that your recovery depends upon this operation. If you won't agree to it, I can do no more for you.' The doctor left, asking Boris to persuade me to reconsider.

Boris looked lost. He talked to me for hours, telling me that I couldn't just throw away all that we had survived this far.

'Boris, listen to me,' I told him weakly. 'You know how much I want children. I'm prepared to risk my life to have them. I will never agree to this operation! I'm sorry.' Boris looked at me in silence for a long time.

Without another word, he got up and left. He was gone for most of that day and night, and finally came back looking pale and exhausted.

'Lilya, I can't bear watching you die. I don't know what I'll do without you,' he cried, and ran to me, holding me close.

'Darling, I won't die, you'll see, I'll get well.' I tried to console him, stroking and kissing him—but despite his protests and entreaties, I remained resolute. I would will myself to get better.

Days grew into weeks. I was still bedridden and my condition had not improved. Boris resigned himself to looking after me when he was in the camp, but he was away much of the time. He managed to earn enough money to feed us through the winter with his sketches of the American soldiers and even some of the local Germans. He managed to buy some paints, which meant that he could paint portraits, which brought in more money than sketches.

By now my illness was well known in the camp. In fact, many of the women would come by and look after me during Boris's absences. One day, one of the Ukrainian women came running to me. 'Mrs Natalenko, I've just heard some wonderful news. There's a gynaecologist in Kaufbeuren. Perhaps he can help you.'

Dr Tamm, the gynaecologist, was an Estonian, also a refugee, who had managed to establish a small practice since arriving in Kaufbeuren. He was already well known in the area because he had treated a number of women successfully. When Boris returned from one of his painting trips I told him what I had heard.

'Lilya, that's wonderful news. I'll get you to him no matter what. It's not as though we have anything to lose,' he said, perhaps a little too bitterly, I thought. My husband was still hoping I would change my mind and have the operation. Five months had passed since I became ill and I couldn't bear to look at myself. I was emaciated, my skin dark and bruised and my eyes lifeless and yellow—all the physical symptoms of kidney disease.

By this stage, I could no longer walk, so Boris begged a local farmer to take us to Kaufbauren, offering to pay him what we could. We arrived at Dr Tamm's cottage clinic unannounced and Boris carried me inside. Luckily the doctor was there. He examined me thoroughly and confirmed the diagnosis of the camp doctor. After hearing my absolute refusal to undergo surgery, he said quietly, 'My dear, I can't promise you miracles but I am willing to try some alternative treatment which may at least arrest the infection. If we can't stop it you have little hope of surviving at all, let alone of having children.'

I was ecstatic. I was willing to undergo anything if it meant there was even a small chance of my having children. Throughout all these months of unbearable pain, my biggest fear wasn't dying—I was almost resigned to it anyway—it was the thought that I might survive but not be able to have children. That would be intolerable. I thought about Ina, and how I had lost her. For some reason, that was the only part of my past I'd never told Boris about and I couldn't bear to tell him now. I remembered those terrible years and the death of my little girl. And now my life seemed to be repeating itself. Perhaps I would never have children, but I had to try. So whatever treatment Dr Tamm recommended for me, I would gladly try it.

The treatment consisted of regular injections of some compound, whose name I never knew, for two weeks. The bleeding eased and I felt slightly better. Dr Tamm stopped the injections for two weeks, then resumed for another week. Then I had a month's respite from the injections altogether. The bleeding stopped completely and I felt some of my strength return. The pain in my back also eased. Then Dr Tamm began diathermy—a method of treatment that passed an electric current through the body. Over the next seven weeks or so I felt better than I had in some time. My colour improved and I put on a little weight, and finally Boris and I began to think I might survive after all.

Our relief was short-lived, however. I lost my appetite again and felt nauseous and unwell most of the time. Boris and I both believed I was dying. Boris brought Dr Tamm back to see me. He examined me thoroughly, asked lots of questions and then, after an almost unbearable silence, looked at me and said, 'Frau Natalenko, you are going to have a baby.' I couldn't believe what I was hearing. My heart almost burst with happiness—I was going to have a baby! Boris was delighted too, but worried about my still-weakened condition.

'Don't worry, Herr Natalenko,' Dr Tamm told him reassuringly. 'Your wife is young and strong, despite what she's been through. As long as she looks after herself, both she and the baby will be fine. I must caution you that her kidneys will never fully recover, but with the proper medical care and attention, she has every chance of a full-term healthy birth.' The doctor gave me a long list of instructions to follow, along with some pills to take, made an appointment for my next visit and left.

CHAPTER TWELVE

The early part of my pregnancy was difficult. At first, I was in a lot of pain again—and I couldn't eat the food served in the camp. It all tasted far too bland. I had incredible cravings; one day I wanted pickled cucumbers, the next I yearned for herrings, fried potatoes and apples. Poor Boris wore himself out going from village to village trying to find food that might satisfy me.

My health began to improve steadily, however. Dr Tamm continued to visit regularly and gave me weekly injections of whatever it was he was using. I've often thought of him over the years and said a prayer for him, because I truly believe that he saved my life. As I grew healthier, my energy returned and so did my interest in theatre. The camp in which we lived was large and divided into sections. We met many talented people—dancers, singers and actors. One evening as we were chatting, I said to Boris, 'Darling, why don't we put on a show and invite all the camps in the area? It could be the best production ever seen here. We'll easily find willing performers.'

Boris thought for a minute, then enthusiastically agreed. 'Why not indeed? I'll direct and you do the choreography. Only are you sure you're up to it?'

I was now four months pregnant and feeling wonderful—better than I had felt in a long time. 'I feel fine, now that Dr Tamm is looking after me so well,' I answered, giving him a hug.

'You know, I'm tired of running and hiding,' Boris said thoughtfully. 'It's about time we enjoyed ourselves and tried to live a normal life. This will be a great challenge for us—and it will help take our minds off what we're going through.' We began to argue about what to present. Boris wanted to stage a musical comedy. I wanted to do a dramatic piece. After some heated debate, we decided on the musical because it would be easier—and we already had a script.

So Boris and I put up announcements around the camp. We were to hold auditions the following week. I was slightly nervous about it, worried that no one would be interested. To my surprise and delight, we were inundated with volunteers, dozens of singers, dancers and actors turning up in eager anticipation.

Rehearsals began and after the usual period of tantrums, arguments and tears, we were ready for opening night. We received a tumultuous welcome; there was standing room only. The audience couldn't get enough and we extended our original season. Our success was the talk of the refugee camps in Bavaria. Those Americans and Germans who came were in raptures and we had full houses night after night. Culturally speaking it was a huge success, so much so that the prevailing local opinion towards refugees improved greatly and we were accorded more respect by everyone.

A few weeks after performances ceased, we were told that the camp was closing down and its inhabitants were to be dispersed to surrounding camps. Boris and I wanted to be sent to Kempten—a camp not far away—but we were moved to Mittenwaldt. Once again, it seemed that fate had intervened in our lives, for this move undoubtedly saved us from the disaster which befell the refugees at Kempten.

Red Army troops, still occupying this part of Germany, surrounded Kempten, herding the Ukrainian refugees into trucks to take them back to the Soviet Union. People tried to escape, fleeing into neighbouring forests, hiding in churches, but to no avail. The Soviets broke down the church doors and dragged men, women and children against their will into the waiting trucks. Many were beaten, others were killed. There were accounts of people committing suicide rather than go back to face Stalin's wrath. The most shocking incident of all was when scores of Ukrainian Cossack men cut open their own stomachs in a mass suicide attempt. Most of them died. All this occurred in front of the Americans and under the eyes of journalists. But still the Americans aided the Soviets in returning the refugees. The Kempten tragedy was brought to the attention of the world, but not before thousands of refugees had been forced to go back to the Soviet Union. We paid dearly for our freedom.

Conditions in Mittenwaldt were atrocious in comparison to Obersdorf. We were housed in deserted army barracks which had been heavily bombed. There were no windows or doors and many walls were missing. Our quarters were divided by bits of torn blanket into tiny, cramped spaces. Boris and I had to share a stretcher. It was impossible to sleep in it at the same time, so we devised a roster system. The stench of hundreds of people crammed together was appalling. There was no privacy at all, and food was strictly rationed. There were no toilets or washing facilities, and people suffered from all sorts of illnesses. We didn't know how we would survive this new hell.

'Boris, I can't have our baby here,' I cried, heavily pregnant by this time. Boris agreed with me.

'Lilya, I have an idea. I still have a few packs of American cigarettes left. I'll go back to Obersdorf and try to trade them for a room somewhere. They should pay the rent for a little while yet.'

'No, you can't leave me here by myself. I'll go mad,' I begged him.

He took me in his arms and said gently, 'It's our only hope. You're in no condition to go wandering about looking for somewhere to live. Please be patient and strong one more time and I'll come back for you soon, I promise.'

I knew he was right but I was beside myself with worry. What if he were caught by the Soviets? What if I had the baby even before he came back? Panic overtook me and I couldn't eat or sleep. I didn't need to worry though—Boris returned after a week, with wonderful news. He had found a room for us in Missenberg, a small village near Obersdorf, and had paid the landlord in advance with his cigarettes; this had secured us the room for a few months. Most importantly, however, Missenberg was close to Dr Tamm.

I was nearly seven months into my pregnancy when we arrived at Missenberg, when I became ill again. Apparently the baby was pressing on a nerve and the pain radiated down my legs. I could barely walk. Dr Tamm ordered me to bed with a hot-water bottle, refusing to give me any painkillers for fear they would adversely affect the baby. He was also afraid that my damaged kidneys could lead to a condition known as eclampsia—a form of convulsion, usually recurrent, occurring especially during pregnancy. He advised Boris to take me to the hospital so that I would be under constant observation during the last few weeks of my confinement. However, I refused to stay at the hospital because conditions there were extremely overcrowded. I preferred to leave my care entirely to Dr Tamm and stay at home.

Two things in particular didn't help my state of wellbeing. We lived in daily fear that we'd come to the attention of the Soviets and be captured. I was also terrified that I'd die during childbirth and leave my baby without a mother.

Boris had to leave me often, sometimes for days on end. He continued to paint portraits of the Americans, especially officers and their wives. He was paid well in food and cigarettes, which he could trade for anything we needed, so our living conditions improved tremendously. He often came back with the latest news gleaned from other refugees. It was almost the end of 1946 and still Stalin's henchmen were hunting down Russian and Ukrainian refugees and any other Soviet prisoners of war in an attempt to satiate Stalin's merciless thirst for revenge. Those of us who had escaped his dictatorship realised he was afraid that the West would hear about his death camps in the north of Russia, his acts of terrorism against his own people, the widespread repression he had orchestrated. It wasn't until the Cold War during the 1950s, when relations between the Soviet bloc and the West became increasingly tense, that the full extent of the atrocities became known.

We heard that many Russian officers of the ROA, the Russian Liberation Army, had been captured, returned to the Soviet Union and publicly executed. Included in this list was my friend, General Vlasov, along with General Trukhin and General Zhilenkov, with whom I had danced that New Year's Eve.

There were daily reports of refugees or Displaced Persons—as we were then known—being caught by the Soviets in broad daylight and in full view of both American and British military. This was happening all around us: in Augsburg, Munich and Kempten, all American- or British-occupied zones. We weren't safe, that was certain, but although we had heard that various countries were willing to accept Eastern European refugees and give them work, I could no longer run. My baby was due any time now. And so we waited.

'God, please help us once more,' I prayed.

I entered hospital at the end of January and on 7 February 1947 our little girl Ksana was born. The labour was horrendous. My pains began at midnight on 5 February; I thought I would die. Because of all my previous complications, Dr Tamm refused to give me anaesthetic or analgesics of any kind. Poor Boris was suffering too, unable to help, and at my bedside almost throughout the ordeal. The pains continued for the entire night of the 5th, all of the next day, and it wasn't until 2.30 am on the 7th that Ksana decided she was ready to come into the world. By that time Boris, exhausted, had dozed off in the waiting room. He was woken by one of the hospital staff to be told that both mother and daughter were doing well.

I stayed in hospital for a few more days while Boris looked for another place to live close by, as our single room in Missenberg was too small for our new family. We moved into a room on a farm owned by a kind German family. Our life took on a somewhat peaceful routine and I renewed my efforts to find Alec, but there was still no news of him.

Compared to the trauma and hardships of the previous few years the next year or so was relatively uneventful. My time was spent looking after Ksana, who was often sick with the childhood diseases that were so common at the time. Boris earned money in a variety of ways, including painting, drawing, radio work and playing chess. He felt rather uncomfortable about using his favourite pastime in this way, because he was a man of principle. By this I mean that while he could easily beat most of the players who liked to play for money, he felt it was unfair to do so, preferring to play against opponents who had a better chance against him. Of course this meant that playing chess for money was much more like gambling than a means of earning a living. There were many players he could easily have beaten, but he would offer to play them on a handicap basis, giving them a significant head start.

In October 1948 our son was born. Since the pregnancy had progressed normally this time, we decided I would have the baby at home. I also didn't want to leave Ksana, who was only eighteen months old, with anyone else while I was giving birth. This time I was in labour for only twelve hours. Boris and a midwife assisted me and again, my baby was born naturally. Boris jokingly told me a few times to hurry up as he was hungry and it was close to dinnertime. (I didn't have the energy to explain that it was hardly up to me!) Our little boy was beautiful. I wanted to call him Alexander after my brother, and Boris agreed, but when he returned from registering the birth he told me that he had changed his mind and named our son Bohdan. His explanation was that since I had prayed constantly during my pregnancy for a safe delivery, he'd chosen this name because it meant 'gift from God'. I was rather upset, but not too surprised—for he had done the same thing in naming our daughter. We had agreed on the name Irina, but she turned out to be Ksana, thanks to Boris's impulsive nature.

After Bohdan's birth, my health almost completely recovered, and I revelled in motherhood. Boris continued to eke out a living painting portraits, while my days and nights were completely taken up with looking after the babies.

And so time went on. The United Nations was still uncertain what to do with those Russians, Ukrainians and other former Soviet citizens who refused to go back to their country. Stalin certainly knew what he wanted to do with them. Even as late as 1953, when Stalin died, refugees from the Soviet bloc were still being deported and serving considerable periods of detention in labour camps. Those were the lucky ones. If there were any evidence of collaboration with the Germans during the war, the penalty still could be, and often was, death. For many years the United Nations seemed to turn a blind eye to this inhumanity, but slowly began to introduce refugee assistance programs. Under these, countries like America, Canada and Australia began to grant Eastern European refugees political asylum.

Our fear of being captured directly by the Soviets or handed over to them by the Allies was still very strong. We were determined not to attract undue attention from the authorities by moving from where we were living. Although our little farmhouse was not ideal, it was more than adequate and, above all, seemed as secure and out of the way as we could hope for.

I wanted to migrate to America where most of the Russian intelligentsia sought to go. Boris thought we should consider Australia, which he had read about as the land of opportunity and where, he said, we would be welcomed with open arms. Little did he know about Australia in the early 1950s! Australia was seen as an emerging nation with opportunities for many, though lacking the cultural vitality of Europe and Russia. This bothered us considerably, but I was more concerned with what Australia had to offer as a place to raise our children than with what it had to offer Boris and me. He bewailed the fact that our children would be raised in a cultural backwater, but I pointed out that their cultural education would be our responsibility in any case. As for a sound general education, we agreed that Australia could provide it as well as any other Western country. Inwardly, I was more than happy about the remoteness of Australia as it also meant remoteness from the Soviet Union of Joseph Stalin. Surely the tentacles of his blood lust would not reach us there and we would finally be safe.

We were called into Augsburg for an interview and waited a month or so before we heard that we had been accepted by Australia and were to go to a transit camp in Wildflecken to await our turn for migration. It was the beginning of 1949.

Our leavetaking from Missenberg was painful. We had grown to love our German landlords—Ksana especially loved Opa and Oma (Grandfather and Grandmother)—and their daughters Babette, Frenzel and Rosette, and they loved her. And leaving the animals was painful for her too—even as a little girl, Ksana showed an extraordinary affinity with animals. I found her in the cowsheds daily, covered in mud and animal droppings. She had names for all the farm animals and Opa almost found it impossible to slaughter any for meat, as Ksana searched endlessly if one of them couldn't be found. She tearfully hugged and kissed all her human and animal friends and even big Max, the bull, roared after us as if he knew that we were never coming back.

The holding camp was little better than the refugee camps we had been in, with thousands of people in cramped quarters. Illness and disease were rife, particularly amongst the children, and the mortality rate was incredibly high. Everyone suffered from malnutrition. The single hospital was inadequate to cater for the thousands of refugees. Its hygiene was dubious and its so-called isolation ward for infectious diseases was situated in the centre of the compound. Despite my best efforts in maintaining hygienic conditions and ensuring that my babies had enough food, it was only a matter of days before Bohdan became critically ill with amoebic dysentery. As soon as any child became ill, the authorities would take the little one to the camp hospital, whether the parents gave permission or not.

I fought with the staff who came to get Bohdan, because I had heard of the many children who died in the hospital, but I was held down while he was taken away. I wasn't allowed to see him and I almost went mad with worry. After three days I could bear it no longer. Despite the protests of the staff, I forced my way into the compound. When I found Bohdan wailing miserably, I was almost paralysed with rage. I took off his nappy, which obviously hadn't been changed for a considerable time, to find it covered in blood. His little bottom was red-raw and dirty. I became like a madwoman. I grabbed him, wrapped him in a blanket and fought my way past the nurses back to our quarters.

Bohdan settled down a little, but I could see that he was still very ill and the bleeding hadn't stopped. I had heard there was a general hospital not far away, so I told Boris to borrow a car. When we got to the hospital we found that the medical registrar was on leave that day and no other doctors were available. I had a little money with me and offered some to the woman at reception in exchange for telling us where the doctor lived. She gave us directions and suggested it would be wiser to admit our little boy right away—he would be looked after while we went to get the doctor.

Dragging Bohdan with us would not help his condition, so I reluctantly agreed, and Boris and I, carrying Ksana, went to look for the doctor. Within an hour or so we found his house. He was a kindly man and agreed immediately to accompany us back to the hospital. I offered to pay him, as we still had a little money left, but he refused.

I sent Boris back to the camp with Ksana while I stayed with Bohdan at the hospital.

I wasn't allowed to stay in the ward with him, so I sat in the street under his window. Whenever I heard his little cry, I would press my face against the glass so he could see me and quieten down. I stayed huddled in the street for two days and two nights, until I was satisfied that he had improved a little, then I walked back to the camp, about 30 kilometres away, to see how Ksana was. I hadn't eaten in all that time and Boris was horrified when he saw me. He begged me to stay but after spending a restless night and attempting to eat something, I headed back to the hospital—again on foot.

Bohdan was a lot better. The doctor told me my baby would have to stay another three or four days and that I should be thankful that I had brought him in when I did. With some of the money he had earned by painting, Boris had bought me a beautiful amethyst ring and necklace. I gave these to the sister in charge, begging her to make sure my little boy was well cared for. (Boris was incapable of saving money. Whenever he earned some, he would splurge it on gifts for the children or me. I loved his generosity, but was constantly frustrated by his total disregard for saving money.) At last Bohdan was allowed to leave the hospital. Boris was able to borrow a car again from the Americans and so he came to take us both back to the camp.

We had to eat our meals communally, for cooking in individual quarters was forbidden. I knew that my babies would be at a greater risk of catching other illnesses if they came into contact with other children so, again, I defied the authorities and found a small hot plate that I could plug into the light socket. Boris would bring home vegetables, chicken and fruit which I cooked and pureed so the children could be fed the kind of diet prescribed by the German doctor.

Despite my care, Bohdan's dysentery returned and now Ksana became ill as well. Again we went to the general hospital where the children recovered, only to fall ill again a few weeks later. Not only did they suffer from dysentery; they also caught whooping cough, glandular fever and measles. Their constant illnesses kept us from going to Australia, as they couldn't pass the medical test. In that year, 1949, my hair turned white.

At the end of January 1950, our turn to migrate came around again, and thankfully both children were well enough to pass the required medical test. We were taken by train to Bremerhaven where our ship, the Italian SS *Castel Bianco*, was berthed. The day of our departure, 22 April 1950, was bitterly cold, even though it was spring. As we walked up the gangplank, I was filled with emotion. We were leaving the first half of our life behind. Goodbye Russia and beloved family buried there. Goodbye Alec, wherever you are. I knew I would never stop looking for him. Farewell Germany. Boris and I stood on board, clutching our children, lost in our separate thoughts. We looked at one another in silence as the ship's horn gave three mournful blasts and we began to move away from land.

Our feelings of anxiety and hope were soon overlaid by the realities of shipboard living. Because of the large number of passengers, the men's quarters were in one part of the ship, separated from the women and children. Food was very plain but, compared to the deprivations most of us had experienced over the past decade, it was more than reasonable and there was no shortage of it. None of us refugees complained, but this was not the case with those paying full fare on the journey. They complained about anything and everything. Particularly hurtful was their open resentment at having to share facilities with those whom they called 'freeloaders'—the subsidised refugees. It was an attitude that was to resurface many times in our new homeland.

As the voyage proceeded, it became clear that getting to Australia was not going to be quite as peaceful as we'd imagined. We passed through the North Sea and the English Channel during relatively calm weather but already we were feeling a little seasick. Then it was announced that we should prepare for a spell of bad weather in the Bay of Biscay. The 'bad weather' turned out to be a full-scale gale. Not only were most of the passengers seasick, including the four of us, but so were most of the crew, who said it was the worst weather they had ever encountered. Eventually the weather cleared and we looked forward to a relatively calm and uneventful voyage. Our children had other ideas.

Ksana had been devoted to animals back in Germany and her interest hadn't waned since then. When she discovered the *Castel Bianco* was constantly escorted by dolphins riding the bow wave she was utterly captivated. Every day she would watch for hours from a safe vantage point on deck, only the tip of her nose showing over the guard rails—but one day I realised that she had moved further than usual towards the bow. Before I could call her, Ksana leaned under the lowest rail and was precariously poised over the ship's edge. In horror I called out, gesticulating wildly as I ran towards her. Thank God that one of the crew, who was fairly close to her, was alerted by my screaming and made a frantic dash across the deck. If he hadn't been so near, Ksana would surely have been lost overboard, for just as he reached her she lost her balance. The man lunged at her and a very lucky three-year-old found herself dangling above the ocean far below, held by her ankles. After this horrific incident, I didn't allow either child to leave my side, but still our guardian angel would be forced to work overtime.

One of the paying passengers was a wealthy American returning from Europe with his wife. They were childless and middle aged and had travelled to Europe with the intention of adopting one of the countless orphans created by the war. Bohdan, or Bobik, as we called him, was a beautiful little boy. He was extremely outgoing, unlike Ksana, who was shy and clingy, and loved to approach people, holding out his hand to greet them. He befriended the American couple and played little tricks on them, like sneaking up from behind, putting his hands over their eyes and surprising them. The American was so taken by Bobik (who, inevitably, became Bob) that he pleaded with us to give him our little boy in return for a large sum of money. In fact he offered us a fortune and, while at first we treated it merely as a joke, it turned out that he was perfectly serious. He even had legal documents drawn up which guaranteed that Bob would be provided with a virtual fortune. Of course we gently refused his offer, but the affair highlighted the way many people perceived refugees. With our few possessions and very limited prospects, they saw us as second-class citizens. While some people, like this American, were very courteous and friendly, others treated us as social and cultural inferiors. Boris and I became absolutely determined that whatever hardships we might encounter in our new homeland, we would ensure that our children received the best possible education and standard of living we could provide.

After landing in Melbourne we were transported to the refugee camp in Bonegilla in Albury, on the border between Victoria and New South Wales. Conditions were dreadful. Hygiene was almost non-existent, the food barely edible and the heat severely oppressive. Then there were those flies! They were everywhere. Swarms of them, in your eyes, in your mouth, just waiting to land on any surface.

Many aspects of camp life were very poorly administered. Those few of us who could speak a smattering of English would gingerly approach the authorities with simple suggestions that could improve conditions without imposing added burdens on the staff. We always received the same response—don't be ungrateful. We were still treated as an irritating inconvenience at best and as unwanted freeloaders by most, and the authorities made it abundantly clear that instead of complaining, we should be grateful to get whatever was offered. So we tried to make the best of our circumstances. We made some friends there, but life in Bonegilla was very transitory. People would leave as soon as they found work outside the camp, their places taken immediately by more and more new arrivals. Boris began looking for work, one of the conditions of the migrant assistance scheme, but before he secured employment, another disaster was to befall us.

Bob was stricken with polio. In the 1950s, being diagnosed with polio spelt either a death sentence or a life of crippling disability. After many weeks of illness and the rapid deterioration of Bob's motor functions, the camp doctor gave us the grave news.

'I'm sorry, but your little boy has poliomyelitis,' he told us with downcast eyes.

My blood ran cold. When would all this end? What would happen to my beautiful Bobik? Boris and I clung to each other, neither of us able to speak. In the coming days, our little boy's condition deteriorated until he was completely paralysed. Boris and I were engulfed in despair. There was nothing we could do and no one to whom we could turn. Boris was an atheist, but I believed in God, knowing that in the face of utter hopelessness so many times before, things had worked out for me in the end. I prayed, as I had done so many times in my life, begging God to save my little son. And once again, my prayers seemed to be answered.

Bob slowly began to regain some movement in his arms and legs. The doctor explained that the partial reversal of symptoms was probably due to the intense physiotherapy he was receiving. At that time, physiotherapy was extremely rudimentary and the only form of treatment for polio. Even though Bob's condition was considered untreatable, he continued improving slowly. Finally the doctor told us that there was a chance, albeit a very slight one, that he had suffered a less severe form of the infection despite his symptoms. This prognosis gave us fresh hope. Once again, providence had intervened in my life and Bob continued his recovery till only a faint trace of stiffness in his legs remained.

Our lives resumed some form of normality for a month or so before Ksana fell seriously ill with diphtheria, soon joined by Bob. The camp was rife with infectious diseases of all kinds and, because there were no isolation facilities, children in particular were very vulnerable. Ksana and Bob were constantly ill—polio, diphtheria, measles, whooping cough, amoebic dysentery amongst their illnesses. Boris and I were almost beside ourselves. We knew that the longer we stayed there, the greater the risk to our children.

One of the conditions of coming to Australia as a Displaced Person was to work in a position assigned by the government. Some people's professional qualifications were recognised, but many could only work as labourers. Since Boris's qualifications were not recognised, he would have to accept work as a labourer in whatever location was assigned to him. This turned out to be at the huge Port Kembla steelworks near Wollongong, in New South Wales.

So on 7 May 1951, Boris left us to travel to Wollongong. The plan was that he would settle into his job, secure some accommodation and send for us as soon as possible. Everything seemed to be going according to plan and Boris wrote to me from a place called Cringila. He had a job at the steelworks and, even though it was a thankless labouring job at the coke ovens, it provided a small but regular wage. The children seemed to be getting stronger and I couldn't wait to join my husband and leave the camp. Then it happened: Boris's letters suddenly stopped. I lost all communication with him.

I was in a strange country with two small children, speaking only a little English, and now my husband had disappeared from my life. I tried to imagine what could have happened. It was inconceivable that Boris had abandoned us after what he and I had been through. Some of the other wives in the camp were convinced he'd left me, but I never, ever considered this a possibility. So I went to the camp authorities. I asked whether they could make some enquiries on my behalf. I should have known better. The authorities weren't in the business of tracking down missing husbands, I was told curtly. If I were so concerned I should go to the police. I thought about this possibility but quickly decided against it. For one thing, I was ignorant of how these affairs were dealt with in Australia. What if I got Boris into trouble by contacting the police? Of most concern to me, however, was my intense desire to retain as much anonymity as possible. Even though it was now six years since the war, we continued to hear about refugees being deported back to the Soviet Union. Obviously Stalin's tentacles were still outstretched.

So that was that. I would find my husband myself. In his earliest letters he told me about the place where he was staying, Cringila, and how small it was. Just like a village. Well, I reasoned, a village was just a few cottages close together, a farm or two and a place where everybody knew everybody else. That's what a village in Russia was like. It should be easy to find him. With the meagre amount of money I had, I packed up, and the children and I set out by train.

After two uncomfortable and tiring days of travel, we arrived in Wollongong. The railway platform was in the middle of a huge industrial area that had to be the steelworks where Boris said he worked. But it was enormous! I would obviously need to find someone who could help me find my husband in this huge complex. After trudging a few kilometres, we came to some houses. I knocked on the door of the first house and a woman came out. It was immediately obvious that we didn't have any language in common. In desperation I pointed at the steelworks and said 'husband', then shrugged my shoulders to indicate that I didn't know where he was. The woman fortunately seemed to understand and asked, 'German? Polish? Russian?' When I replied 'Russian', she pointed in the direction of a nearby corner store and made me understand that I should ask there.

Ksana and Bob were almost asleep on their feet, but I urged them to continue a little further. When we reached the store, I discovered the storekeeper was actually Yugoslav, but since there are enough words similar to both languages, I made some progress. He told me that one of his neighbours was Ukrainian and led us around the corner to meet him. This was a godsend. Perhaps this Pavel might know Boris. After all, how many other Ukrainians could there be in a small village in Australia? Pavel didn't know Boris, but insisted we stay with him and his wife while he made enquiries. The children and I took a much-needed rest while Pavel went out for a few hours. His wife, Olga, fussed around us, feeding us and offering us a bed in their modest cottage. The children fell asleep immediately. I lay down next to them, their soft breath on my cheek, and thought about our plight. Would I ever see my husband again? Soon I too was fast asleep. My dreams were troubled, with random images flashing through them. From somewhere far away, I heard my name being called. 'Lilya, Lilya.' It was Boris. Half-conscious, I imagined that he was rousing me, shaking me gently by the shoulders. 'I can't go on, Boris, I can't keep running any more,' I muttered, believing myself to be back in Germany, deep in some forest or other, running, always running.

'Wake up, darling, it's me!' Still dazed, I looked up. My God! He wasn't a dream. It really was my Boris. I hugged him and began to cry.

'I can't believe it,' I said, clutching him. 'Here I was looking for you and it was you who found me.'

Boris and Pavel had a mutual acquaintance with whom Boris worked. As soon as Pavel had told this acquaintance about me, he put two and two together and ran to tell Boris that his family was looking for him.

'But why did you stop writing to me?' I asked, puzzled.

'Darling, what are you talking about?' he responded. 'Your letters stopped over a month ago. I've been worried sick that something had happened to you or the children. I was just waiting for some rostered days off work and then I was going to visit you to make sure that everything was all right.'

We couldn't understand what could have happened, as my friends at the camp were still receiving their mail.

'Anyway, it doesn't matter now that we are back together,' he said, 'and with the money I've been sending you, we can look for a larger flat somewhere in this area.'

'Boris, what money? I haven't received any money from you,' I replied with a sinking feeling in the pit of my stomach.

We realised what must have happened. Boris had been sending me cash with his letters. All incoming and outgoing mail was sorted and distributed by camp staff. Since no one else's mail was missing, we understood that the thief must have spotted the money in Boris's letters and helped himself to it. To evade detection, he'd simply withheld both sets of letters.

I was hugely upset at this revelation, but at least our family was together again and we could begin the next phase of out lives. We thanked Pavel and his wife and Boris took us to his living quarters, which turned out to be a poky one-room fibro shanty. The children slept in the single bed, Boris and I on a mattress on the floor, borrowed from his landlord. We needed to find more suitable accommodation as soon as possible. But how, and where should we start looking? We had next to no money, only enough for food and the current rent. We had no belongings, only the clothes we were wearing. I had to wash daily because we barely had a change of underwear.

Boris had met some Russian people who lived not far away in Thirroul, immigrants from China who had been in Australia for some years and could speak a little English. My hopes soared. Surely they would be able to help us. Few people had telephones in those days and we certainly didn't, so off we went by train to Thirroul, unannounced. At Thirroul station I asked Boris where we were going from there. Well! Boris was as disorganised as ever, and had managed to lose the address. He did remember that the street name was Ocean Street or River Road or Spring Road—something to do with water, anyway. Despite my rising frustration, I thought it was at least a start.

After three hours or so of trudging up and down the hills of Thirroul we were still no closer to any street that had anything to do with water. I could have wept with disappointment. Not so Boris. As usual, he was still optimistic. It didn't matter that we couldn't find his new Russian friends, he told me, we would look for accommodation ourselves.

'Lilya, we'll just go up to one of these houses and ask for a room. Look how large they are,' Boris said confidently.

I didn't think anyone would welcome two such bedraggled strangers and two little children into their home, but swallowed my reservations in the face of such enthusiasm. We walked up the path of the closest house. An old gabled wooden house with a wide verandah running right around, it looked cheerful and inviting. Boris knocked on the door. A man came out and looked at us with a hesitant smile.

'Hullo, me Boris. She wife, Lilya. This—children. You—big house. We live here, yes?'

I was extremely embarrassed, especially when I caught the look of utter stupefaction on the man's face. There was a long pause while he simply stared at us. I could happily have disappeared into the ground; I didn't know where to look. To my amazement, he gestured for us to come inside. Boris led in his strange little brigade with total assurance. The man introduced himself as Mr Williams and called his wife. After all the introductions, made in broken English, Mr Williams and his wife offered us tea and brought out biscuits and lemonade for the children. I couldn't believe our good fortune in stumbling across such friendly people so early in our search for accommodation. I'm sure that neither of the Williams couple had intended sharing their house with boarders—especially ones who spoke no English and had two little children—but it seemed they wanted to help us. They led us to the back of the house where there were two rooms with a separate entrance off the verandah. My senses were swimming. Could this be possible? Do such good people exist? My mind went back to

Germany, to the people who'd taken us in when Boris and I were on the run. Obviously they did.

The next day Mr and Mrs Williams took us on a walking tour of the neighbourhood and into the township of Thirroul, which boasted a small corner store, a butcher's shop, a hotel and a public school. I was overwhelmed by their generosity but Boris took it all in his stride and said matter of factly, 'See, Lilya. I told you it would be all right.'

Like Blanche Du Bois in Tennessee Williams' play *A Streetcar Named Desire*, I have always depended on the kindness of strangers. This has not been by design, because I have always tried to be self-reliant, but without the generosity of others I would never have survived the many precarious situations in which I found myself throughout my life. The Williamses were the kind of people who restore one's faith in humanity.

CHAPTER THIRTEEN

Life in Thirroul was very quiet. I knew that our situation was only temporary. We needed more permanent accommodation, preferably closer to Wollongong, so that Boris wouldn't have a long trip to the steelworks at all times of the day and night. His meagre wage was barely sufficient for living expenses. I couldn't go out to work with two little children to care for, so Boris supplemented his labourer's earnings by painting portraits. He was beginning to be known as a talented portraitist and people quite often introduced him to potential clients.

After six months or so, we sadly said our goodbyes to the Williams couple. Boris and I had grown to love them dearly and so had the children. I would never forget their kindness as long as I live, I thought, as we walked down the path for what was possibly the last time.

We relocated to a tiny two-room flat in East Corrimal, much closer to the steelworks than Thirroul. It wasn't too far from the railway station for Boris and was fairly close to a school for Ksana and Bob, now five and four respectively. They slept in the single bed, head to toe, and Boris and I had a double bed for the first time in our lives. Our existence became easier.

One day Boris came home from work with a stranger in tow. 'Lilya, this is John. I told him that he could stay with us till he found a job and somewhere to live,' he told me cheerfully. I looked at him aghast, wondering where on earth he imagined this John could be accommodated.

'But Boris, we only have enough room for ourselves. What are you thinking of?' I said. During this exchange John sat calmly, smoking a cigarette.

'Look, he can sleep in the laundry,' Boris replied, and with that led John out to the back to the tiny laundry. Over the coming months my husband brought home many such guests—homeless men who were down on their luck. When I resisted, he would remind me how kind people such as the Williamses had been to us and deep down I admired him for his selflessness. But it wasn't my churlishness that put a stop to this practice. Our landlord told Boris flatly that if he brought home any more vagrants, he would be out on the street himself.

It was particularly hot that year, 1953. The temperature was frequently above the century mark, remaining high into the night. Looking down the dirt street towards the lagoon gently flowing into the sea, all I could see was a shimmering haze. The waves seemed to dance on the horizon. Our little flat became intolerable at night, the porous brick walls having drunk in the heat of the day. On nights like these, Boris and I would take the children and sleep at the beach, the sand warm beneath our bodies. We weren't the only ones to seek relief in this way. Many people from our neighbourhood also slept at the beach, their bodies half in and half out of the lagoon to escape the oppressive heat.

By the end of that year, we managed to buy a block of land a few streets away. We paid fifty pounds for it. Boris was half-hearted about owning anything, claiming that only American capitalists were landowners. I, on the other hand, was ecstatic, knowing that now we would at last live like normal human beings, not like stray animals. Together with some Russian and Ukrainian friends we had made, we began to build our nest—a three-room dwelling. I helped dig the foundations, carried bricks and mixed the concrete. At last our home, such as it was, was ready. We proudly carried the few possessions we now had to our new home. We had no telephone, no car, no television set, no sewerage, nor any appliances other than a small electric stove. Bread and milk were delivered by horse and cart, as was the ice for our state-of-the-art ice-cooler. I did the washing in an open tub, heating the water over an open fire. Today, such living conditions would seem archaic, but to us it was sheer bliss compared to the deprivations of the past.

Our family was becoming more and more accustomed to the Australian way of life and diet. Late one afternoon, I was cooking 'tea'. The children had come home from school and Boris from work. Our dining-cum-lounge room also served as a kitchen and when I needed to use the stove I had to stand across the only doorway out of the room. The potato chips were sizzling nicely in their pot of oil. I called everyone to dinner. Boris and Bob sat down, but at the last minute Ksana decided to run outside to check on our dog, Topsy. She ducked under my outstretched arm to get through the door. The next few moments seemed to happen in slow motion. Ksana bumped my arm and, no matter how I tried, I couldn't hang onto the pot. The entire contents splashed down over my little girl's face. Before my eyes, her skin began to fry and peel off in layers. Some of the burning oil also made its way into her hair and the smell of burnt skin and hair was sickening. I grabbed her and, with Boris, dashed to one of our neighbours who had a car.

Ksana was rushed to the emergency ward in the local hospital and treated for third degree burns to her face and head. My poor baby was in hospital for three months. Her entire head and face were tightly bandaged, and these bandages had to come off daily, the burns treated and new bandages applied. The doctors were undecided whether to do skin grafts, but luckily a visiting specialist from Sydney was called in as a consultant. He told us that because she was so young—only seven—her scars could recede into her hairline with time. Thankfully they did. She was left with only one large scar on her forehead, but since she wore her hair with a fringe even that scar was not visible.

Boris was not happy in this new country and became morose and taciturn. He was understandably frustrated and grew bitter about having to spend his life as a labourer under dangerous and unhealthy conditions. Whenever I suggested that we should think about building a bigger house, he accused me of succumbing to Western materialism. Of what value were material possessions, he would say, when we were deprived of all our cultural and professional values? Obviously the cultural life we had known before the war was no longer available to us. I understood his intense frustration and shared the same feelings, but I was more practical. I was relieved that we had an opportunity to create a future for our children. But Boris couldn't be convinced. His answer to everything became 'return to the Soviet Union'.

I could never accept that Boris seriously believed this to be a real possibility. He knew as well as I did the folly of such a move. After the West was alerted to the true nature of Stalin, following the Berlin blockade crisis of the late 1940s, information about the Soviet Union had become increasingly available. The expatriate Ukrainian community was intensely active politically and kept track of all the corrupt and inhumane activities of the Communist regime, so there was lots of evidence for the argument against going back. But Boris wouldn't be convinced. His bitterness was sometimes so great that even rational argument couldn't appeal to his enormous intelligence. This placed a huge strain on our marriage and caused us to argue bitterly and frequently.

Matters between us became even worse upon Stalin's death in 1953. Boris felt that now the monster was dead, there must surely be improvements within the Soviet Union that would allow us to return. I begged him to wait and see who would take over. In the event, most of Stalin's cronies remained in power; thus nothing really changed. Ultimately Boris conceded that going back with the children could have placed them, let alone us, in danger. It was his love for the children that kept him working at a job that he detested and which undoubtedly contributed to his ill health later. Tragically, there was a solution of sorts at hand that could have opened up greater opportunities for both of us, but neither Boris nor I recognised it at the time. Only years later, after his death, did I realise that this solution had always been within reach—learning English.

One of the greatest difficulties Boris and I had faced during the war was not knowing the language needed. We both spoke Russian and I picked up a smattering of German, but neither of us could speak or understand English, a lack which left us at the mercy of circumstance. Had we been more fluent in either German or English, we would have better understood how to avoid hazardous situations and been able to talk our way out of more predicaments. We didn't realise that when we got to Australia, language would still play such an important role in determining our destiny.

I was more willing than Boris to learn English, for I accepted that Australia was to be our permanent home. Boris looked upon our life here as temporary, although he had no plans for a final destination. Gradually I picked up more and more English while Boris still knew only a handful of words. Without English, we had no hope of resuming our careers in the theatre. It should have been obvious that bridging the language barrier was the key to regaining our former professions. It should have been, but it wasn't.

There were some limited opportunities for non-English speaking migrants to learn the language, but in those days we were not in a position to avail ourselves of them. Boris was a shift-worker and I had two small children to look after. We just weren't able to attend classes in the few timeslots offered. So Boris continued to languish in a mind-deadening job, in an extremely unhealthy work environment. In the early 1950s, pollution control and work safety ethics were not priorities on anyone's political agenda. Stupidly, we resigned ourselves to a way of life we thought inescapable. Only many years later did I understand the enormity of our lack of judgement. Had we made the effort we could have profoundly altered the circumstances of our new life. Boris and I could have become involved in developing theatre. Perhaps we could have obtained positions teaching Russian or working in the Department of Foreign Affairs as translators. The possibilities were enormous. It was only our vision that was so tragically limited.

I had abandoned any theatrical ambitions and, because my English was so basic, was forced to do whatever menial jobs came my way to supplement Boris's small wage. I cleaned people's houses, worked in a fish and chips shop and took in sewing.

Over the years there were, however, some funny incidents related to our difficulties with English. One morning Boris happened to be at home so I asked him to buy the groceries. Normally I would have done it myself, but I was busy with the washing. I carefully wrote out a list for him in English so that if he couldn't find a particular item, he could show someone what he wanted. My spelling was rather poor, because of the non-phonetic peculiarities of the language, but it was adequate. Ever since I had known him, Boris had been a keen chess player. In fact, 'keen' doesn't adequately describe his attitude to chess: 'fanatical' would be more accurate. How else would you describe someone who could become so involved that he risked being killed during an air raid on Berlin, rather than abandon an interesting game to seek refuge in a bomb shelter? Anyway, I made the mistake of trying to communicate with Boris while he was engrossed in analysing a game. So he either ignored my shopping list or misplaced it or both. He arrived at the shops armed only with a hazy memory of the English names of the items he required and a vague understanding of this alien language.

Milk, butter and some other basic items presented little difficulty. He simply pointed them out on the shelves or went over and selected them himself. So far, so good. But now it was time to obtain an item I needed to make soup—an item not on the shelves, an item with the power to instil fear into the heart of a simple butcher and turn a customer into a raving madman—chicken giblets.

'Good-day mate, what would you like?'

Boris paused, unable to remember even the word 'chicken'.

'What would you like?' repeated the butcher, more slowly and more loudly. It's strange how many people think foreigners have hearing difficulties. Boris paused again. Suddenly, he tucked his hands under his armpits and started flapping his elbows to the accompaniment of various chicken-like sounds.

'Coo-coo-ri-coo,' Boris sang.

Well, this butcher was not so simple that he didn't recognise an impression of a chicken—even a foreign chicken—when he saw and heard one. So, full of confidence in his interpretation of the display before him, he suggested, 'Ah, chicken. You want chicken.'

You might have thought that here was a golden opportunity for Boris to say yes, then point out the actual part of the chicken he wanted. But not my Boris. Instead, he said dramatically, 'No, no chicken!' He looked at the butcher, pointed to his stomach and began making strange gestures.

The butcher was now totally confused. If what he was witnessing was not meant to be a chicken, then what on earth was it? And why was chicken-man now clutching at his stomach as though he had been shot? The mystery deepened.

Boris suddenly had an inspiration. He grabbed the knife which the butcher had placed on the counter when the show began and began to improvise something that probably very few butchers have witnessed—a customer performing self-evisceration in the shop. Of course, Boris did not wish to confuse the butcher so he alternated this with his previous impression of a chicken, albeit a crazy knife-wielding chicken which occasionally made a slash at its throat to indicate it was no longer of this world.

Perhaps Boris overdid the noises or didn't flap his wings quite the right way. It might even have been the knife. In any case the butcher not only didn't fetch any chicken giblets, he indicated he wanted Boris to put the knife down and get out of his shop. He also kept repeating some phrase with the word 'police' in it. This was a word that Boris recognised only too well, in any language. Exhausted by his stage-show, my chicken giblet-less husband returned home in exasperation, cursing the lack of understanding of simple improvisational drama in parts of the local community.

'Next time,' he said bitterly, 'make sure you give me a list written in English!'

Boris's problems with English were a reflection of his general outlook towards life in Australia. He fought against assimilating in any way. We spoke Russian at home—the children were both fluent speakers—but it was clear to me that they would need to become proficient in English as well.

Our home in Corrimal reminded me of my own home in Russia. Nearby, there were extensive tracts of bushland and a wonderful coastal lagoon. This was an ideal environment for our children to grow up in, just as my own environment had been. So when it was time for the children to begin school, Boris and I were optimistic that at least this aspect of life in Australia would present no problems.

On the first day of the school year, I accompanied Bob and Ksana to East Corrimal Public School, about two kilometres away. Many children walked there on their own, for in the fifties few parents had any serious concerns about the safety of their children away from home. Traffic was far less heavy; child abductions were rare events that only happened somewhere else in the world. For about three weeks everything seemed to be going well. The children told us what they did during the day and appeared fairly happy. Progressively they became less talkative, but Boris and I simply assumed that they were becoming familiar with their routine and didn't feel there was much to report. But at the end of the first month we received a strange letter from the school, asking us to explain why neither Bob nor Ksana had been in attendance for almost three weeks. Were we aware that the law made attendance compulsory? Of course we were, but we had no idea where our children had been for those three weeks!

What had happened was that both Ksana and Bob had become more and more distressed at school. Because they couldn't speak any English, they were teased and bullied by the others constantly. In addition, Bob was called names and bullied because of his slight limp, the legacy of the polio attack. Ksana had attempted to defend him, but in the end had decided that avoiding the situation was the simplest solution. Her plan was simple. They would leave home as though going to school, and spend the day hiding in neighbouring bushland. When they heard the other children going home, they would return home too. Boris and I were heartbroken. We blamed ourselves for bringing the children here. Perhaps, had we gone back home as Boris wanted, our children would have been happier. No sooner had I entertained such a thought than I dismissed it. Neither of us would ever have seen our children grow up.

When we raised the matter of bullying with the school, we received a patronising, even hostile response. In those days, schools were far less aware of issues such as tolerance and multiculturalism. We were made to feel that these problems were of our own making because we didn't encourage the children to speak English at home. As for the teasing and bullying, it was 'natural' for Australian children to feel uncomfortable with children from different backgrounds. So while the bullying was not openly condoned, it was understandable as far as the school was concerned. We innocently suggested that in our view it was the school's task to teach our children English. The school took the view that it could hardly be expected to perform miracles when it didn't receive any cooperation at home. We were made to feel like second-rate people and third-rate Australians. It was a humiliating and painful experience and a reminder of our outcast and fugitive status during the war years.

Thankfully a new public school was about to be opened in our own neighbourhood and we hoped our children's education could begin afresh there. Bellambi Public School had been built to cater for the large influx of people to the Illawarra due to the employment needs of the Port Kembla steelworks. This school had a large proportion of migrant children, so we hoped that Ksana and Bob would fit in. Ksana was shy and introverted but settled down extremely well to her studies. She adored her teachers, Mr Walker, Mr Williams and Mr Burke. Bob was somehow more precocious and outgoing and preferred physical activities to schoolwork. However, both began to produce very good academic results. Ksana, especially, turned in incredible work. Two of our closest Russian friends, Sasha and Anatole, encouraged our children by giving them rewards for achieving well at school. Sometimes the rewards were monetary, more often in the form of books. Ksana must have cost them a small fortune because she came first in every subject, year after year. No one could recall any student achieving so consistently well. She read a great deal and became a very good writer. So good, in fact, that she got herself into trouble for it.

Boris and I always made time for our children. We spent hours reading to them or simply re-telling the classics with which we were so familiar. So it came as no surprise that the principal contacted us to let us know that Ksana was to receive a special award for story writing. Her story exhibited a level of sophistication that was beyond the teaching experience of the school staff, particularly from a student of primary school age. A day or so later, Ksana brought home a note saying that the principal would like to meet us. The next day Boris had a rostered day off, so we set out for the meeting together.

We were thrilled that our daughter had distinguished herself. When the principal ushered us in, we were puzzled that he seemed very uncomfortable. Because of the extraordinary quality of Ksana's story, he told us, he had circulated it amongst the staff members. One of them was fairly sure that it wasn't original, though he couldn't recognise the author. So the principal asked Ksana where she'd got the idea. When she told him that she had just made it up, he decided to ask us whether we knew anything about the matter.

Boris began by asking about the story itself. It was produced and, with some difficulty because of our poor English, we started to read it. After just a few minutes, we began to laugh. A bemused principal waited patiently for us to explain.

'Of course it was a good story,' I said, 'because it was one of O'Henry's best.'

'Oh, so you are familiar with this story?' said the principal and then paused, realising that this implicated his star pupil in front of her parents.

'Of course,' we both replied. 'Isn't everybody? It is one of the best-known stories in American literature today; in fact, in world literature. It is called "The Gift of the Magi".'

'Haven't you read it?' I asked, politely but somewhat incredulously.

'Well, I probably did, some time ago,' said an embarrassed principal, 'but I don't remember it. Anyway, the issue is whether or not Ksana copied it, even though she denies it.'

'Ksana did not copy this or any other story,' I said quietly. 'We tell our children many stories all the time. Most of them are taken from the classics. Sometimes we read them from the original when we have the text in Russian; at other times we just relate the story from memory. I can assure you we do not have a copy of O'Henry in Russian so we must have just related the story to her. I think it's very likely that Ksana had forgotten it could have been someone else's story. After all, many of our stories are also made up as we go along.'

The principal seemed a little surprised, then relieved. 'Well, I guess that explains it,' he said. 'I'll just make sure I ask Ksana to write her stories from her imagination alone from now on. Thank you both for coming in to see me and for straightening out this little mystery. And thank you for taking such an interest in the education of your children. It helps us a lot when children are supported by their parents at home.'

He stood up, stretching out his hand to bid us goodbye, then noticed Boris still sitting, quite obviously deep in thought, because his brows were drawn together as happened when he was concentrating. 'Moment please, Mr…' he said.

With my help, Boris asked why it was that only one teacher recognised that Ksana's story was not original. Didn't they read any books? If they knew so little about English literature, they presumably knew nothing about European and world literature. Of course, these questions alluded to the principal as well. Putting all this forward in a polite and friendly manner, Boris finally asked to see the school library.

The principal tried to explain that there was no formal requirement for teachers to have a wide reading knowledge. They simply needed teaching qualifications from a recognised institution. This raised further questions in both our minds, but we didn't press the matter further. It was now almost lunchtime, so the principal agreed to take us to the library. What we found there came as a severe shock.

The library was a converted classroom, with shoulder-height bookshelves around three walls. It couldn't have contained more than 1500 books at most—but it was the range of titles that disturbed us even more. Admittedly, we found *Robinson Crusoe, The Adventures of Tom Sawyer* and *The Adventures of Huckleberry Finn, The Adventures of Marco Polo*, some works by Jules Verne and *A Children's Picture Book of Shakespeare*. But the remainder included dozens of children's first readers, *Boy's Own* and *Girl's Own* annuals, *Bumper Book of Sports* and the like. I tried to point out what authors should be included in a children's library. Boris was more to the point.

'Rubbish,' he proclaimed with a broad sweep of his hand. 'Ninety-nine per cent rubbish.'

Before the principal could respond, Boris asked me to tell him we would provide a comprehensive list of the titles that belonged in a primary school library. Of course, we were naive about Department of Education policy and funding. The principal, however, thanked us both for our interest and said he would welcome any suggestions we cared to make. It could have been a hollow promise made simply to placate us. It wasn't.

Over the next few months the principal made a concerted effort to acquire many of the titles we listed. He took us seriously and was impressed by our concern. But, as he later confided to us, what most impressed him was the extent of our knowledge. He admitted that when he first met us he thought of us as a simple migrant family and was apologetic that he might have given the impression of looking down on us. We became good friends and he introduced us to other teachers at the school, particularly those who were teaching Ksana and Bob. Through our friendship he learnt that Boris was an artist. The school was still new and had not acquired any art works other than some second-rate prints. Boris offered to paint some pictures for the school, but what the principal really wanted was some significant work concerning Australia's early history. Moreover he insisted that Boris be paid, so he negotiated with the Department of Education to formally appoint Boris as 'designated artist'. Not only was this achieved but, within a few months, Boris received a commission from the State Premier himself to do a large oil painting depicting Captain Arthur Phillip's first landing at Sydney Cove. I clearly remember this as Ksana, Bob and I had to model all the characters because Boris insisted on painting from real life. The friendships and associations we formed with the staff at Bellambi Public School were to last for many years.

The next three or four years passed fairly uneventfully. Ksana graduated from Bellambi Public School as dux and went on to secondary education at Corrimal High School, also close to home. Bob finished primary school a year later and also went on to Corrimal High. As a prerequisite to enrolling in high school Bob and Ksana were required to sit for an IQ test. Both passed easily, but Bob was deemed to have the highest IQ in the school's history.

Boris and I began to notice Ksana's waning interest in her schoolwork. By now, she had begun piano lessons and was demonstrating a technical brilliance beyond her years. She practised daily for hours at a neighbour's house, because we couldn't afford to buy a piano. Her keyboard talent was becoming known to others, as she played at some local concerts. One day, she came home from high school with a letter from one of her favourite teachers, Mrs Beryl Robinson. Mrs Robinson had heard Ksana play and found out that we didn't have a piano at home—and had bought one for her as a present. Such friendship between teacher and pupil seems unthinkable in today's world. Yet again I found that a guardian angel was helping us. We became very close to the Robinsons and grew to love them dearly. They took us with them on weekend excursions to places such as the Minnamurra Rainforest and on picnics. We have never forgotten Mrs Robinson's incredible generosity and when she passed away not long afterwards, we were all devastated.

We also became good friends with another teacher, an exceptional man who became a lifetime friend. Vincent Rees taught English and History and was the most gifted teacher at the school in our view. He had been an actor but, unable to maintain a reasonable living in the theatre, had become a teacher. His skills with drama were the keystone of his teaching brilliance. Ksana and Bob loved his lessons, which were always full of improvisation and other theatrical techniques. Boris and I admired him enormously and went to see him teach during school open days. Long after our children left school he visited regularly, often staying till the small hours of the morning discussing our mutual passion—the theatre.

As proud of our daughter as we were, Boris and I were nevertheless worried about her worsening grades. Asked whether she was experiencing problems at school, Ksana's reply was that she just wasn't interested in anything but her music. In fact, it took a great deal of persuasion, not to mention argument, to keep her at school until she graduated. Boris and I knew only too well that an artistic career was difficult to sustain and that it didn't offer many career opportunities, especially here in Australia. Had Ksana grown up in Russia, I have no doubt that she would have succeeded in being a concert pianist.

A Russian Memoir

At home, the arguments with Boris continued. Boris hated his labourer's job, hated where we lived, hated everything about our new lives. I understood that it was not really any of these things that he hated—it was the frustration of not being able to pursue a career that used his enormous talents that made him so bitter. He would disappear for days at a time, playing chess. I was torn—I definitely didn't want to return to the Soviet Union but it was difficult watching Boris as he became more and more depressed and remote. Many years later, Ksana told me that her lasting memory of her father was of him sitting at the kitchen table with his head in his hands.

Boris had also begun losing weight. He wasn't eating properly, claiming he had lost his appetite. I begged him to go to the doctor, but he always managed to find some excuse to delay the visit. Finally, I persuaded him to make an appointment. The doctor ordered some tests on the spot and told us to return for the results in a week. I was not really worried, thinking he was probably suffering from stress-related symptoms. But at the end of that week the news couldn't have been worse: Boris had advanced-stage cancer. There was nothing anyone could do. This was in February 1965, and by the end of July in the same year Boris passed away. He was only 56 years old.

Despite all our disagreements, Boris was the love of my life. We had gone through so much together and I had looked forward to reaching old age with him. Now he was gone. Why him? Why Boris? If it hadn't been for the children, I definitely would have ended my life at this point. I had no energy left to struggle, no strength of will. Both children were grief-stricken. Ksana was eighteen and Bob sixteen. I felt I should have helped them more in coping with their grief, but I was too immersed in my own misery.

That year Ksana left home to study at the Conservatorium of Music in Sydney. Bob was in his last year at school and Boris's death derailed his academic progress. His final school grades were considerably lower than his potential, though still good enough to earn a university scholarship, which subsidised his fees but certainly didn't fully cover them. Boris wasn't entitled to any superannuation and he had no life insurance, so there was no money coming in except from what I earned by taking in sewing. Still, I managed to pay for Bob's continuing education and helped Ksana financially whenever I could. Somehow we survived.

And so, slowly, life returned to some sort of normality. I stopped looking for personal happiness and lived entirely for Ksana and Bob—their achievements became my achievements; their happiness, my happiness. Bob seemed to have inherited Boris's eclectic nature. At the University of Wollongong he became a perennial student. Over a period of twenty years he studied Arts, Philosophy, Science and Mathematics, graduating with an Honours degree in English, another Honours degree in Philosophy, and a degree in Mathematics. Like Boris, he had a love for all learning and found it almost impossible to restrict his interest to one particular field. I was proud that I was able to uphold my promise to continue educating the children. Bob went on to work at the University, in both administration and lecturing part-time in Philosophy and Education.

Ksana, also sharing Boris's restless nature, which would continue to plague her for most of her life, didn't know what she wanted. Although she was an extremely gifted pianist, she couldn't settle down to one pursuit. After finishing at the Sydney Conservatorium of Music, she went on to become a music teacher at a local high school. Having aroused the interest of the local Department of Education with many award-winning theatre productions with her school students, Ksana was deployed from classroom teaching and became a consultant to teachers in both music and drama. From here she went on to lecture at the University of Wollongong in Theatre Studies and, after resigning in 1982, went to live in Hong Kong and Singapore, where she toured several Australian productions, including *Jesus Christ Superstar*.

Upon her return to Australia in 1985, she worked in radio and television as a media consultant for the next fifteen or so years. Currently she is adopting dogs with special needs and is rehabilitating them.

I continued taking in sewing and also taught ballroom dancing in my home. In retrospect, I laugh at the memory of my dance students learning the steps of the tango or rumba as we navigated our way around my modest kitchen table.

A local high school asked me to take some classes in Russian with senior students. I enjoyed this immensely and began giving private lessons at home. Consequently, my English improved considerably.

When Boris and I first moved to the Illawarra in the early fifties, we naturally became part of the local Russian community as well as the Sydney one. Boris and I would often perform dramatised readings of Russian literature. I particularly loved reading excerpts from Tolstoy's *Anna Karenina*, while Boris preferred doing comic routines. So although we desperately missed the rich cultural life we had left behind, we tried to replace it as best we could in our new homeland.

After Boris died, I was totally preoccupied with raising my children. In a state of intense grief, I functioned robotically in my daily life. The theatre played a secondary role to that of mother for a number of years. Gradually, though, I resumed my association with the theatre, teaching at the National Institute of Dramatic Art as well as acting in and directing various productions. I became heavily involved with the theatrical productions of the Russian community in Sydney.

Even though travelling to Sydney by train became more and more difficult as severe osteoporosis restricted my mobility, I thoroughly enjoyed participating in the many theatrical productions of well-known Russian plays and operettas. I met several other Russian migrants living in Sydney, also ardent lovers of the theatre, who were to become my friends for life. Sergei Korshun, a brilliant actor himself; Anton Gurchenko, gifted director and much-loved associate; Tanya Porotikova; Mischa Dubinin; Kolya Apolonov; Valya and Sofia Aronsky; Alyssa and Leonid and Moussa Paschenko—I love all of you and treasure our times together. Of course there were many others who were just as important to me in my theatrical life in Australia. Vince Rees, actor, director, theatre critic and brilliant teacher, you passed away far too soon and left a huge gap in the cultural life of Wollongong.

I still missed Boris dreadfully, even after all these years, talking to him daily and reliving our happiest times together—and there had been many happy times for us, despite the terrors of our earlier life. I know that Boris would have enjoyed seeing our children mature into the compassionate and intelligent people that they have become. He would have been as proud of them as I am.

I also continued to miss my brother Alec, always wondering what had happened to him. Ksana had been in touch with the International Red Cross, which helped locate family members of refugees, but I was never confident that their enquiries would lead to any concrete results. Then one day Ksana told me Alec's wife and daughter had been found. They were living in Moscow. Would I like to be put in touch with them?

I thought for several days about what I would say to them, trying to steel myself for the inevitable emotional trauma that awaited me, but finally the time came to simply make the call. After the usual glitches and delays in making an overseas phone call at that time, a voice answered, 'Yes. I'm listening.'

'Hello, this is Lilya. Lilya Makarova.' There was nothing but silence.

'Lilya. Alec's sister.'

More silence, then some muttering in the background, then finally, 'What Lilya? Where are you calling from?'

I realised I hadn't even mentioned I was calling from Australia. I began to explain when it suddenly dawned on the other party what this call signified. I was talking to my niece—Alec's daughter Ina—who was there with her mother Larissa, and her Auntie Gina, whom I'd also known in Smolensk. Everybody was overcome with emotion and the ensuing conversation was a mixture of crying, interruptions and confusion. It is impossible to adequately describe the effect of trying to compress half a century of hope and despair, of loss and longing, of struggle and achievement, into a single telephone conversation. I recall feeling incredibly elated and drained at the same time; but I had finally made contact with the only members of my pre-war family who remained alive as far as I knew. They had also tried to find Alec in Russia, but to no avail. He just vanished. Despite our continued efforts, we failed to find any trace of him.

Ina came to Australia the following year, just after her mother died. I came outside to greet her when she arrived with Bob from the airport. We hugged one another for the longest time, unable to speak, choking back our tears. Over the next three months we sat up until the early hours of the morning, relating our life stories to each other. In 1991 the collapse of the Soviet system took place following the spectacular disaster of Gorbachev's perestroika. He had tried valiantly to rebuild Communism, but the underlying structure was so rotten and corrupt that it was bound to collapse. Needless to say, I wanted Ina to give me all the details about modern life in Russia. The more I found out, the more obvious it became that for most Russians, life under the new system had not markedly changed. The needs of ordinary people still remained the last item on the political agenda. The fall of Communism, for which I had been praying for so many years, had come as something of an anti-climax, as Ina made it clear that all the old bureaucratic difficulties remained. Eventually, the dreaded moment arrived when I had to part with her. It was heartbreaking when Ina left to return to Russia but we vowed to meet again somehow.

Unfortunately, by the time I saw Ina again, my health had completely deserted me and I had suffered a heart attack and several strokes. My darling niece returned to visit and help take care of me. I was not overly concerned that my health was so poor, nor did I fear dying. I simply regretted that so many years had passed without our knowing of each other's existence or sharing our lives together. Finding Ina meant that my life had come full circle and I had much to be grateful for. I had learned that every moment in life was precious and should be lived to the full.

My greatest concerns were not for myself, but for Ksana. How would she react to my inevitable passing? I spent many hours talking with Bob, who clearly understood that all my struggles had been for the sake of my children. More than anything, I wanted them to be happy—that was what had given my life meaning. But would Ksana be able to accept this and not be lost in grief? She and I had become as close as mother and daughter could possibly be. Thankfully, she and Bob were also very close and I knew they would continue to care for each other after my passing.

Bob and I spent many hours discussing these and other personal and philosophical matters. I found that I was genuinely interested in the cosmological and scientific questions that occupied his mind so frequently. Here I was, into my eighties, taking notes while Bob explained the workings of differential and integral calculus! I even tackled the exercises he set for me with relish. Not only that, but I got most of them right. My old nemesis, mathematics, was not the monster I had always imagined it to be. What a pity that life is so short. There is so much to learn, and so much wonder and amazement to experience.

And now, as I approach the end of my life and look back over the years, I thank God for what He has given me: two children whom I adore and who love me; a husband who was devoted to our children and who loved me unconditionally; three wonderful grandchildren, Taras, Xenia and Alex, who mean the world to me; a reunion with Ina, my brother's only child, after a lifetime apart; and the theatre, my beloved theatre, which provided me with riches even beyond my expectations. Of course in my life there have been times of great unhappiness and sheer despondency, times when only an instinctive sense of self-preservation kept me going. My heart still aches for my mother, who died so young; for my father and my beloved uncle, both executed during the war; for my beautiful and adored first baby girl, who died needlessly from malnutrition; and for Alec. Despite all this, I have never felt bitter. In fact, my resolve to live life to the full imbued me with a sense of wonderment at the simple things in life: the delicate beauty of a rose growing in the garden, or waking to a new day. Having realised long ago that life is transient, I grasped at it passionately—the good and the bad.

Boris has already visited me in my dreams, beckoning me. I know that I have only a little while left here and feel at peace, knowing that I have achieved most of the things I set out to do.

EPILOGUE

At 6.30 am on 3 January 1998, at the age of 83, my darling mother passed away at home, surrounded by her family—my brother Bob and his family, myself and Ina. I don't think that she ever gave up her will to live—that indomitable will that had enabled her to survive the great tragedies of her life. It was simply that she had resigned herself to the inevitability of her condition. She faced death with the same courage with which she had faced life. But I was inconsolable. How could I go on without her? Ina stayed on for another month or so before returning to Moscow, and she and I would sit in the room where Mum had spent most of her time, staring at each other blankly, both of us racked with grief. Bob, ever the philosopher, tried hard to console me by reminding me of the rich legacy our mother had left us.

A few months after Mum's death, while I was going through her things, I came across a tape. It was entitled 'Ludmila, 1989'. Having absolutely no recollection of what it contained, I played it. My mother's voice resounded across the room, as clearly as though she were there with me. As I listened closely, I remembered the context in which the tape was recorded. I had tried to persuade Mum to write her memoirs as far back as 1989, even to the point of haranguing her. She had resisted strongly, mainly because she felt that her story was not unique but also because she couldn't face reliving certain incidents. I cried, I cajoled, telling her that her story was indeed unique—unique to her. Finally, she relented, but we had to overcome yet another hurdle. Mum didn't know where to begin or how to organise her thoughts. I suggested that I ask a journalist friend of mine to interview her, in a kind of oral history style. We made four tapes, outlining major incidents in her life. From there, Mum began the task of writing about her life. She wrote in Russian and in longhand. It was a slow process, taking more than five years to complete, but at last an autobiography took shape. Mum was actually working on the finishing touches when she passed away.

With the help of Ina and one of our Russian friends, Bob and I began the mammoth task of translating Mum's story into English. That process alone took over a year. Finally, the entire manuscript was rewritten, retaining Mum's voice throughout.

And so it was that we were able to put these memoirs together—the remarkable story of a remarkable woman. Through this book, I hope that her voice will live on, an inspiration to others who find themselves in difficult situations and a reminder of the rich cultural tapestry that Australia has become.